PRAISE FOR A(

I've had the privilege of reading more than two dozen titles in the digital accessibility space. *Accessible Communications* is one of the most well-rounded and strategically aligned books I've come across for communications professionals and content creators. This book isn't just a guide; it's a strategy for embedding accessibility into modern communications. I highly recommend it for any communications professional serious about reaching and respecting all audiences.
Crystal Scott, CPWA, Founder of the Accessibility Book Club

What makes this book stand out is how it models what it teaches. It communicates with clarity, compassion and purpose – meeting the reader where they are and guiding them gently, yet confidently, through the complex world of accessible communication. This book offers insights and tools that are valuable for anyone committed to reaching, engaging and respecting diverse audiences. A must-read for those who want to elevate their craft while honouring the full spectrum of human experience.
Priya Bates, ABC, MC, IABC Fellow, President, Inner Strength Communication Inc, co-author of *Building a Culture of Inclusivity*

Buy this book if you want to ensure your corporate communication is impactful and implemented in the most inclusive way. You'll get a road map for making accessibility a strategic advantage, helping you to engage better, reduce organizational risk and build brand reputation. Demystifying laws and standards and packed with advice on how to avoid missteps through testing, training and continuous monitoring, this is a straightforward action plan for equitable communication. A recommended read for anyone in the creative industries and management teams who believes accessibility is a shared endeavour.
Sarah Waddington CBE, CEO of the Public Relations and Communications Association (PRCA)

Accessible Communications is your go-to book to learn about accessibility and inclusivity from the experts. Lisa Riemers' and Matisse Hamel-Nelis' inspirational and practical guide will fundamentally change how you view information. The advice, checklists and guidance are incredibly valuable, you'll want to keep this book within reach.
Rachel Miller, Founder, All Things IC, and author of *Internal Communication Strategy* **and** *Successful Change Communication*

It's such a good read. I didn't expect to be hooked on a book I thought to be a reference guide for my work. As practical as it is, I was delighted to think new thoughts as Lisa Riemers and Matisse Hamel-Nelis laid out the way forward, supported by genuine insights and robust references. Review your house style guide against chapters 4 and 5.
Wedge Black, intranet content consultant

Lisa Riemers and Matisse Hamel-Nelis have written an insightful, clear and useful guide to accessible communications. This warm and charming duo reframes accessibility as a driver of innovation. Their approach makes it easy to understand the challenges people face in communication. Then they provide detailed guidance, tools and case studies to clarify their points. The takeaways, the tools, the checklists are practical and clear. So many 'I didn't know that' moments; I can't wait to get started!
Kari E. McLean, MS-IMC, CMP

Practical, clear, and long overdue. *Accessible Communications* is packed with practical advice on what accessibility really means, why it matters, and how to get it right — without jargon, judgement or overwhelm. What I especially appreciated is how actionable it is. Whether you're writing an email, creating a video or posting to social, the authors offer concrete examples and common pitfalls to avoid. If you're a communicator who wants to reach more people, avoid costly mistakes and build trust through inclusive, thoughtful content, this is the handbook you didn't know you needed.
Sharon O'Dea, Co-founder, Lithos Partners

A must-read for all communicators. *Accessible Communications* is a practical guide that offers clear, actionable steps and frameworks to help you embed accessibility and inclusion into everyday practice.
Ann-Marie Blake, Co-Founder, True Communications

If you feel like you don't know how to 'do' accessibility, or how to talk about it with others, this is the book you need. It's practical, it's easy to follow and it's just so interesting. You'll soon feel confident that your content is more inclusive and is all the better for it.
Christine Cawthorne, Director, Crocstar

This book will help you remove barriers, build bridges, enhance engagement and above all reach your audience to deliver your messages. This book should become a standard for every person that includes communications as part of their work. If you want your ideas, concepts and words to be understood by all, this book shares how and why to reach that goal. In our world where voices and needs are diverse, this book reminds us that accessible communication is essential.
Samantha Evans, CAE, ICE-CCP, MBA, Certification Director, IAAP/G3ict and Accessibility Advocate

It's finally here – a practical guide to making your communication truly accessible and inclusive. Lisa Riemers and Matisse Hamel-Nelis have compiled everything you need to know to enhance the power of your communication – not just for people with disability, but for everyone who engages with your work. Forget boring theory, instead think helpful tools, tips and case studies that demonstrate how important accessible communication is. Whether you're a strategic communicator by profession, or someone who communicates as part of your job (which is everyone!), this book will open up your eyes to opportunities to reach even more people in ways that cut through.
Melanie Loy, SCMP, Founder and CEO, Hey Mel! Communications & Training

Accessible Communications

Create impact, avoid missteps and build trust

Lisa Riemers and Matisse Hamel-Nelis

Publisher's note

Every possible effort has been made to ensure that the information contained in this book is accurate at the time of going to press, and the publishers and authors cannot accept responsibility for any errors or omissions, however caused. No responsibility for loss or damage occasioned to any person acting, or refraining from action, as a result of the material in this publication can be accepted by the editor, the publisher or the author.

First published in Great Britain in 2026 by Kogan Page Limited

All rights reserved. No part of this publication may be reproduced, stored or transmitted by any means without prior written permission from Kogan Page, except as permitted under applicable copyright laws.

Kogan Page
Kogan Page Ltd, 2nd Floor, 45 Gee Street, London EC1V 3RS, United Kingdom
Kogan Page Inc, 8 W 38th Street, Suite 90, New York, NY 10018, USA
www.koganpage.com

EU Representative (GPSR)
Authorised Rep Compliance Ltd, Ground Floor, 71 Baggot Street Lower, Dublin D02 P593, Ireland
www.arccompliance.com

Kogan Page books are printed on paper from sustainable forests.

© Lisa Riemers and Matisse Hamel-Nelis 2026

The moral rights of the authors have been asserted by them in accordance with the Copyright, Designs and Patents Act 1988.

ISBNs
Hardback   978 1 3986 2186 2
Paperback   978 1 3986 2184 8
Ebook   978 1 3986 2185 5

British Library Cataloguing-in-Publication Data
A CIP record for this book is available from the British Library.

Library of Congress Cataloging-in-Publication Data
2025028152

Typeset by Integra Software Services, Pondicherry
Print production managed by Jellyfish
Printed and bound by CPI Group (UK) Ltd, Croydon, CR0 4YY

CONTENTS

List of figures and tables xi
About the authors xii
Foreword xiii
Preface xvii
Acknowledgements xxii

PART ONE
Laying the groundwork: Understanding the fundamentals of accessibility, legislation and building an accessible culture

01 The foundation: Understanding the basics of accessibility and disability 3

What is disability? 3
The global context: Disability in numbers 5
The models of disability 6
The foundation of accessible, user-centred communication 9
The foundation of digital accessibility 11
A primer on assistive technology 12
D&I, DEI, IDEA or ABIDE: What's the difference? 15
Practical examples in organizations 17
References 19

02 What you need to know to be compliant: Standards, guidelines and laws 22

The business and ethical case for compliance 23
The business case: Why accessibility makes sense 24
The ethical case: It's the right thing to do 26
The Web Content Accessibility Guidelines (WCAG): The backbone of digital accessibility 27
Beyond the web: Standards for documents and multimedia 30

Key accessibility laws and regulations worldwide 33
Challenges and common pitfalls in compliance 48
References 53

03 Creating a strategic cultural shift towards accessibility 59

Defining a culture of accessibility 60
Building the foundations for change 63
Creating an accessibility action plan 67
Embedding accessibility in daily workflows 71
Training and awareness: Building accessibility knowledge and confidence 75
Measuring and sustaining progress: Keeping accessibility front and centre 79
References 85

PART TWO
Putting it together: A practical guide on embedding accessibility into your workflow

04 Creating content with plain and inclusive language in mind 89

Plain language principles 95
Experts prefer plain language 101
How to write about statistics and numbers 104
Readability levels, formulas and caveats 106
The difference between plain language and easy reading 108
Writing that meets your users where they are 109
Inclusive language: Words matter 111
Practical tips for implementing inclusive language 115
References 120

05 Writing for and creating an accessible web presence: The basics 124

Writing for the web: How people read differently online 125
Hyperlinks: Making navigation clear and meaningful 130
Visual accessibility: How to make images meaningful for everyone 134

Bringing it all together: A holistic approach 138
Visual design: Accessibility beyond alt text 139
Test with your audience 143
References 144

06 Getting started with accessible documents 148

A quick overview: Types of documents and why accessibility matters 148
Text documents: Simplicity meets functionality 150
Structuring slide decks for accessibility 155
Making spreadsheets accessible 158
Accessible graphs, charts and data visualizations: Turning numbers into inclusive stories 162
Accessible PDFs: Designing for universal access 165
Tools and resources for document accessibility: Simplifying the path to inclusion 172
Real-world examples of accessible documents in action 177
Accessible documents as a foundation of communication 179
References 181

07 Creating accessible social media content 186

The importance of accessible social media content 186
The fundamentals of accessible social media 191
Accessible images and graphics 194
Building inclusive social media experiences through captioning and audio accessibility 199
Writing inclusive copy for social media 202
Platform-specific accessibility tips 206
Common pitfalls and how to avoid them in accessible social media content 212
References 218

08 Making videos and podcasts for everyone 223

Planning for accessibility in videos and podcasts 224
Video accessibility 229
Open versus closed captions and when to use them 232
Audio descriptions: Post-production versus integrated 237
Visual accessibility 243

Accessible video players: YouTube, Vimeo and beyond 248
Creating accessible podcasts 253
Transcripts: The cornerstone of accessible podcasting 259
Accessible podcast players: Making sure everyone can listen 265
Key takeaways 269
References 270

PART THREE
Looking towards the future

09 Future challenges and opportunities: How to stay ahead of the curve 277

The next frontier: Emerging technologies and accessibility 277
The role of inclusive design in the future of communications 285
Chapter wrap up 286
Wrapping up the book: The bigger picture 287
References 287

Checklists 290

A checklist for plain language 290
Accessible social media content checklist for communicators 290
Accessible video content checklist 292

Index 295

LIST OF FIGURES AND TABLES

FIGURES

Figure 3.1	Accessibility is everyone's responsibility 72
Figure 4.1	X-ray, not imaging; when official terms don't match user needs you end up with patchy workarounds 99
Figure 4.2	78 per cent of people prefer a longer, helpful explanation 101
Figure 5.1	Home working trends 138
Figure 6.1	Document metadata in an MS Word file 153
Figure 8.1	Engagement by week 230

TABLES

Table 4.1	Complex vs clear words 97
Table 6.1	An example of an inaccessible table 153
Table 6.2	A more accessible table 153
Table 8.1	A quick guide to the differences between post-production and integrated described 242

ABOUT THE AUTHORS

Lisa Riemers is an independent communications consultant and accessibility advocate who helps clients connect their people and tell their stories. Based in London, Lisa advises large and complex organizations including world-leading universities, charities, insurers, business-to-business (B2B) companies and the UK government.

Matisse Hamel-Nelis is an award-winning communications and digital accessibility consultant and a PR professor at Durham College. Based in Toronto, Canada, she also founded and hosts the PR & Lattes podcast and is the past Chair of the Diversity, Equity and Inclusion (DEI) Committee for the International Association of Business Communicators (IABC).

FOREWORD

Humans are hardwired to communicate – to share ideas, connect with others and build understanding across cultures, languages and abilities. Yet, too often, the messages we craft, the content we create and the information we share exclude the very people we're trying to reach. This isn't intentional; it's simply the result of systems and practices not designed with everyone in mind from the start.

I've spent my career at the intersection of communication, technology and human connection. As someone who works with organizations to tell their stories and connect their people, I've witnessed first-hand both the existing barriers and the transformative power of making accessibility a priority. Too often, I've seen well-meaning communicators approach accessibility as something to check off a compliance list when, in reality, it's about ensuring every voice can be heard and every message can be received by all.

When Matisse first approached me about writing this foreword, I knew immediately this was a book the communications industry desperately needed. What struck me most about the authors' approach is their demystifying accessibility while focusing squarely on what matters most: genuine human connection.

In my work across government agencies, multinational corporations, and non-profits, I've seen the full spectrum of accessibility implementation – from organizations that view it as an afterthought to those that embed it into their DNA. The difference is stark. When accessibility is integrated from the beginning, communications become stronger, clearer and more impactful for everyone. It's not about creating multiple versions of content; it's about building better content from the start.

This book brilliantly addresses what I believe is the central challenge of our time: creating communications that truly serve everyone. Lisa and Matisse don't just tell you what to do; they provide the framework for understanding why accessible communication matters on multiple levels – ethical, legal, and business. They've taken what can feel like an overwhelming topic and broken it into manageable, actionable guidance that mid-level communicators can implement immediately in their daily work.

What makes this book particularly valuable is its practical approach. Rather than theoretical concepts, you'll find real-world examples reflecting the communications challenges professionals face daily. Whether crafting an internal email, creating a social media campaign, or developing a company-wide presentation, this book provides the tools and knowledge to make your communications accessible without sacrificing creativity or impact.

As someone who bridges the gap between technical capabilities and human needs, I've learned that accessibility is fundamentally about removing barriers – not adding complexity. The authors understand this deeply. They recognize that when we design for accessibility, we create better experiences for everyone. A clearly structured document helps all readers, not just those using screen readers. Captions on videos benefit not just viewers with hearing loss but also those watching in noisy environments, non-English users, and those with learning disabilities. Plain language serves everyone, regardless of cognitive ability or educational background.

The timing of this book couldn't be more critical. We're at a pivotal moment where legislation is expanding, technology is evolving rapidly, and organizational culture is shifting to embrace inclusivity in all its forms. Yet, many communicators still lack the confidence or knowledge to navigate this landscape effectively. This book fills that gap, providing both the foundational understanding and the practical skills needed to create truly accessible communications.

What impresses me most about Lisa and Matisse's work is their recognition that accessibility is an ongoing journey, not a destination. It is never a 'one and done'. They've created a resource that acknowledges both the current regulatory landscape and the evolving nature of best practices. This forward-thinking approach ensures the guidance remains relevant as standards develop and new challenges emerge.

Having worked with diverse teams across various organizations, I've seen how accessibility can transform workplace culture. When communicators prioritize inclusivity, it creates a ripple effect throughout the organization. Teams become more collaborative, innovations multiply as diverse perspectives are valued, and the quality of all communications improves dramatically.

This book also addresses something often overlooked in accessibility discussions: the business case for inclusive communications. Accessible communications expand market reach, enhance brand reputation, and build customer loyalty. When people feel seen and included, they become advocates for your organization. Conversely, exclusionary communications can damage relationships and create significant reputational risk in our increasingly connected and digital world.

To the readers of this book: you hold in your hands more than just a guide to accessible communications. You possess a road map for creating meaningful connections with every audience you serve. Whether you're a communications manager seeking to upskill your team, a content creator looking to expand your capabilities, or a business leader wanting to ensure your organization's messages truly resonate, this book will transform your approach to communication.

As you begin this journey, remember that accessible communication is not about limitations – it's about possibilities. It's about expanding the reach of your message, amplifying diverse voices, and building trust with every interaction. It's about recognizing that when we remove barriers for some, we create opportunities for all.

The path to accessible communications may seem daunting at first, but with this book as your guide, you'll discover it's achievable and rewarding in ways you might not expect. Every email that reaches more people, every document that's clearer to understand, every video that includes everyone – these small victories compound into transformative change.

I encourage you to approach this book not as another set of rules to follow but as an invitation to rethink how we connect with one another. Let it inspire you to question assumptions, challenge existing practices, and imagine new possibilities for inclusive communication. The insights within these pages can shape not just your communications but the culture of your organization.

As Lisa and Matisse demonstrate throughout this book, creating accessible communications is ultimately about respect – respect for diversity, respect for individual needs, and respect for the fundamental right of all people to access information. It's about choosing inclusion over ease, clarity over convention, and connection over convenience.

Accessible communication is a life-long passion. Born with profound hearing loss, I understand deeply how accessibility transforms lives. My decades in disability advocacy have shown me that accessible communication isn't just about inclusion but human dignity. When I champion captioning in universities, courts, and theatres, I advocate for the transformative power of inclusion that benefits those with hearing loss and everyone in our diverse society.

The future of communication is accessible; with this book, you have everything you need to help create it. The question is no longer whether accessible communications matter but how quickly we can make them the standard rather than the exception. I invite you to join this essential movement and discover how accessibility can elevate everything you create.

This book is your companion on that journey – use it well, share what you learn and watch as your communications transform from good to exceptional, from reaching some to reaching all. The impact you'll create extends far beyond any single message; you'll build bridges of understanding that strengthen communities, advance organizations, and affirm the dignity of everyone who encounters your communications.

Welcome to the future of inclusive communication. Welcome to a world where everyone's voice matters and every message connects. Welcome to accessible communications.

Lorin MacDonald (She/Her)
Human rights lawyer and disability advocate and Member of the Order of Canada

PREFACE

Have you been in a situation recently where you weren't able to read or understand the information in front of you? Why is it that some designers seem to prioritize a certain style over making things usable?

When quirky design trumps usability

Have you found yourself squinting while trying to read the ingredients on some packaging?

How about trying to read a children's book that has letters and words jumping all over an image – while trying not to fall asleep yourself, as you read by night light?

Perhaps you've been in a restaurant which has low lighting – and a menu with a beige, tiny italic font, on a cream background. Whatever vibe the designers were going for in that lovely candlelit restaurant was completely ruined by people getting their phone torches out to select their starter.

When corporate guidelines don't take user needs into account

One of my favourite things I like to spot are those handwritten signs hastily stuck to menus, or added to official signage, to answer questions or signpost people to the information they need. At a hotel I struggled to find the toilets, as the signs on the dimly lit wall were black, in an unreadable swirly font, on a dark red background. The black and white, hastily laminated poster that accompanied it with a big arrow saying 'toilets', showed that staff were continually interrupted by people asking for directions.

Perhaps you're in a position where you can influence your corporate guidelines. Or, at least, learn how to apply them in a more accessible way.

What this book is about

This book is not (just) about inclusivity. This is a book about how to make your information easier to read. It's about how to increase the reach of your communications. How to make sure the people reading your content know what they need to do next. It's a practical guidebook designed to help you make sure that all that work you've done doesn't go to waste and can be consumed by your audience.

Whether you're a communications professional, or someone who sends reports, writes presentations, runs a podcast, creates social media content or sends emails, this book is a guide to make your messages clearer for everyone. The WHO estimates that one in three of us will need assistive technology, ranging from glasses to mobility scooters, in our lifetimes.[1] We are all only ever temporarily not disabled, and making communications accessible makes it easier for everyone to get the information they need.

Handling objections

Sometimes it's easy to think that accessibility isn't relevant to us. You're already considering that it might be, as you're reading this (congratulations!).

Some actual objections I've heard over the last 18 months include:

- 'But I don't think we have anyone with accessibility needs who works in my organization' – from someone who wasn't aware of what constitutes a need, or that people don't necessarily disclose their access requirements to their colleagues and employers. Accessibility is not an edge case – and we've got plenty of statistics to back up this up in Chapter 1.

- 'Our legal team say we're not covered by the public sector regulations so we won't bother' – from an organization who would rather ignore the other legislation and keep paying to settle claims from people who complain, rather than focusing attention on making services that are easier to use for everybody. Inaccessible websites, communications and services can be an expensive headache to remedy – and there's more on this in Chapter 2.

- 'I'm too busy, I already have too much to do.' As Alexa Heinrich pointed out, making your information accessible isn't extra work, it means that without, for example, alternative text on your images, it's not finished.[2] Inaccessible content means that fewer people are able to see it; for a small amount of time up front you could potentially be reaching many more people! Part 2 of this book has loads of practical tips and techniques to embed accessibility into your workflow.

A bigger impact to more people

Accessible communications open up information to a bigger audience. They make your messages more impactful, and don't need to be a compromise on design or functionality.

This is a book about how to make our communications have a bigger impact to more people, without excluding anyone along the way.

In it we go deep. We dive right into relevant legislation, as well as talking about building accessibility into our workflows.

We go broad. We're looking across the channels that professionals use every day to communicate – from PowerPoint presentations (my fave) to cracking accessible PDFs (one of Matisse's particular areas of expertise).

We talk Big Picture about building a culture of accessibility, about the business case for it, and how it's so much more than just a DEI (Diversity, Equity and Inclusion) initiative that's an SEP (Douglas Adams's 'somebody else's problem' – something that people manage to avoid by assuming it's not their responsibility).[3]

We talk tactics. Whether your entire role is about communications, or you're regularly called upon to send emails, write reports or use social media yourself, there'll likely be at least a chapter for you.

Collaborating across time zones

I first met Matisse Hamel-Nelis at the World Conference of the International Association of Business Communicators in New York City. We hit it off immediately; I was blown away by her expertise and deep understanding of, among other things, how to make PDFs that are actually accessible for people. At the time, we also both had pink hair.

We ended up hanging out together around the event and online since, geeking out about all sorts of stuff around accessibility. We don't always agree on absolutely everything – and something we've learned through writing this book together is that there may be regional or local variations to advice and the way things are managed.

When we get together to talk about these things we get a better product at the end. I have learned so much from working with Matisse, and I cannot wait for you to do the same.

Making the complex more simple

When I first started talking to people about this book, one of the things that people often said to me was 'oh, you mean it's about easy read language?' While easy read is something that we'll talk about in our chapter on plain and inclusive language, there's a lot more to it. Even experts prefer plain language – something that my sometimes colleague and co-conspirator Christine Cawthorne proved in her research with Christopher Trudeau.[4]

User-centred communication

As a communications professional who also works in user-centred content design (sometimes referred to as UX writing), I see them as two aspects of a remarkably similar discipline. Both are about providing the right information, in the right format, to the right people, at the right time. The driving objectives and corresponding processes may differ, but the fundamental principles are the same.

- The best marketing and communications campaigns are targeted to your audience.
- The best websites and digital services are designed with user needs in mind.
- The best campaigns have had user insights, and the best digital products and services have had extensive user testing.

Communications may have another 'user' to take into account. Internal communications folks may consider the organization as a user. This is information that the organization needs to make available, to ensure that all employees have access to it, whether they think they need it personally or not.

User-centred content folk are laser-focused on making sure user needs are met, while external marketing and communications folks might be more concerned about creating those user needs – and desires – in the first place.

Both are looking to make it easier for people to do the thing or buy the thing – as Kotler and Keller suggest, marketing is about making products which meet the needs of users – profitably.[5]

Progress over perfection

Working as a communications professional can be tiring. It can feel like we're always trying to keep up with a frantic pace, and that the work we're doing isn't necessarily making a difference. Accessibility can feel like another thing to keep on top of, but we're here to help. This book is designed to break down complex concepts into practical steps you can start to do right now. With each step you'll be working towards communications that better meet the needs of your audience.

We're all at different stages of learning. Maybe you're right at the start of your accessibility journey, or maybe you'll find something that you don't necessarily agree with in this book. Different users have different needs and the things that help some people might have a detrimental impact on others. We won't always know that of course, unless we actually seek and act on user feedback.

What we can all hopefully agree on is that we're trying to make our communications better than before. We can strive for excellence while being satisfied that we're making progress – and work together to make more impactful communications for everyone!

References

1 Global Report on Assistive Technology, World Health Organization, https://iris.who.int/bitstream/handle/10665/354357/9789240049451-eng.pdf (archived at https://perma.cc/T22M-Z5J4)
2 'I hate when folks make writing alt text sound like extra work. It's not extra work. It's missing work. Without alt text, your content is unfinished.' LinkedIn, www.linkedin.com/posts/alexaheinrich_i-hate-when-folks-make-writing-alt-text-sound-activity-7224421821675188227-jVbt/ (archived at https://perma.cc/PR9V-XVRZ)
3 D Adams (1982) *Life, the Universe and Everything*. 'An SEP is something we can't see, or don't see, or our brain doesn't let us see, because we think that it's somebody else's problem. That's what SEP means. Somebody else's problem. The brain just edits it out, it's like a blind spot.'
4 C Trudeau and C Cawthorne. The public speaks, again: An international study of legal communication, *University of Arkansas at Little Rock Law Review*, 40 (2), https://lawrepository.ualr.edu/lawreview/vol40/iss2/3 (archived at https://perma.cc/SS45-J6T7)
5 P Kotler and K L Keller (2016) *Marketing Management*, 15th ed., Pearson Education

ACKNOWLEDGEMENTS

From Matisse:

I'd first like to thank my brilliant partner-in-crime and co-author, Lisa Riemers. Your insight, dedication, patience, and all-round great energy made this book not just possible, but a joy to create together. I honestly am so grateful you said yes to writing this with me!

To my husband, Peter, thank you for your endless support, encouragement, and for holding everything together through the long days and even longer nights. And to my parents, thank you for always believing in me and cheering me on every step of the way. This book is as much yours as it is mine.

To the incredible team at Kogan Page: thank you, Donna, for believing in this project from the beginning and championing its value, and Bobbi-Lee for your positivity, encouragement, and guidance every step of the way. And to everyone else behind the scenes, thank you for helping bring this book to life and into the hands of readers who need it most.

From Lisa:

I would first like to thank my brilliant co-author, Matisse Hamel-Nelis. Your enthusiasm, drive, patience, subject matter knowledge and generally being fun to work with has literally made this book possible. Thanks to our brilliant editorial team at Kogan Page; Donna for seeing the value in and championing the project, Bobbi-Lee for being incredibly positive and supportive, and everyone else for helping us get this book into your hands.

Thank you to Christine Cawthorne who has been a brilliant supporter, trainer, sometimes co-conspirator and mentor who helped me understand a lot more about user-centred content design. Thanks to Jeanette Rosenberg OBE who helped me realize the importance of finding allies to champion accessibility. To Sharon O'Dea, who has led the way in many areas of my working life and is a force to be reckoned with. To Wedge Black who, among many things, first showed me how to write a good hyperlink. To Elizabeth Buie who helped me see the importance of using adequate colour contrast. To Rob Finch, who proved that content can always be improved. Thank you to my husband, Nick Ashton, who provides an excellent sounding board and has kept me sane, fed and watered. Thanks to Katherine Appleford, Jenni Field, Shimrit Janes, Howard Krais, Helen Lippell, Rachel Miller, Suzie

Robinson, Monique Zytnik, and all the brilliant authors I know who've given time and advice on the writing process.

We'd also like to thank the brilliant accessibility advocates and our communications network, who frequently share their knowledge, experience and support. This includes Advita Patel, Alexa Heinrich, Ann Knettler, Ben Luby, Eduvie Martin, Eric Eggert, Gail Spivak, James Buller, James Robertson, Lorin MacDonald, Kari McLean, Kathryn Kneller, Kathryn Prosser, Kaye Moors, Laura Parker, Lauren Pope, Meryl Evans, Paige Hoveling, Rachael Pearson, Rachel Edwards, Sarah Winters, Sheri Byrne-Haber, Simon Monger, Simon Thompson, Susi O'Neill and Tiffany Yu.

PART ONE

Laying the groundwork: Understanding the fundamentals of accessibility, legislation and building an accessible culture

Creating a truly inclusive and accessible environment begins with a solid foundation. Accessibility isn't just about adding features to accommodate people with disabilities; it's about embedding inclusivity into the core of how we communicate, collaborate and operate. Accessibility makes good business sense. It helps us reach more people, can enhance the reputation of our organizations, and helps avoid risks.

To achieve this, we must understand the 'why' behind accessibility, the laws that govern it, and the cultural shift required to make it a standard practice rather than an afterthought.

This section is your starting point. We'll dive into the fundamentals of accessibility, breaking down complex legislation like the Americans with Disabilities Act (ADA), the Accessibility for Ontarians with Disabilities Act (AODA), and the European Accessibility Act (EEA) into clear, actionable insights. Beyond compliance, we'll explore how building a culture of accessibility can strengthen teams, foster innovation and enhance brand reputation.

Whether you're a seasoned professional or new to accessibility, this section will equip you with the knowledge and mindset to champion inclusivity in everything you do. By laying the groundwork now, you'll be ready to tackle the practical strategies and tools covered in the chapters ahead.

What you can expect in this part of the book

- Chapter 1 establishes the essential framework for creating accessible and inclusive communication strategies, providing a comprehensive introduction to the principles and practices of accessibility.
- Chapter 2 explores the accessibility standards, guidelines and laws that professional communicators need to understand and apply to their work.
- Chapter 3 explores how organizations can embed accessibility into their core values by fostering a cultural shift. By prioritizing accessibility as a cultural cornerstone, organizations can enhance their brand reputation, deepen audience trust, and ensure their communications genuinely connect with everyone. This chapter provides actionable strategies to make accessibility a shared responsibility and a natural part of organizational identity.

01

The foundation: Understanding the basics of accessibility and disability

Accessibility isn't just about meeting legal obligations – it's about making content, tools and experiences easier and more inclusive for everyone. While often thought of in the context of disability, it extends far beyond that, benefiting all users by improving clarity, usability and engagement.

In this chapter, we lay the essential foundation for understanding disability and accessibility, particularly as they relate to communications.

We'll explore:

- the definition of disability
- the global context
- how that applies to accessible communications
- principles of digital accessibility
- understanding assistive technology
- the importance of D&I, DEI, IDEA and ABIDE

Understanding these foundational concepts helps us to effectively apply accessibility principles. Throughout this book, we'll build on this knowledge, demonstrating how these principles can be integrated into real-world communication practices – ensuring that the messages we craft, the tools we use and the stories we tell are accessible to all.

What is disability?

When considering the needs of our users, there are a variety of considerations. In this book, we're defining disability as a physical, mental, or sensory condition making it harder for someone to do everyday things or interact with the world around them. We're also going to discuss the different types of disabilities, neurodiversity and situational disabilities that may affect how our audience interacts with our information.

What is the difference between a visible and an invisible disability?

The difference between visible and invisible disabilities is in how apparent they are to others:

- **Visible disabilities** are those you can easily notice, like if someone is using a wheelchair or wearing a prosthetic limb.
- **Invisible disabilities**, on the other hand, aren't immediately obvious, like chronic pain, mental health conditions or learning disabilities.

Both types of disabilities impact daily life, but because invisible disabilities aren't as easy to spot, people who have them often face unique challenges in getting the understanding or accommodations they need.[1]

Situational disabilities

All of us may from time to time be affected by the environment that we're in. How often have you been to a restaurant and struggled to read the menu because of low-light conditions, or tried to read a book to a child while using a night light? Perhaps you've attempted to pick up a message in a loud environment, or you've worked on a corporate device that has no speakers, or a low-quality screen. Maybe you've got someone waiting for the answer on a phone call, and you're trying to look up some key information while they're waiting impatiently for an answer and talking to you, increasing your cognitive load. These examples show how the world around us can impact what we're able to do – and are more common than you might think.

Disabilities can be situational, temporary or lifelong, but the real challenge often comes from the barriers society creates, like inaccessible spaces or a lack of understanding.

Neurodiversity

People with neurodiversity also have accessibility considerations that we need to take into account; from the language we use, to the format and colour of communications. Some neurodivergent people may not consider they have a disability – and this book isn't about to define what is and isn't classified as such. What we want to do is help people understand how to make their communications more useful, usable and used.

At its core, disability is about how well (or poorly) our world is set up to include everyone. Throughout this book, we'll be providing guidance on how to adjust your communications so that they are accessible for all.

The global context: Disability in numbers

The World Health Organization estimates that 1 in 3 of us[2] will need assistive technology, ranging from glasses to mobility scooters, through to digital tools like screen readers, in our lifetimes.

> KEY POINTS
>
> An estimated 1.3 billion people worldwide, or 1 in 6 of the global population, are living with some form of disability, and that's just those who identify as such.
>
> This includes:[3]
>
> - 3.2 per cent identify as having some form of low vision or blindness
> - 6 per cent identify as being deaf or having some form of hearing loss
> - 2.6 per cent identify as having an intellectual disability
>
> In the UK, where Lisa is from, approximately 1 in 4 people[4] are registered as having some sort of disability. In Canada, where Matisse is based, 27 per cent of people are classified as disabled.[5]
>
> It's estimated that 1 in 10 people have dyslexia.[6]
>
> Approximately 1 in 12 men (8 per cent) and 1 in 200 women are colour-blind[7] – and while many may not identify as having a disability, they do have a need to access information in a format that does not rely on colour. (See more in Part 2.)

As communicators, we need to understand that disabilities, whether physical, sensory, mental, or intellectual, affect how people engage with the world and access information.

With the population ageing and chronic health conditions on the rise,[8] our responsibility to communicate inclusively will only grow.

The economic impact of exclusion and the role of communication

Excluding people with disabilities from education and the workforce doesn't just create social inequality – it also carries a huge economic cost. The World Bank estimates that this exclusion can cost countries up to 7 per cent of their GDP.[9]

People with disabilities represent an emerging market larger than China, with over one billion people. When you add their friends and family, that number jumps to 3.3 billion, collectively controlling over $13 trillion in annual disposable income. This is a market that touches 73 per cent of global consumers, and it's a group whose experiences and interactions with products and services can shape the future of design and innovation.[10]

£274 billion a year[11] is the estimated spending power of families with at least one disabled person, in the UK alone. In Canada, the purchasing power for Canadians living with disabilities is over $55 billion a year.[12] If we exclude people from accessing our information, we're closing off potential customers and reducing the size of our potential market.

Companies that centre disability in their consumer insights and product design aren't just meeting a moral obligation, they're positioning themselves for larger returns.

By designing with these experiences in mind, businesses can unlock new ways to create value and attract this powerful cohort of consumers. In a market that rewards innovation, placing accessibility at the heart of your brand isn't just inclusive – it's a strategic advantage.

The models of disability

Disability can be understood in different ways, and how we define it shapes how we approach accessibility and inclusion. There are models of disability which demonstrate different lenses through which society views and deals with disability. Each model reflects a set of beliefs and attitudes, shaping everything from policies to how we design spaces and treat people with disabilities. The way we think about disability can either create barriers or help break them down, and these models guide how we approach inclusion, accessibility and equity.

> **KEY POINTS**
>
> The main models of disability are:
>
> - the medical model
> - the social model
> - the biopsychosocial model
> - the charity model
> - the human rights-based model

Medical model of disability

The medical model[13] can be considered as looking at disability as something 'wrong' within a person, seeing it as a 'defect' that needs to be fixed or cured for someone to live a good life.

In this view, healthcare and social service professionals are given the power to try to 'correct' these conditions. But for many people with disabilities, especially those with significant limitations or high support needs, disability is an important part of their identity. It affects how people connect with their families and communities. When society treats disability as something negative or broken, it can lower self-worth, making disabled people feel like an essential part of who they are is something to be fixed.[14]

This negative view of disability often comes through in subtle messages – from the media, our communities, and even healthcare professionals. These can be well-meaning, like inspirational stories about people with disabilities doing basic everyday tasks or praising non-disabled people for simple acts of kindness. But these messages often come with low expectations, which can limit opportunities for people with disabilities.

Other times, we see messages that play on people's fears of becoming disabled, associating disability with weakness or dependency. And sometimes, the push to 'normalize' through treatments focuses on fixing something society deems undesirable, rather than truly improving a person's quality of life or their ability to participate in the activities they choose.[15]

Social model of disability

The social model of disability[16] completely reshapes how we think about disability. Instead of seeing it as something wrong with a person, it shows us that the real issue is the barriers and attitudes society creates. Sure, physical barriers, like inaccessible buildings, are part of the problem, but it's also the stereotypes, discrimination and lack of inclusive policies that hold people back. This model puts the responsibility on society, not the individual, to change.

Disability isn't just about someone's medical condition – it's about how the world around them responds to it. An impairment is simply a medical fact, but a disability happens when society fails to make accommodations. The answer isn't to 'fix' people; it's to remove the obstacles standing in their way. That means creating spaces that are accessible, passing laws that account for everyone's needs, and making sure educational systems include all students. It's about empowering people to live fully, instead of focusing on 'curing' what makes them different.

The social model pushes for universal design, accommodations, and breaking down discrimination through education and systemic change. When we value all abilities, we open ourselves up to the richness that diversity brings.

As writer Alison Kafer said, 'To eliminate disability is to eliminate the possibility of discovering alternative ways of being in the world.'[17]

Biopsychosocial model of disability

The biopsychosocial model of disability combines both the medical and social perspectives to look at the whole person. This model says we can't just focus on biology to understand someone's condition – we also need to consider their mental and social factors.

It encourages a more holistic, person-centred approach to care, considering how these three factors interact:

- **Bio**: Refers to the medical condition or physical disability.
- **Psycho**: Involves thoughts, emotions and behaviours, like coping strategies and mental health.
- **Social**: Includes external factors like work, family and economic circumstances.

It's the foundation for the World Health Organization's International Classification of Functioning, Disability and Health (ICF), although some critics of the model argue that disability should focus more on societal changes rather than health factors.

Ultimately, this model helps provide a more complete understanding of disability by considering how a person's physical, emotional and social worlds impact their daily life.[18]

Charity model of disability

The charity model views people with disabilities as individuals who need care, protection and support from others, often seeing them as victims or objects of pity. This perspective focuses on their disability as their defining trait and assumes that society knows what's best for them.

While this model comes from a place of goodwill, it can unintentionally promote a paternalistic attitude, treating people with disabilities as passive or helpless. By focusing on dependency and charity, it reinforces negative stereotypes rather than recognizing the capabilities and independence of people with disabilities.[19]

Human rights model of disability

Finally, the human rights model recognizes disability as a natural part of human diversity that should be respected and supported. People with disabilities have the same rights as everyone else, and disability should never be an excuse to deny or limit those rights.

This model is rooted in the United Nations Convention on the Rights of Persons with Disabilities, developed in 2006 by people with disabilities to promote equality worldwide.[20]

Which model should we use?

As communicators, we play a powerful role in shaping how society views people with disabilities, so it's crucial to be mindful of the models of disability in our work.

The charity model, for example, often portrays people with disabilities as victims, which can unintentionally reinforce harmful stereotypes of helplessness and dependency. However, organizations like the International Committee of the Red Cross are aware of the challenges and offer specific guidance, including the use of imagery, in their ethical content guide.[21]

The medical model focuses on disability as something to be fixed, which reduces the person to their disability, ignoring their individuality and strengths.

The social model and human rights-based model offer a much more uplifting perspective. These models recognize that disability isn't just about physical or mental impairments – it's about the barriers society creates.

As professional communicators, embracing the social model and human rights model in our work is key. We should avoid pity-driven language and instead highlight the strengths, rights and contributions of people with disabilities.

This approach not only fosters inclusion but ensures that our messaging respects and empowers all members of our community.

The foundation of accessible, user-centred communication

Now that we have a base understanding of disability, disability models and the global context of disability, we're ready to move on to building our foundation on accessible, user-centred communication.

Communications professionals may already know about the importance of targeting messages to their audience. Thinking about the desired outcome, rather than outputs of communication is something that is often discussed, particularly when we're considering elevating our communications strategy and profile. Thinking about the right message, to the right people, at the right time, is vital to successful communication – and so is the right format. To truly unlock the value of our communications, we need to make sure that information is available to all users, whatever their needs, while considering the environment in which they are accessing that information.

Using the right format

When considering the right format, and the channels through which that information is delivered, ask yourself: Is that better delivered via text? Would images and graphs help, or is this something that might be better delivered via a presentation or video? It may well be a combination of these – both to reinforce your messaging, but also make the content accessible to those who may otherwise not be able to read it.

Knowing your audience, using the right language and format for them – and providing alternative formats where appropriate – will help make sure your message is not lost.

Whether you're selecting a colour palette for your charts and graphs, or applying brand guidelines to a new social media campaign, considering whether the colour contrast, font size, etc, is usable by your audience is key. (Read more about this in Part Two.)

Environmental context

We touched already on the idea of situational disability. Most people are not browsing your website, reading your direct mail or digesting your report in perfect conditions. As communicators we need to make sure our messages meet users where they are.

Testing with your audience

The only way we can really know if our communication is accessible to those who need it is to simply test it. Testing with your users is a vital part of making sure you are making your information accessible. Not everyone with the same disability will have the same response – and it may depend on how they're accessing your information too.

The foundation of digital accessibility

Many of the channels used to communicate with audiences are now online. There are specific standards and guidance that can be applied to digital communications.

What is digital accessibility?

Digital accessibility means making sure that everyone, regardless of ability, can easily access and interact with websites, apps and online content. It's about designing digital spaces that work for all users, including people with disabilities, whether they use screen readers, voice commands, or need adjustable font sizes.

At its core, digital accessibility is about inclusion. It's about ensuring that no one is left out or limited in how they connect with the online world. It's not just about checking off boxes; it's about creating a better, more usable experience for everyone.[22]

From work and education to shopping and staying connected with friends and family, the internet is an essential part of daily life. If we're leaving people out because they can't access digital content, we're contributing to their exclusion from opportunities and connections.

In other words, digital accessibility is key to inclusivity.

The core principles of digital accessibility

At the heart of digital accessibility there are four key principles known as POUR – Perceivable, Operable, Understandable and Robust.[23]

These principles guide how we create digital content that everyone can access and use, no matter their abilities or the technology they rely on.

Let's dive into what each means.

Perceivable

Imagine trying to read an article on a website but the text is hidden behind an image, or watching a muted video without any captions. For some users, this is a daily reality.

The principle of perceivability ensures that information is presented in ways that can be read by all. This means providing alternative text for images, captions for videos, and making sure text can be read by screen readers. It's about making sure no one misses your content because they can't see, hear or otherwise perceive it.[24]

Operable

We all interact with websites differently. Some people use a mouse, others rely on a keyboard, and many use voice commands or other assistive technologies. The principle of operability ensures that your digital content is designed so that everyone can navigate and interact with it, no matter how they access the web.

Think of it as making sure your website's doors are open to all, whether someone is using a mouse, a keyboard or a switch device.[25]

Understandable

Even if content is perceivable and operable, that doesn't matter if it's confusing or unclear. The principle of understandability is all about making sure that users can easily comprehend your content and how to navigate through it.

This means using clear, straightforward language, designing predictable navigation, and providing help when needed. You want users to feel confident and comfortable, not frustrated or lost, when engaging with your digital content.[26]

Robust

The digital world is constantly evolving, with new devices and technologies emerging all the time. The principle of robustness ensures that your content can adapt to these changes.

It's about making sure your digital presence works across a variety of browsers, devices and assistive technologies, both now and in the future.[27]

For professional communicators, POUR is more than just a set of technical guidelines – it's a way of thinking about inclusivity in the digital space.

Whether you're crafting a website, writing an email or producing a social media post, keeping POUR in mind helps ensure that everyone can engage with your message.

A primer on assistive technology

Assistive technology (AT) is a term which refers to any tool or device that helps people with disabilities navigate and interact with the world around them. It's not new – people have been wearing glasses to help them see better for hundreds of years – although glasses-wearers may not consider themselves to have a disability (and indeed would not necessarily be classified as such either).

Imagine trying to navigate a website without being able to see it; assistive technology makes that possible. It's not just about making content accessible; it's about enabling people to actively participate in the digital world.

From screen readers that convert text into speech, to voice recognition software that allows users to control a computer without a keyboard, assistive technology lets users access digital information in a format that works for them.[28]

Whether someone has a physical, sensory or cognitive disability, AT can provide them with the tools they need to engage with digital spaces, services and information.

Not all users of technology will have the same level of technical skill, digital literacy or physical ability, and may use tools in different ways. Understanding and integrating AT considerations into our content ensures that we're reaching as many people as possible, no matter their abilities.

Types of assistive technology

Assistive technologies help break down barriers and make the internet a more inclusive place, where more people can access information and interact with websites, apps and digital content – and, increasingly, the physical world around them.

Screen readers

Screen readers turn written text into speech, making websites and digital content more accessible to people with various disabilities, including neurodiversity and sight loss.

With commonly used[29] tools like JAWS (Job Access With Speech) and NVDA (Non-Visual Desktop Access), users can navigate an entire website through voice, with descriptions of text, images, buttons and links.[30]

Even mobile devices have built-in screen readers, like VoiceOver on Apple and TalkBack on Android, making the digital world even more accessible on the go.[31]

Screen magnifiers

Screen magnifiers are sometimes used by people who have low vision or are partially sighted. These tools, like ZoomText, enlarge everything on the screen – text, images and even icons – so that users can read and interact more easily.[32]

Many modern operating systems, like Windows and macOS, come with built-in screen magnification tools to help users adjust their view for comfort and clarity.

Speech recognition software

Speech recognition software offers a hands-free way to interact with digital content. Tools like Dragon NaturallySpeaking allow users to control their computers, type documents and browse the web using only their voice.

This is especially helpful for individuals who have difficulty using a keyboard or mouse. With voice commands, they can compose emails, conduct searches and navigate through websites.[33]

Text-to-Speech (TTS)

Text-to-Speech (TTS) software is another powerful tool for people with visual impairments or learning disabilities. Instead of reading, users can have web content read aloud to them. Tools like NaturalReader and Kurzweil 3000 convert text into spoken words, helping users engage with written content, such as articles, reports or e-books, without the need to rely on visual reading.[34]

Keyboard alternatives

For individuals who have difficulty using traditional keyboards, there are many alternative input devices that can make navigating online spaces more manageable. Switch systems allow users to control a computer with a single button or switch, while on-screen keyboards let users type by selecting keys with a mouse or other pointing device. Some users may also rely on eye-tracking systems, which enable them to move the cursor and select options simply by looking at the screen.[35]

Braille displays

For some users who are deaf, blind or Deafblind, refreshable braille displays can be indispensable. These devices convert on-screen text into braille characters that users can read by touch. As they move through a web page, the braille display refreshes to show the new content, allowing users to access information online, without sound or visuals.[36]

Challenges and innovations in assistive technology

Assistive technology can help people navigate digital information, but users still face some real challenges every day.

The good news? There are many considerations being made to help with constantly breaking new ground, showing us just how much more is possible.

Challenges in assistive technology

While assistive technology has come a long way, it's not without its issues. One of the biggest challenges is cost. High-end devices, like advanced screen readers, speech recognition software or eye-tracking systems, can be expensive and out of reach for many users. This often leaves people relying on outdated or limited tools, which may not fully meet their needs.

Another issue is compatibility. Not all websites or apps are designed with AT in mind, making them difficult or even impossible for some users to navigate. Despite increasing awareness of digital accessibility, many platforms still don't fully support assistive technologies, leaving users frustrated and excluded from certain online experiences.

Complexity can also be a challenge. Some tools require a steep learning curve, especially for first-time users or those who are less tech-savvy. Navigating these systems can be overwhelming without the right support and training, which further complicates access for those who need it most.

And last, there's the issue of limited customization. Assistive technology often adopts a one-size-fits-all approach, which doesn't account for the unique needs of every user. A tool that works well for one person may not be suitable for another, yet customization options are often limited or inaccessible.[37]

As technology evolves, we're starting to see advances in AI-generated alternative text, improved automated transcription services and new ways of interacting with content. As this technology becomes more mainstream, we will hopefully see a reduction in cost, to make these more accessible for all. For more about the future, read Chapter 9.

D&I, DEI, IDEA or ABIDE: What's the difference?

Now that we've explored disability, accessibility and assistive technology, it's time to understand how they intersect with the broader world of DEI (Diversity, Equity, and Inclusion).

Creating inclusive spaces isn't just about checking boxes; it's about ensuring that everyone, regardless of ability, has equal opportunities to engage, contribute and thrive. When we talk about accessibility, we're adding an essential piece to the DEI puzzle, ensuring that inclusion truly means everyone.

With that in mind, let's break down some of the key terms and acronyms which often seem to be used interchangeably.

Diversity and Inclusion (D&I)

At its core, Diversity & Inclusion (D&I) is about recognizing and valuing differences – whether those are based on race, gender, age, abilities or experiences – and creating an environment where everyone feels welcome and respected.

Diversity is all about the mix of people in the room, while inclusion is about making sure everyone has a voice and feels valued once they're there.

Diversity, Equity & Inclusion (DEI)

Diversity, Equity & Inclusion (DEI) adds a critical layer to the conversation: equity. While diversity focuses on bringing different people together, and inclusion ensures they feel valued, equity is about fairness. It's ensuring that everyone has the support they need to succeed, even if it means different people need different types of assistance.

Inclusion, Diversity, Equity & Accessibility (IDEA)

When you see Inclusion, Diversity, Equity & Accessibility (IDEA), accessibility is added to the mix, making sure that the environment – whether it's physical, digital or cultural – is designed so everyone, regardless of ability, can participate.

IDEA acknowledges that true inclusion isn't possible unless we eliminate the barriers that keep people with disabilities from fully engaging with the world around them. In the digital space, this means making sure websites, apps and tools are accessible to all.

Accessibility, Belonging, Inclusion, Diversity, and Equity (ABIDE)

While ABIDE includes many of the elements from D&I and DEI, the focus on belonging makes it special.

Belonging goes deeper than inclusion – it's about creating a space where people don't just feel welcome but truly feel like they're an essential part of the team. It's the difference between having a seat at the table and knowing that your voice matters when decisions are made.[38]

The role of accessibility in creating inclusive spaces

Regardless of your preferred acronym, accessibility isn't just an add-on, it's a core component of creating truly inclusive environments.

Whether we're focusing on diversity or creating a sense of belonging, accessibility is the key that ensures everyone, no matter what their abilities are, can fully participate and contribute.

In frameworks like DEI, accessibility ensures that equity truly exists by providing everyone with the tools they need to succeed. In IDEA and ABIDE, accessibility is integrated from the start, making sure that inclusion isn't just a check box but a lived experience where everyone can participate meaningfully. Belonging, in particular, thrives when accessibility is embraced.

People don't just feel included, they feel like they belong and matter.

Practical examples in organizations

So, how do we make this real in the organizations we work with and for? Let's look at a few ways accessibility can be woven into these frameworks:

Physical accessibility

Organizations might ensure their buildings are fully accessible, with ramps, elevators and accessible restrooms. However, it's more than that, it's about providing adaptable workstations and ensuring all employees have access to the spaces they need to thrive. Work needs to be done to make sure all departments in an organization consider accessibility throughout the workplace. (See more in Chapter 3.)

From a communications perspective, physical accessibility is about having clear and inclusive signage that prioritizes giving people the information they need over style choices. It's about making sure posters are clear and easy to read – even if they're printed at a local depot using their black-and-white printer. It's about ensuring your offline channels of communication are usable in the environment they're read in, which might include providing options to increase – or decrease – the sound in audio announcements, to take account of people's needs and preferences. (See more in Part 2.)

Digital accessibility

This could mean making sure your company website, intranet and employee apps are accessible to people using screen readers or other assistive technologies. It's about closed captions for videos, ensuring your PDFs are screen-reader friendly, and offering multiple ways for people to engage with digital content. (See more in Part 2.)

Belonging and accessibility

Think about hosting team-building events where all employees can fully participate, regardless of ability. This might involve creating flexible participation options – whether virtual or in-person – that accommodate everyone's needs. It's not just about ensuring access but creating a culture where every employee knows they belong. (See more in Chapter 3.)

KEY TAKEAWAYS

This chapter laid the groundwork for understanding accessibility, emphasizing its critical role in creating inclusivity for everyone.

In summary:

- Accessibility isn't just about accommodations for people with disabilities, but making things easier and more usable for everyone.
- What is disability?
    - Defined what is disability and explored the differences between visible and invisible disabilities.
    - Explored the various disability models and how they may impact how we communicate.
    - Took a closer look at disability and accessibility from a global context.
- Accessible, user-centred communication uses the right format and considers the environment our users are in.
- Not all people with the same disability have the same needs – it's vital to test with our users.
- Digital accessibility is built around four foundations:
    - Perceivable
    - Operable
    - Usable
    - Robust
- Assistive technology (AT) tools like screen readers, braille displays and speech recognition software help people to interact with our communications.
- While there are barriers to entry for some assistive technology, we're starting to see a reduction in costs for some types of assistance.
- There are four key frameworks which organizations may be using:
    - Diversity & Inclusion (D&I)
    - Diversity, Equity & Inclusion (DEI)
    - Inclusion, Diversity, Equity & Accessibility (IDEA)
    - Accessibility, Belonging, Inclusion, Diversity and Equity (ABIDE)
- Organizations need to consider how to accommodate physical disabilities, make their digital channels accessible and foster a culture and approach of belonging.

References

1. Visible vs. invisible disabilities: Why it matters in the workplace, Forbes, www.forbes.com/sites/dianewiniarski/2023/10/17/visible-vs-invisible-disabilities-why-it-matters-in-the-workplace/ (archived at https://perma.cc/79WA-MYAK)
2. Disability, World Health Organization, www.who.int/news-room/fact-sheets/detail/disability-and-health (archived at https://perma.cc/MZ77-JPJK)
3. Disabled people in the world: Facts and figures, Okeenea, www.inclusivecitymaker.com/disabled-people-in-the-world-in-2021-facts-and-figures/ (archived at https://perma.cc/B3EJ-HD4W)
4. Family Resources Survey: Financial year 2022 to 2023, GOV.UK, www.gov.uk/government/statistics/family-resources-survey-financial-year-2022-to-2023/family-resources-survey-financial-year-2022-to-2023#disability-1 (archived at https://perma.cc/K4ML-Y9QP)
5. The disability rate in Canada increased in 2022, Statistics Canada, www.statcan.gc.ca/o1/en/plus/5980-disability-rate-canada-increased-2022 (archived at https://perma.cc/CF7E-C48F)
6. Dyslexia, British Dyslexia Association, www.bdadyslexia.org.uk/dyslexia (archived at https://perma.cc/66Y3-RK83)
7. Colour Blind Awareness, www.colourblindawareness.org/ (archived at https://perma.cc/25KP-B4YR)
8. Health topics – Disability, World Health Organization, www.who.int/health-topics/disability#tab=tab_1 (archived at https://perma.cc/B6DB-5N4N)
9. Inclusion of persons with disabilities is crucial for the sustainable development of Latin America and the Caribbean, World Bank Group, www.worldbank.org/en/news/press-release/2021/12/02/la-inclusion-de-las-personas-con-discapacidad-clave-para-el-desarrollo-sostenible-de-america-latina-y-el-caribe (archived at https://perma.cc/PWL4-EGDF)
10. Macro/market study annual report 2020, Return on Disability, www.rod-group.com/research-insights/annual-report-2020/ (archived at https://perma.cc/7HC9-NTPX)
11. Accessibility and disability: UK research and statistics, Scope, https://business.scope.org.uk/accessibility-and-disability-facts-and-figures/ (archived at https://perma.cc/AC2T-GCGN)
12. Inclusivity and accessibility: A smart business decision, Ontario Chamber of Commerce, https://occ.ca/inclusivity-and-accessibility-a-smart-business-decision/ (archived at https://perma.cc/7EJ3-M52W)
13. Disability in higher education, Office of Developmental Primary Care, University of California San Francisco, https://odpc.ucsf.edu/clinical/patient-centered-care/medical-and-social-models-of-disability (archived at https://perma.cc/9PN5-3E3E)

14 Y H Jung, S H Kang, E C Park and S Y Jang. Impact of the acceptance of disability on self-esteem among adults with disabilities: A four-year follow-up study, *International Journal of Environmental Research and Public Health*, 19 (7), 3874, doi: 10.3390/ijerph19073874 (archived at https://perma.cc/KB56-YQZL)

15 Disability in higher education, Office of Developmental Primary Care, University of California San Francisco, https://odpc.ucsf.edu/clinical/patient-centered-care/medical-and-social-models-of-disability (archived at https://perma.cc/KLW8-QYQ5)

16 Disability in higher education, Office of Developmental Primary Care, University of California San Francisco, https://odpc.ucsf.edu/clinical/patient-centered-care/medical-and-social-models-of-disability (archived at https://perma.cc/S5AX-TMXZ)

17 A Kafer (2013) *Feminist, Queer, Crip*, Indiana University Press, Bloomington, Indiana, p. 83

18 Conceptual models of disability and functioning, Physiopedia, www.physio-pedia.com/Conceptual_Models_of_Disability_and_Functioning (archived at https://perma.cc/78T5-5EWA)

19 What are models of disability, Christian Blind Mission, https://participation.cbm.org/why/disability-participation/models-of-disability (archived at https://perma.cc/F3NE-62D8)

20 Human rights model of disability, National Institute of Health, www.ncbi.nlm.nih.gov/books/NBK378951 (archived at https://perma.cc/V5GK-3LPD)

21 Ethical content-gathering for public communications, International Committee of the Red Cross, www.icrc.org/en/article/ethical-content-gathering-public-communications (archived at https://perma.cc/RH2B-FYPK)

22 Digital accessibility, UC Berkeley, https://dap.berkeley.edu/learn/what-digital-accessibility (archived at https://perma.cc/NJ5J-R3Z9)

23 Introduction to understanding WCAG 2.0, W3C, www.w3.org/TR/UNDERSTANDING-WCAG20/intro.html (archived at https://perma.cc/N9G2-PKWD)

24 Accessibility principles, W3C, www.w3.org/WAI/fundamentals/accessibility-principles/ (archived at https://perma.cc/K52D-SCJW)

25 Accessibility principles, W3C, www.w3.org/WAI/fundamentals/accessibility-principles/ (archived at https://perma.cc/K52D-SCJW)

26 Accessibility principles, W3C, www.w3.org/WAI/fundamentals/accessibility-principles/ (archived at https://perma.cc/K52D-SCJW)

27 Accessibility principles, W3C, www.w3.org/WAI/fundamentals/accessibility-principles/ (archived at https://perma.cc/K52D-SCJW)

28 Assistive technology, World Health Organization, www.who.int/news-room/fact-sheets/detail/assistive-technology (archived at https://perma.cc/ZA7Y-ETZZ)

29 Screen readers, CNIB Foundation, www.cnib.ca/en/screen-readers (archived at https://perma.cc/H266-DK48)
30 Screen readers, CNIB Foundation, www.cnib.ca/en/screen-readers (archived at https://perma.cc/X8TL-YVAW)
31 How do blind and visually impaired people use a mobile phone? Life of a Blind Girl, https://lifeofablindgirl.com/2019/02/03/how-do-blind-and-visually-impaired-people-use-a-mobile-phone/ (archived at https://perma.cc/YLY3-K3XX)
32 Screen magnification, RNIB, www.rnib.org.uk/living-with-sight-loss/assistive-aids-and-technology/computers/screen-magnification/ (archived at https://perma.cc/9VUW-UAZK)
33 The role of assistive technology in digital inclusion, Level Access, www.levelaccess.com/blog/assistive-technology/ (archived at https://perma.cc/7UM7-5KAV)
34 Assistive technology, Disability Insider, https://disabilityinsider.com/product/text-to-speech/ (archived at https://perma.cc/C9AF-UZYF)
35 Keyboard and mouse alternatives and adaptations, AbilityNet, https://abilitynet.org.uk/factsheets/keyboard-and-mouse-alternatives-and-adaptations (archived at https://perma.cc/P87X-RFNP)
36 Braille displays and note takers, CNIB Foundation, www.cnib.ca/en/braille-displays-and-note-takers (archived at https://perma.cc/MZ7K-QTQT)
37 Assistive technology, World Health Organization, www.who.int/news-room/fact-sheets/detail/assistive-technology (archived at https://perma.cc/28K3-GKM3)
38 What is Diversity, Equity & Inclusion (DEI)? InclusionHub, www.inclusionhub.com/articles/what-is-dei (archived at https://perma.cc/7ZFU-84WZ)

02

What you need to know to be compliant: Standards, guidelines and laws

Accessibility might seem like a maze of rules and regulations, but at its heart, it's about creating spaces – digital or otherwise – where everyone can participate and thrive. For professional communicators, understanding the standards, guidelines and laws that shape accessibility is not just about avoiding legal pitfalls; it's about demonstrating your commitment to inclusion and leading by example.

This chapter is your essential guide to the frameworks that govern accessibility, breaking down what you need to know. Whether crafting accessible content, developing an inclusive website, or planning events that welcome everyone, compliance provides the foundation for effective, ethical communication.

We'll start by demystifying the most important standards you'll encounter, like the Web Content Accessibility Guidelines (WCAG). These internationally recognized guidelines set the bar for digital accessibility and provide a roadmap for making your websites, apps and digital materials usable for people of all abilities. You'll learn more about the four core principles of WCAG – Perceivable, Operable, Understandable and Robust (POUR) – and how they translate into actionable steps for your work.

Next, we'll explore accessibility laws and regulations worldwide, from the Americans with Disabilities Act (ADA) in the US to the Accessible Canada Act (ACA) in Canada and the European Accessibility Act (EAA). Each has its own requirements and nuances, and we'll unpack what these mean for communicators. Whether your audience is local or global, knowing the legal landscape ensures your work meets the mark.

But accessibility isn't just about digital spaces – it's about every interaction and touchpoint. That's why we'll also touch on standards like PDF/UA for accessible documents and guidelines for creating inclusive physical spaces and events. Compliance stretches across formats and platforms, and this chapter will help you connect the dots.

Of course, compliance is only one piece of the puzzle. While it provides the baseline, accessibility is about going beyond the minimum to create experiences that genuinely work for everyone.

By the end of this chapter, you'll have a solid grasp of the key standards and laws you need to know and practical tips for applying them in your day-to-day work. Whether you're just beginning your accessibility journey or looking to strengthen your expertise, this chapter sets the stage for creating communications that are not only compliant but also inclusive, impactful and future ready.

Let's dive in and start building a stronger foundation for accessible communications.

The business and ethical case for compliance

Accessibility compliance isn't just about ticking boxes or following rules; it's about people. It's about ensuring everyone can engage with your content, connect with your brand, and not feel excluded from your story regardless of their abilities.

Let's explore why compliance matters, from understanding its purpose to embracing its ethical importance to recognizing the clear business benefits.

What compliance is really about

Accessibility laws and standards aim to make sure that everyone, regardless of their abilities, has equal access to information, services and opportunities. At their core, these guidelines are about removing barriers that can exclude individuals from participating fully in society.

For communicators, this means creating content, platforms and experiences that work for everyone. Compliance goals are not limited to technical check boxes; they emphasize usability, clarity and inclusivity. When you align your communications with accessibility standards, you build bridges connecting you to audiences who might otherwise be left out.

Accessibility is about making the world a little easier to navigate for everyone. Whether it's designing a website that works seamlessly with screen readers, adding captions to your videos, or ensuring documents are easy to read and navigate, these efforts collectively empower people to engage with your brand, message or organization.

The business case: Why accessibility makes sense

Accessibility isn't just a nice thing to do; it's also smart business.

> ### ACCESSIBILITY ISN'T AN EDGE CASE
>
> - **1 in 6** or 16 per cent of the global population has a significant disability – and that's just those who identify as such.[1]
> - **1 in 4** or 24 per cent of people in the UK,[2] 28.7 per cent in the USA[3] and 27 per cent in Canada[4] are classified as having a disability.
> - **1 in 3** – the World Health Organization (WHO) estimates 1 in 3 of us will need assistive technology, ranging from glasses to mobility scooters, in our lifetimes.[5]

Reach more people

According to the WHO, an estimated 1.3 billion people worldwide live with a significant disability – that's approximately 16 per cent of the global population.[6] In the UK,[7] US[8] and Canada,[9] it's estimated that one in four people are disabled. These statistics only capture those who identify as such, too – the true number may be much higher.

By making your communications accessible, you're not just meeting legal requirements, you're opening your message to a vast audience. Let's not forget that accessibility features, like captions or transcripts, are helpful to everyone, from non-native speakers to busy parents multitasking during your webinar. And the WHO also estimates that one in three of us will need assistive technology, from glasses to mobility scooters, in our lifetimes.[10]

Non-compliance also has significant opportunity costs. By failing to make websites, apps or content accessible, organizations effectively exclude a significant portion of the population, missing out on potential customers, clients or users. It's estimated that consumer companies with inaccessible websites and digital strategies lose up to $6.9 billion a year in revenue.[11]

For instance, if an online retailer's checkout process isn't keyboard navigable, users with mobility impairments may abandon their carts, leading to lost sales. Similarly, if a video campaign lacks captions, it alienates users who are deaf or hard of hearing, reducing the campaign's overall impact and reach.

Making accessibility a priority isn't just a defensive strategy; it's a forward-looking investment. Accessible practices signal that your organization is proactive, inclusive and innovative. For example, companies like Microsoft have embraced accessibility as a cornerstone of their brand identity. Their ongoing commitment to accessible products and services prevents legal and reputational risks and strengthens their market position as a leader in inclusivity.

Future-proofing your brand means recognizing that accessibility is not a trend but a fundamental aspect of business in a diverse and interconnected world. By prioritizing compliance now, you're not just avoiding trouble; you're building resilience, fostering trust and positioning your brand for long-term success.

Avoid risks

The biggest risk many organizations have faced in this area is a financial one – non-compliance can have a significant financial and reputational cost.

Non-compliance with accessibility standards often leads to lawsuits, and the financial repercussions can be steep. For instance, in the US, organizations that fail to meet the Americans with Disabilities Act (ADA) requirements for digital accessibility have faced costly lawsuits. Whether damages are awarded in the court case or not, managing a legal challenge can be costly. Deque Systems determined that a simple and quickly settled digital accessibility lawsuit could cost the defendant an estimated $350,000.[12]

In 2024 alone, there were roughly 4,280 digital accessibility lawsuits filed in the US.[13] Beyond the courtroom, the court of public opinion can be just as punishing. Inaccessible digital platforms can lead to bad press and a perception that an organization doesn't value inclusivity. For example, when major e-commerce platforms or ticketing sites are called out for inaccessibility, the backlash often extends to social media, with hashtags like #AccessibilityFail trending and public trust eroding.

HIGH-PROFILE ACCESSIBILITY LAWSUITS

Consider the following cases:

- In 2018, Fox News Network was sued for its website having barriers for people with disabilities, particularly those with sight loss.[14]
- In 2019, Domino's Pizza faced legal action after its website and app were found to be inaccessible to a blind user. The lawsuit went to the Supreme

Court, and while the company ultimately settled, the legal fees and negative publicity were substantial.[15]

- In 2019, Beyoncé's official website, under the name Parkwood Entertainment, came under scrutiny for being inaccessible to users with sight loss[16] drawing widespread media attention.
- In 2019 and 2020, Rhianna's Fenty Beauty also came under fire for having an inaccessible website for people with sight loss.[17, 18]
- In 2022, US bookstore giant Barnes & Noble faced a class action lawsuit for having an inaccessible website.[19]
- In 2023, toy company Hasbro had a class action lawsuit brought by Luis Toro, claiming the company failed to make its website fully accessible to and independently usable by people with sight loss.[20]

Enhance your reputation

When you show you care about accessibility, people notice. It's a chance to set your brand apart as inclusive, forward thinking and socially responsible. In a world where audiences pay more attention to what brands stand for, accessibility sends a powerful message about who you are.

Coles Supermarket in Australia faced legal action in 2015 over accessibility issues on its online shopping platform, highlighting significant gaps in accommodating customers with disabilities. The lawsuit served as a wake-up call, prompting the retail giant to reassess its approach to inclusivity.[21] Today, Coles has transformed its practices, earning recognition as a leader in access and inclusion for Australians with disabilities. By implementing robust accessibility measures across its digital platforms and in-store experiences, Coles has addressed past shortcomings and set a benchmark for other organizations.[22] This turnaround underscores the importance of proactive efforts in creating a genuinely inclusive customer experience.

The ethical case: It's the right thing to do

Beyond legal mandates, accessibility is an ethical commitment to inclusion and equity. It's about acknowledging that diverse abilities are part of the human experience and ensuring your communications respect and reflect that diversity.

Think about how often we rely on technology in our daily lives – whether it's reading a website, attending a virtual event or watching a video.

For someone with a disability, even a small oversight, like missing captions or poor colour contrast, can create significant barriers.

Compliance, then, is not just about avoiding lawsuits; it's about showing that your organization values all people. When you prioritize accessibility, you send a powerful message: 'We see you, we value you, and we want you to be part of our story.'

For professional communicators, this commitment translates to creating content that doesn't exclude. It's a chance to lead by example and foster a culture of respect and empathy that extends far beyond your audience to your internal teams, clients and the broader community.

The Web Content Accessibility Guidelines (WCAG): The backbone of digital accessibility

The Web Content Accessibility Guidelines (WCAG) (we usually say it out loud as wuh-cag, but some say wi-cag)[23] are central to creating an inclusive and accessible digital landscape. These guidelines provide a global standard for accessibility, helping organizations ensure their digital content is usable by everyone, including people with disabilities.

WCAG isn't just something for developers or your technical team. While some of the criteria may need to be implemented by your digital team, understanding and adhering to the principles for your digital communications means that your content can be accessed by everyone.

To understand WCAG's transformative impact, let's explore its history, principles and practical implications for communicators.

Introduction to WCAG: History, purpose and global adoption

WCAG was first introduced in 1999 by the Web Accessibility Initiative (WAI) of the World Wide Web Consortium (W3C). Its purpose was clear: to create a framework that developers, designers and communicators could follow to make web content more accessible. Over the years, WCAG has evolved, with major updates like WCAG 2.0 in 2008 and WCAG 2.1 in 2018, reflecting technological advancements and changing user needs.[24]

Globally, WCAG has been embraced as the gold standard for digital accessibility. It is referenced in legislation and policies such as the Americans with Disabilities Act (ADA) in the US, the Accessibility for Ontarians with Disabilities Act (AODA) in Canada, and the European Accessibility Act (EAA). This widespread adoption underscores its role as a universal accessibility benchmark.[25, 26]

The four principles of accessibility (POUR)

At the heart of WCAG are four guiding principles known as POUR: Perceivable, Operable, Understandable and Robust. These principles outline the foundational elements of accessible design, ensuring digital content meets diverse user needs.[27]

THE FOUR PRINCIPLES OF ACCESSIBILITY (POUR)

Perceivable: Ensuring all content can be experienced

Content must be presented in ways that users can perceive, regardless of sensory impairments. This principle includes providing:

- text alternatives for images and multimedia, such as alt text and captions
- adaptable content that works across various devices and screen sizes
- time-based media alternatives, like transcripts for audio content and audio descriptions for videos

By addressing perceivability, communicators ensure no user is excluded from accessing information.[28]

Operable: Designing interfaces everyone can navigate

Operability focuses on ensuring users can interact with content seamlessly. This involves:

- keyboard navigation which allows users to navigate without a mouse
- enough time for users to read or interact with content, such as adjustable time limits on forms
- avoiding content that could trigger seizures, like flashing animations

The operable design ensures that individuals use content using assistive technologies like screen readers or switch devices.[29]

Understandable: Making content clear and predictable

Content should be easy to understand. This involves:

- readable text with plain language principles and intuitive navigation
- predictable functionality, avoiding unexpected behaviours like sudden pop-ups
- input assistance, offering clear instructions and error suggestions

Understandable content builds trust and confidence, especially for users with cognitive disabilities.[30]

Robust: Creating adaptable content for future technologies

Digital content must be robust enough to work with current and future technologies. This includes:

- using clean, semantic HTML that aligns with web standards
- ensuring compatibility with assistive technologies, such as screen readers and braille displays

Robust content guarantees long-term accessibility as technologies evolve, making it a cornerstone of inclusive digital design.[31]

WCAG levels (A, AA, AAA): Decoding conformance

WCAG defines three levels of conformance – A, AA and AAA – to categorize the extent to which digital content adheres to accessibility standards.

Level A: Basic accessibility

Level A sets the minimum standard for accessibility. Meeting Level A ensures critical barriers, like missing alt text or non-navigable interfaces, are addressed. While essential, Level A compliance alone often falls short of delivering a fully inclusive experience.[32]

Level AA: Practical accessibility

Level AA is the most commonly targeted conformance level[33] balancing inclusivity and feasibility.[34] It includes features like:

- adequate contrast ratios for text and backgrounds
- providing captions for live videos
- designing forms with clear labels and instructions

For communicators, Level AA ensures digital content is usable by the broadest audience while maintaining reasonable technical implementation requirements.

Level AAA: Enhanced accessibility

Level AAA represents the highest level of accessibility and is often considered aspirational. Examples include:

- providing sign language interpretation for multimedia
- ensuring expanded contrast ratios for text and images
- offering multiple ways to navigate content, such as site maps or table-of-contents links

While achieving Level AAA compliance is ideal, it's not always practical for every project. Communicators should aim for AAA features where they align with audience needs.[35]

Why WCAG matters for communicators

For professional communicators, WCAG provides a roadmap for creating content that has the potential to resonate with their whole online audience. By integrating POUR principles and striving for Level AA or higher, communicators can:

- enhance brand reputation by demonstrating a commitment to inclusion
- make it easier for everyone to access and engage with your content
- avoid legal risks associated with non-compliance
- expand audience reach, particularly among the 1.3 billion people worldwide living with disabilities

WCAG as a strategic advantage

WCAG is more than a set of technical guidelines; it's a framework for fostering inclusivity in the digital space. By embracing its principles and conformance levels, communicators can ensure their content is accessible, impactful and future-ready. In doing so, they meet compliance requirements and contribute to a more equitable digital world.

Beyond the web: Standards for documents and multimedia

Accessibility is not limited to websites. It encompasses various forms of communication, including documents, multimedia, print materials and even

PDF/UA (Universal Accessibility): Standards for accessible PDF documents

PDFs remain a widely used format for reports, forms, brochures and presentations, but they often pose significant accessibility challenges if not designed with inclusivity in mind. The PDF/UA (Universal Accessibility) standard ensures that PDF documents are usable by all, including individuals relying on assistive technologies like screen readers or braille displays.[36]

Key features of PDF/UA compliance

While we'll expand on these key features in Chapter 6, it's important to understand what makes your documents PDF/UA compliant:

- Tagged content: Properly tagged text, images, and tables enable screen readers to interpret the document's structure.
- Logical reading order: Content is organized to be navigated intuitively, ensuring that users with visual impairments can follow the flow of information.
- Alternative text for images: Clear alt text conveys the meaning and context of images and graphics for all users, regardless of how they access the information.
- Form accessibility: Interactive forms include labelled fields and keyboard-navigable elements, enabling users with disabilities to complete forms independently.

Why it matters

PDF/UA compliance is critical for ensuring that essential documents, such as contracts, annual reports or policy papers, are accessible. Providing this information in an alternative format like HTML helps make it easier for people to access information. Where PDFs are seen as necessary formats, communicators should incorporate accessible PDF practices into their workflows and utilize tools like the PDF Accessibility Checker (PAC) to validate compliance.[37]

Multimedia accessibility guidelines: Applying accessibility to videos, podcasts and more

With the rise of video and audio content in communications strategies, ensuring accessibility for multimedia is no longer optional; it's an expectation. Multimedia accessibility guidelines provide actionable steps to make videos, podcasts and other media formats inclusive.

Key accessibility features for multimedia

- Captions and subtitles: Real-time captions and subtitles ensure that videos are accessible to deaf and hard-of-hearing audiences.[38] Tools like YouTube, Rev and Adobe Premiere streamline the captioning process.
- Audio descriptions: For visually impaired users, audio descriptions narrate important visual elements in videos, ensuring they can follow the content fully.
- Transcripts: Detailed transcripts for podcasts and videos allow audiences who prefer or require text-based content to engage with the material.
- Visual accessibility: High-contrast visuals, large text sizes, and avoidance of flashing elements help make multimedia content clearer and safer for all viewers, including those with low vision or photosensitive epilepsy.

We'll be going more in-depth on these topics in Chapter 8.

Print materials and physical spaces: Accessibility outside the digital world

While digital content takes centre stage in many communications strategies, accessibility considerations for print materials and physical spaces remain equally important. For organizations that rely on in-person interactions or traditional media, inclusivity must extend beyond screens.

Accessible print materials[39]

- Readable fonts and layouts: Use clear, sans-serif fonts (e.g. Arial or Verdana) and maintain a font size of at least 12 points to improve readability.
- High-contrast design: Ensure sufficient contrast between text and background colours to enhance visibility.

- Braille and large print options: Providing materials in braille or large print formats allows individuals with visual impairments to access the content.
- Clear language: Plain language principles make printed materials understandable to a broader audience, including those with cognitive disabilities.

We'll go more in-depth on these topics in Chapters 4 and 6.

The importance of a holistic approach

Accessibility spans multiple mediums. Creating accessible PDFs, multimedia, printed materials and physical spaces builds an inclusive environment for everyone. For professional communicators, understanding and applying these standards is not just about meeting legal requirements; it's about building trust, equity and connection with diverse audiences.

By embracing these practices, organizations position themselves as leaders in accessibility, ensuring their messages can resonate with everyone, regardless of format or platform.

Key accessibility laws and regulations worldwide

Understanding the global legal landscape of accessibility is essential for communicators who operate in a connected, digital-first world. Accessibility laws and regulations vary by region, but they share a common goal: ensuring people with disabilities have equal access to information, products and services.

Here's an in-depth look at the key accessibility frameworks worldwide and their implications for professional communicators.

Americans with Disabilities Act (ADA): Overview

The Americans with Disabilities Act (ADA), signed into law in 1990, is one of the most comprehensive civil rights legislations addressing the rights of individuals with disabilities. It prohibits discrimination and ensures equal opportunities in all areas of public life, including employment, education, transportation and public accommodations. For communicators, understanding the ADA's scope and its evolving interpretations is critical for ensuring compliance and fostering inclusivity.[40]

A closer look at the ADA

The ADA is divided into five titles, each addressing different areas of public life:

1. Title I: Employment protections.
2. Title II: Public services and state/local government programmes.
3. Title III: Public accommodations, including businesses and non-profits.
4. Title IV: Telecommunications.
5. Title V: Miscellaneous provisions.

For professional communicators, Title II and Title III are the most relevant. Title II requires state and local governments to make their services accessible, while Title III extends these obligations to private businesses, particularly regarding physical and digital public-facing spaces.[41]

Digital accessibility and Title III

Although the ADA was written before the digital age, courts and policymakers have increasingly interpreted Title III to include digital spaces, such as websites, apps, and other online platforms. Businesses categorized as 'public accommodations' (e.g. retailers, hotels, healthcare providers and educational institutions) must ensure their digital properties are accessible to individuals with disabilities.

This interpretation has resulted in a growing number of lawsuits and legal challenges related to inaccessible websites. The Department of Justice (DOJ) has clarified that the ADA applies to digital content, emphasizing the need for accessible websites and mobile applications to ensure equal access.[42]

Title II regulatory updates and online accessibility

The updated Title II regulations, outlined in documents such as the DOJ's latest interpretations, reiterate the importance of ensuring accessibility for state and local government programmes. These guidelines require clear communication, accessible formats, and auxiliary aids to accommodate people with disabilities, such as:

- text-to-speech technologies
- closed captioning for videos
- properly structured HTML for screen readers

These measures highlight the ADA's broader intent: removing barriers to physical or digital participation.[43]

ADA and WCAG: The unofficial standard

While the ADA itself does not specify technical standards for digital accessibility, the Web Content Accessibility Guidelines (WCAG) have become the de facto benchmark. Courts and regulators often reference WCAG 2.1 Level AA as the standard organizations should meet to ensure compliance.[44]

KEY TAKEAWAYS FOR COMMUNICATORS

Legal relevance: ADA compliance for digital properties is not explicitly codified, but failure to adhere to WCAG standards can lead to lawsuits. Over 4,600 ADA-related website accessibility cases were filed in 2023 alone, underscoring the legal risks of non-compliance.[45]

Expanding reach: Beyond legal obligations, ensuring digital accessibility allows businesses to engage a broader audience. Over 70 million adults in the US live with some form of disability, representing a significant market segment.[46]

Future-proofing: As digital accessibility laws evolve, organizations adhering to WCAG today position themselves for smoother compliance with potential future regulations.

By aligning with ADA requirements and embracing accessibility as a core value, communicators not only reduce legal risks but also build stronger, more inclusive connections with their audiences.

Accessible Canada Act (ACA)

The Accessible Canada Act (ACA), enacted in 2019, is a groundbreaking federal law designed to eliminate barriers and promote accessibility for people with disabilities across Canada. It aims to create a fully accessible Canada by 2040, focusing on systemic change to ensure inclusion and equity in federally regulated sectors. For communicators in Canada, or in global teams which include Canadian audiences, understanding the ACA's provisions is vital to aligning messaging, platforms and practices with its accessibility objectives.[47]

A closer look at the ACA

The ACA applies to federally regulated organizations, including:

- federal government departments and agencies
- Crown corporations
- transportation industries (airlines, railways and ferries)
- banking and telecommunications sectors

Its primary goal is to identify, prevent and remove barriers that hinder people with disabilities in communication, employment, transportation and access to goods and services.

Seven priority areas

The ACA targets barriers in seven key areas, several of which directly impact communications:[48, 49]

1. Employment: Inclusive hiring practices and accessible workplace policies.
2. Built environment: Barrier-free physical spaces.
3. Communication and technology: Accessible websites, documents and communication channels.
4. Transportation: Accessibility in federally regulated transportation services.
5. Procurement: Accessible goods and services in government purchasing.
6. Programmes and services: Equitable access to government programmes and services.
7. Information and communication: Clear, accessible and inclusive communications.

Accessibility standards and planning

The ACA requires federally regulated entities (Government of Canada entities, including departments and agencies; Crown corporations, every portion of the federal public administration designated under subsection 7(3) of the ACA, the Canadian Forces, parliamentary entities, and federally regulated private sector entities) to develop and implement accessibility plans.[50] These plans must be proactive, addressing barriers and detailing measures for compliance. Additionally, organizations must consult people with disabilities when creating accessibility plans, ensuring their lived experiences guide decision-making.

Progress reporting and feedback
Organizations must report on their progress towards achieving accessibility goals and establish mechanisms for receiving and addressing public feedback on their accessibility practices.

Enforcement and oversight
The ACA includes robust enforcement mechanisms to ensure compliance, including:

- The Accessibility Commissioner: Responsible for investigating complaints and issuing compliance orders.
- The Canadian Transportation Agency (CTA): Enforces accessibility in transportation.
- The Canadian Radio-television and Telecommunications Commission (CRTC): Oversees accessibility in broadcasting and telecommunications.[51]

Implications for communicators
For Canadian communicators, the ACA emphasizes the importance of accessible communication strategies across all platforms. Key implications include:

- Digital accessibility: Websites, mobile apps and digital content must be perceivable, operable, understandable and robust, aligning with Web Content Accessibility Guidelines (WCAG) 2.1 Level AA.
- Inclusive content: All public-facing documents, media and messaging must be accessible. This includes providing alternate formats, such as large print, braille or audio, upon request.
- Consultation and collaboration: Communicators should actively engage with people with disabilities to ensure their insights inform messaging and design.
- Transparency: Accessibility plans and progress reports must be clearly communicated to the public, showcasing organizational commitment to inclusion.

The ACA and the broader Canadian accessibility landscape
The ACA complements provincial legislation, such as the Accessibility for Ontarians with Disabilities Act (AODA), providing a unified framework for accessibility across Canada. While the ACA governs federal organizations, its principles and standards set an example for non-regulated entities to follow, fostering a culture of accessibility nationwide.

The ACA is not just about compliance; it represents a vision for an inclusive society where accessibility is a shared responsibility. By addressing systemic barriers and fostering collaboration, it creates opportunities for individuals with disabilities to participate fully in Canadian life.

By embracing the principles of the ACA, communicators in Canada can help foster an inclusive culture that aligns with national goals and sets a standard for accessible communications worldwide. Through thoughtful planning and proactive implementation, accessibility becomes not just a legal obligation but a cornerstone of effective and equitable communication.[52]

Accessibility for Ontarians with Disabilities Act (AODA) and Canada's provincial accessibility legislation: Building a nation of inclusion

Canada is a leader in accessibility, with its provinces and territories enacting laws to ensure equal access and participation for people with disabilities. Among these, the Accessibility for Ontarians with Disabilities Act (AODA) stands out as one of the most comprehensive. Yet, it is vital to recognize the broader accessibility framework across the country, as various provinces have their own unique legislation aimed at fostering inclusion.[53]

AODA: Ontario's blueprint for accessibility

Enacted in 2005, the AODA aimed to create a fully accessible Ontario by 2025. It mandates organizations in both the public and private sectors to identify, prevent and eliminate barriers to accessibility.

The AODA sets accessibility standards in five key areas:

1 Customer service: Ensuring services are accessible to people with disabilities, such as offering alternative communication methods or accommodating service animals.
2 Information and communication: Requiring organizations to provide accessible formats and communications, including websites that meet Web Content Accessibility Guidelines (WCAG) 2.0 Level AA.
3 Employment: Enforcing accessible hiring practices and workplace accommodations.
4 Transportation: Making public transit systems inclusive, from signage to seating arrangements.
5 Built environment: Addressing physical barriers in buildings and public spaces.

Organizations must file compliance reports, outlining their progress towards meeting AODA standards. Compliance isn't optional – Ontario's Ministry of Seniors and Accessibility actively enforces the legislation through audits and inspections.[54]

Failure to comply with AODA standards can result in significant penalties:

- For corporations: Fines of up to $100,000 per day for each day of non-compliance.
- For individuals or unincorporated organizations: Fines of up to $50,000 per day for each day of non-compliance.
- For directors or officers: Personal liability for fines if it's shown they failed to take reasonable precautions to prevent the organization's non-compliance.[55]

These penalties underscore the importance of integrating accessibility into organizational policies and practices.

Why AODA matters to communicators

For communicators, the AODA emphasizes the importance of accessible messaging across all platforms:

- Digital accessibility: Websites and online materials must meet WCAG standards, ensuring they are usable for people with visual, auditory, cognitive and motor disabilities.
- Accessible content: Public-facing documents, social media posts and videos must be designed with inclusivity in mind, offering alternative formats when requested.
- Internal communication: Employers must ensure that workplace communications are accessible, fostering an inclusive culture.

Other provincial accessibility legislation in Canada

While the AODA is a leading example, other provinces have enacted accessibility laws that reflect regional priorities and needs. Here's an overview:

Manitoba: The Accessibility for Manitobans Act (AMA) Passed in 2013, the AMA aimed to make Manitoba fully accessible by 2023. Like the AODA, it establishes standards in areas such as customer service, employment, and information and communication. Non-compliance can result in administrative penalties or fines, emphasizing the importance of adherence.[56]

Nova Scotia: Accessibility Act Nova Scotia's Accessibility Act, passed in 2017, aims to make the province accessible by 2030. It emphasizes collaborative policy-making with individuals with disabilities and sets standards for education, employment and the built environment. Enforcement includes public reporting and compliance orders.[57]

British Columbia: Accessible British Columbia Act Enacted in 2021, this act establishes a framework for identifying and removing barriers in public and private sectors. Non-compliance can result in sanctions, including monetary penalties, making adherence a legal obligation.[58]

Quebec: Act to Secure Handicapped Persons in the Exercise of Their Rights Quebec's Act, originally passed in 1978 and revised over the years, focuses on promoting equal opportunities for people with disabilities. Enforcement mechanisms include mandatory reporting and public accountability for public sector organizations.[59]

Other efforts across Canada In 2025, it's noted that other efforts are being made across Canada to be more accessible, including:

- Saskatchewan, Newfoundland and Labrador: Developing accessibility legislation with a focus on removing barriers in public spaces, services and employment.[60]
- Prince Edward Island. While this province currently lacks specific accessibility legislation, it encourages inclusive practices through human rights codes and provincial policies.
- Yukon, Northwest Territories and Nunavut: Accessibility efforts are governed primarily by territorial human rights legislation, focusing on eliminating discrimination.

Aligning with provincial legislation: What communicators need to know

For communicators, provincial accessibility laws highlight the need to ensure content is accessible and inclusive:

- Understand regional standards: Familiarize yourself with the specific accessibility requirements in your province or territory, as they may differ significantly.
- Create accessible digital content: Whether under the AODA, AMA, or another framework, prioritize WCAG compliance for websites, documents and social media.

- Engage with local communities: Consult with people with disabilities in your region to ensure your messaging resonates and meets their needs.
- Promote accessibility beyond compliance: Use your platform to advocate for accessibility as a value, not just a legal requirement.

As provincial and federal accessibility laws evolve, communicators have a unique opportunity to lead the charge in fostering inclusion. By aligning with legislation like the AODA and leveraging best practices across Canada, you can ensure your messaging reaches and resonates with all audiences. Accessibility isn't just a legal obligation; it's a chance to build trust, enhance brand reputation and champion equity in every interaction.

European Accessibility Act (EAA): Shaping accessibility standards in the EU

The European Accessibility Act (EAA), adopted in 2019, is a pivotal piece of legislation to harmonize accessibility requirements across the European Union (EU). By establishing common standards for products and services, the EAA seeks to remove barriers for individuals with disabilities, enhance the accessibility of the internal market, and promote inclusion. Its broad scope encompasses a wide array of industries and communication channels, making it a significant consideration for communicators and businesses operating within the EU.[61]

A comprehensive framework for accessibility

The EAA complements and extends existing EU accessibility legislation, including the EU Web Accessibility Directive. While the Web Accessibility Directive primarily applies to public sector websites and mobile applications, the EAA extends accessibility requirements to private sector services and products. This expansion ensures that accessibility is not limited to government entities but becomes a standard practice for businesses catering to the public.[62]

Key areas of applications

The EAA applies to a range of products and services, including but not limited to:[63]

- E-commerce platforms: Online stores must ensure their platforms are navigable and usable by individuals with disabilities, meeting WCAG standards for digital accessibility.

- Digital banking services: Banking apps and online platforms must be designed to accommodate users with disabilities, ensuring secure and accessible transactions.
- Public-facing websites: Companies must provide accessible web content to comply with the EAA's requirements.
- Ticketing machines and ATMs: Physical devices must incorporate accessible design, such as tactile interfaces and audio guidance.
- Consumer electronics: Smartphones, computers and other devices must be designed with accessibility, including features like screen readers and adjustable font sizes.

Harmonized standards for the EU market

One of the EAA's primary goals is to create a unified set of accessibility standards across the EU. This harmonization is crucial for businesses that operate in multiple member states, as it simplifies compliance by eliminating the need to navigate varying national regulations.

The EAA mandates compliance with recognized accessibility standards, such as WCAG 2.1 Level AA for digital content. Specific requirements include:[64]

- Perceivable content: Ensuring that text, images and other content can be easily perceived by users, including those with visual or auditory impairments.
- Operable interfaces: Designing navigation systems and interactive elements that can be used by individuals with motor or cognitive disabilities.
- Understandable design: Creating content that is clear and easy to comprehend, reducing complexity for all users.
- Robust compatibility: Ensuring that products and services work seamlessly with assistive technologies like screen readers and braille displays.

Implications for professional communicators

For communicators working within the EU, the EAA presents both challenges and opportunities. Understanding and implementing these requirements is essential for maintaining compliance and delivering accessible, inclusive content.

Key considerations for communicators

- Accessible messaging: Digital campaigns, websites and apps must meet WCAG standards to align with EAA requirements.

- Inclusive customer service: Providing accessible communication channels, such as live chat with screen reader compatibility or email support in accessible formats, is critical. While the specific product or platform design may be outside the scope of regular communications activities, working with product teams to ensure the accessible formats are also on brand is something to consider.
- Cross-border consistency: For businesses operating in multiple EU countries, harmonized standards simplify the process of creating universally accessible content.[65]

Alignment with the EU Web Accessibility Directive

The EAA builds upon the foundation laid by the EU Web Accessibility Directive, which came into effect in 2016. While the directive focuses on the public sector, the EAA extends similar obligations to private enterprises, ensuring a broader reach.[66]

Key differences and complementary goals

- The Web Accessibility Directive mandates that public sector websites and mobile apps meet WCAG 2.1 Level AA standards.
- The EAA broadens this scope to include private sector services, such as e-commerce, banking and telecommunications.

Together, these laws ensure that accessibility is a priority across all sectors, creating a more inclusive digital landscape for EU citizens.

Enforcement and penalties

The EAA requires member states to incorporate its provisions into national law, with full compliance effective from 28 June 2025. Enforcement mechanisms include regular audits, response to user complaints and penalties for non-compliance. Fines and corrective actions vary by country, but the overarching goal is to incentivize adherence and ensure accessibility becomes the norm.[67]

Global significance of the EAA

The EAA's harmonized approach to accessibility sets a benchmark for other regions, positioning the EU as a leader in inclusive design. For multinational organizations, aligning with EAA standards can serve as a best practice, even in markets where accessibility regulations are less stringent. It not only ensures compliance within the EU but also enhances brand reputation and demonstrates a commitment to inclusion on a global scale.

Looking ahead: The role of communicators

As the EAA continues to shape accessibility standards in the EU, communicators have a critical role to play. By prioritizing accessibility in their own content and influencing standards – both internally and with suppliers – they can help bridge gaps and foster a culture of inclusion.

Understanding the EAA and aligning with its principles is not just a legal obligation; it's an opportunity to lead the way in creating a more equitable digital future.

The Equality Act 2010 (Great Britain), Disability Discrimination Act 1995 (Northern Ireland) and UK Public Sector Accessibility Regulations

The Equality Act of 2010 (EQA) is the cornerstone of disability rights legislation which applies to England, Wales and Scotland. The EQA replaced the 1995 Disability Discrimination Act (DDA) across the UK, with the exception of Northern Ireland.

The Equality Act prohibits discrimination against people with the protected characteristics that are specified in section 4 of the Act. Disability is one of the specified protected characteristics, and both acts prohibit discrimination based on disability across goods, services and employment.[68]

You may have heard the phrase 'reasonable adjustments' used in conversation; essentially communicators need to take accessibility needs into account in all that they do, where it is possible to do so.

Under the Public Sector Bodies (Websites and Mobile Applications) (No. 2) Accessibility Regulations 2018, public sector organizations are required to meet WCAG 2.2 Level AA standards for their websites and mobile applications.[69]

Key features of the regulations:

- Accessibility statements: Public sector websites must publish an accessibility statement outlining their compliance status and steps being taken to address any shortcomings.
- Regular audits: Organizations are encouraged to monitor their digital content for accessibility and make improvements as needed.

The Equality and Human Rights Commission (EHRC) oversees compliance with the EQA in Great Britain, the Equality Commission for Northern Ireland oversees the DDA in NI, while the Government Digital Service (GDS) monitors public sector adherence to the WCAG-based regulations. Non-compliance can lead to investigations, reputational damage and potential legal actions.

Other regional accessibility regulations: A global perspective

Accessibility standards and laws vary widely across regions, reflecting local contexts and priorities. While the EEA in Europe aims to standardize accessibility standards across its member states, the ACA in Canada supplements the provincial standards.

Below is an overview of how Australia, Japan and Ireland approach accessibility, with a focus on their legal frameworks and digital content requirements.

Australia: Disability Discrimination Act (DDA) of 1992

Australia's Disability Discrimination Act (DDA) is a landmark piece of legislation that mandates equal access to goods, services and facilities for people with disabilities. Although the DDA does not specifically address digital accessibility, the Australian Human Rights Commission has clarified that websites and online services fall under the Act's scope.[70]

Key requirements and standards:

- The DDA emphasizes equal opportunity, meaning businesses and organizations must ensure their digital content is accessible to all users.
- The Australian government considers WCAG 2.1 Level AA the benchmark for meeting accessibility obligations under the DDA.
- The National Transition Strategy has been instrumental in guiding Australian organizations, particularly in the public sector, towards compliance with WCAG standards.

Complaints about non-compliance can be lodged with the Australian Human Rights Commission. Organizations found in violation may face legal consequences, including fines or mandated corrective actions.[71]

Japan: Basic Act for Persons with Disabilities

Japan's Basic Act for Persons with Disabilities provides a broad framework for ensuring accessibility and inclusion. Although the Act does not impose strict legal mandates for private organizations, it establishes principles that encourage accessibility in various sectors, including digital communication.

The key accessibility initiatives:

- The JIS X 8341-3 Standard, aligned with WCAG, provides specific guidelines for making web content accessible in Japan.
- Public sector organizations and many private companies voluntarily adopt WCAG 2.1 Level AA standards as a best practice to ensure inclusivity.[72]

In Japan, accessibility often intersects with cultural values of harmony and respect. Organizations prioritize user-centred design, focusing on making content usable for diverse audiences, including older adults, given Japan's ageing population.

Ireland: Disability Act 2005 and Public Sector Accessibility Directive

Ireland has made significant strides in promoting accessibility through the Disability Act 2005 and its alignment with broader European Union accessibility initiatives. The Act establishes obligations for public bodies to ensure that their services, including digital content, are accessible to people with disabilities.

As part of the EU, Ireland complies with the Web Accessibility Directive, which mandates that public sector websites and mobile apps meet WCAG 2.1 Level AA standards.

Key provisions include:

- Public sector focus: The directive requires Irish public bodies to ensure their digital platforms are accessible, publish accessibility statements, and implement mechanisms for user feedback.
- Legislation extension: The Disability Act extends to private organizations that provide services to the public, emphasizing the importance of equal access.

The National Disability Authority (NDA) oversees accessibility compliance in Ireland. Complaints about non-compliance can lead to investigations and potential sanctions, emphasizing the importance of adhering to accessibility standards.[73]

Global accessibility trends and implications

As accessibility standards evolve, global trends are emerging that influence local regulations and best practices. Key trends include:

- Harmonization of standards: With WCAG serving as the de facto global standard, countries increasingly align their regulations with its guidelines. Communicators can benefit from adopting WCAG Level AA universally to ensure compliance across jurisdictions.
- Focus on private sector accountability: Governments worldwide are extending accessibility obligations to private businesses, making it essential for communicators to prioritize accessibility in all digital assets.
- Increased litigation: High-profile lawsuits, particularly in the US, highlight the risks of non-compliance. Staying ahead of accessibility requirements is not just about inclusion; it's also about mitigating legal exposure.
- Technological advancements: Tools and platforms are evolving to make accessibility easier to implement, such as automated testing software and AI-driven captioning services. Communicators should leverage these innovations while maintaining human oversight.
- Global inclusion initiatives: International organizations like the United Nations emphasize accessibility as a fundamental human right. Communicators must consider how their work contributes to a more inclusive digital world.

Why this matters for communicators

Compliance with accessibility laws and regulations is not just about avoiding fines or lawsuits; it's about creating meaningful connections with diverse audiences.

By understanding and adhering to global accessibility requirements, professional communicators can:

- enhance brand reputation by demonstrating a commitment to inclusion
- expand their reach to include the 1.3 billion people worldwide living with disabilities
- build trust and loyalty among all stakeholders, showcasing a dedication to equitable practices

In an increasingly connected world, accessibility compliance is not just a legal obligation; it's a strategic advantage that sets forward-thinking communicators apart. By staying informed and proactive, you can ensure your work is inclusive, impactful and future-ready.

Challenges and common pitfalls in compliance

Creating accessible communications is an essential goal for modern organizations, but achieving compliance is not without its hurdles. While accessibility laws and guidelines provide a clear framework, the journey to compliance is often fraught with challenges. Misunderstanding legal requirements, over-reliance on automation, and balancing creativity with compliance can all create roadblocks for even the most well-intentioned teams.

Let's unpack these challenges and explore strategies to overcome them.

Misunderstanding legal requirements

Accessibility laws and guidelines, while detailed, can sometimes be difficult to interpret or apply. Misunderstanding these requirements is a common pitfall that can lead to unintentional non-compliance.

Common misconceptions

One-size-fits-all assumption:

Many organizations mistakenly believe that compliance with a single standard, such as WCAG, automatically fulfils all legal requirements. However, different jurisdictions may have unique mandates, such as the AODA in Ontario or the ADA in the US, which require a more nuanced approach.

Confusing accessibility with usability:

While accessibility ensures that content is available to individuals with disabilities, usability focuses on the overall ease of use for all users. Misunderstanding this distinction can result in designs that technically comply with standards but fail to provide a truly accessible and usable experience.

Assuming accessibility is a one-time fix:

Compliance is often treated as a project with a defined endpoint rather than an ongoing commitment. Accessibility requirements evolve and failing to update regularly and audit content can result in lapses over time.

How to avoid missteps

Education and training:

Invest in training for teams to ensure they fully understand the specific accessibility laws and standards relevant to your region and industry.

Legal consultation:

Engage legal experts or accessibility consultants who can provide clarity on complex regulations and help align your practices with the latest requirements.

Continuous monitoring:

Implement a process for regular audits to ensure compliance is maintained as technology and standards evolve.

Test with and listen to your audience:

Different people have different access needs. Testing your communications with your audiences will help you understand their specific requirements and make sure your communications have the biggest impact.

Over-reliance on automation

Automation tools can be invaluable for identifying accessibility issues, but they are not a cure-all and not all tools are created equal. Over-reliance on these tools can result in superficial fixes that leave deeper issues unresolved.

Limitations of automation

Partial coverage:

Automated accessibility checkers can identify errors like missing alt text, improper heading structures or contrast issues, but they cannot evaluate the context or effectiveness of the fixes. For example, an automated tool might flag an image without alt text, but cannot determine whether the provided alt text conveys the image's purpose effectively.

Lack of nuance:

Automation cannot assess subjective aspects of accessibility, such as whether language is clear and inclusive or whether a multimedia description provides meaningful context.

False positives and negatives:

Automated tools are not always accurate, sometimes missing critical issues or flagging elements as problematic when they are not. This can create a false sense of security or lead to unnecessary adjustments.

False claims of effectiveness:

In 2025, the Federal Trade Commission ruled that New York-based accessiBe was making inflated claims about their accessibility software.[74] The company claimed that their software 'can make any website compliant with WCAG', which was proven to be false; they were also found to be misrepresenting online reviews as being impartial.[75]

The role of human oversight

Manual testing:

Combine automated checks with manual testing by individuals trained in accessibility. This ensures a thorough evaluation of both technical and experiential aspects of content.

User testing:

Involve people with disabilities in the testing process to gain insights into real-world accessibility challenges and confirm that your solutions work effectively for your audience. Different users have different levels of technical awareness and digital literacy and may use the same assistive technology differently.

Continuous improvement:

Use automation as a starting point, but rely on human expertise to refine and validate the results.

Balancing compliance with creativity

For many communicators, accessibility compliance can feel like a constraint on creativity. The perception that adhering to strict guidelines stifles innovation is a common challenge, but it doesn't have to be true.

The perceived tension

Design constraints:

Accessibility standards may require changes to visual designs, such as increasing font sizes, ensuring colour contrast or simplifying layouts. These adjustments can feel limiting to designers aiming for visually striking content. However, making visuals have a clearer contrast makes them easier to read for everyone.

Content simplification:

Writing in plain language and avoiding jargon can be seen as diluting the sophistication of messaging, particularly for high-level or technical audiences. We'll talk more about this in the next chapter, but it's been proven that even technical audiences prefer plain language.[76]

Multimedia accessibility:

Adding captions, transcripts, or audio descriptions can increase production time and costs, which may deter creative teams from incorporating these elements into their workflows. However, it's easier than ever to provide transcripts and descriptions and they help more people access your media – and there's more on this in Chapter 8.

Strategies for harmonizing compliance and creativity

Embrace accessibility as a creative challenge:

Instead of viewing accessibility as a limitation, treat it as an opportunity to innovate. For example, designing with simplicity and clarity often leads to more engaging and user-friendly experiences for all audiences.

Leverage inclusive design principles:

Incorporate accessibility into the creative process from the start. Collaborating with accessibility experts and end users during brainstorming and prototyping phases can inspire fresh ideas that prioritize inclusion.

Find flexibility within standards:

Accessibility guidelines provide a framework but leave room for interpretation and creativity. Experiment with layouts, typography and multimedia elements that meet standards while still reflecting your brand's unique voice and style.

Overcoming challenges: A path forward

Navigating the complexities of accessibility compliance requires a balanced approach that combines technical expertise, creativity and a commitment to inclusivity. By addressing misconceptions about legal requirements, using automation as a tool rather than a crutch, and reframing accessibility as a driver of innovation, organizations can overcome these common pitfalls.

Ultimately, accessibility is about creating connections, ensuring that everyone, regardless of ability, can engage meaningfully with your content. By embracing this mindset, communicators can achieve compliance while delivering impactful, inclusive and creative experiences that resonate with all audiences – and ultimately increase the potential audience size too!

This chapter started by considering the business and ethical case for compliance and why it's important. It brought together the essential standards, laws and strategies that form the foundation of accessibility compliance in communications. It tackled challenges like overreliance on automation and balancing creativity with compliance. This helps build a road map to make your communications accessible, inclusive and impactful.

Summarizing the standards

We examined the major accessibility standards and laws that guide inclusive practices:

- WCAG (Web Content Accessibility Guidelines): The global gold standard for digital accessibility, anchored in the principles of Perceivable, Operable, Understandable and Robust (POUR). These guidelines outline the necessary steps for creating web content that works for everyone, regardless of ability or technology.
- PDF/UA (PDF Universal Accessibility): The benchmark for creating accessible documents, ensuring PDFs are navigable and usable by assistive technologies.
- ADA (Americans with Disabilities Act): US legislation requiring equal access in both physical and digital spaces, emphasizing the importance of compliant websites and public-facing platforms.
- AODA (Accessibility for Ontarians with Disabilities Act): A progressive framework mandating clear compliance timelines and reporting requirements for accessibility in Ontario.
- EAA (European Accessibility Act): The EU's harmonized approach to accessibility, applying to public and private sectors alike.
- The Equality Act 2010 (Great Britain), Disability Discrimination Act 1995 (Northern Ireland) and UK Public Sector Accessibility Regulations: How Great Britain and Northern Ireland are reducing disability discrimination and making public services more accessible to all.
- Other regional regulations: Accessibility laws in Australia, the UK, Ireland and Japan, showcasing both alignment with global goals and unique regional priorities.

Together, these standards and laws create a shared vision of removing barriers and ensuring equitable access for everyone.

Pitfalls and challenges

Compliance isn't without its hurdles, and this chapter highlighted some of the most common pitfalls:

- Misunderstanding legal requirements: Many organizations struggle to translate abstract legal language into actionable steps.
- Over-reliance on automation: Automated tools are invaluable but require human oversight to address nuances and context-specific needs.

- Balancing creativity with compliance: Navigating the tension between producing engaging, innovative content and adhering to accessibility standards is an ongoing challenge.

By identifying these challenges, we provided strategies to overcome them, ensuring your path to compliance is clear and effective.

Looking ahead

Accessibility standards continue to evolve alongside advancements in technology and changes in societal expectations. Here's how you can prepare:

- Stay current: Follow updates to WCAG and PDF/UA standards while monitoring new legislation in key markets.
- Leverage innovation: Adopt emerging tools like AI-driven captioning and assistive technologies to enhance accessibility.
- Embed accessibility in strategy: Make accessibility a core element of every project, ensuring workflows are adaptive and future-proof.

This chapter emphasized that accessibility isn't just about compliance – it's about creating inclusion, building trust and expanding your reach. By understanding the standards, navigating the challenges and taking actionable steps, you're not just meeting requirements – you're becoming a leader in accessible communications. Together, we can ensure that every message truly resonates with all audiences, no matter where or how they engage.

References

1 Disability, World Health Organization, www.who.int/news-room/fact-sheets/detail/disability-and-health (archived at https://perma.cc/6R5W-H5YE)
2 UK disability statistics: Prevalence and life experiences, UK Parliament, https://commonslibrary.parliament.uk/research-briefings/cbp-9602/ (archived at https://perma.cc/6ZMV-KN34)
3 Disability impacts all of us infographic, Centre for Disease Control and Prevention, www.cdc.gov/disability-and-health/articles-documents/disability-impacts-all-of-us-infographic.html (archived at https://perma.cc/S7G7-2RCZ)
4 The disability rate in Canada increased in 2022, Statistics Canada, www.statcan.gc.ca/o1/en/plus/5980-disability-rate-canada-increased-2022 (archived at https://perma.cc/P7ZP-3LRW)
5 Assistive technology, World Health Organization, www.who.int/news-room/fact-sheets/detail/assistive-technology (archived at https://perma.cc/APL4-69XR)
6 Disability, World Health Organization, www.who.int/health-topics/disability#tab=tab_1 (archived at https://perma.cc/S9B2-ZZV2)

7. Family Resources Survey: Financial year 2022 to 2023, www.gov.uk/government/statistics/family-resources-survey-financial-year-2022-to-2023/family-resources-survey-financial-year-2022-to-2023#disability-1 (archived at https://perma.cc/MB7N-SYSB)
8. CDC data shows over 70 million U.S. adults reported having a disability, Centers for Disease Control and Prevention, www.cdc.gov/media/releases/2024/s0716-Adult-disability.html (archived at https://perma.cc/V987-E2R6)
9. Statistical Information Service, StatCAN Plus, The disability rate in Canada increased in 2022, www.statcan.gc.ca/o1/en/plus/5980-disability-rate-canada-increased-2022 (archived at https://perma.cc/WP9U-3ZYH)
10. 2.5 billion people need assistive technology globally, Assistive Technology Factsheet, World Health Organization, www.who.int/news-room/fact-sheets/detail/assistive-technology (archived at https://perma.cc/8DPP-YAJ6)
11. R Wettemann and T White. The internet is unavailable, Nucleus Research, https://cdn2.hubspot.net/hubfs/153358/Nucleus-The%20Internet%20is%20unavailable.pdf (archived at https://perma.cc/5MDJ-XEPR)
12. The true cost of website inaccessibility, Corporate Compliance Insights, www.corporatecomplianceinsights.com/cost-website-inaccessibility/ (archived at https://perma.cc/3JGX-4DXS)
13. A look into 2024 ADA compliance lawsuits, AudioEye, www.audioeye.com/post/look-into-2024-ada-compliance-lawsuits/ (archived at https://perma.cc/5ZH3-RAX4)
14. Fox News website not accessible to blind, class action says, Top Class Actions, https://topclassactions.com/lawsuit-settlements/lawsuit-news/fox-news-website-not-accessible-blind-class-action-says/ (archived at https://perma.cc/SG87-BDUA)
15. Supreme Court hands victory to blind man who sued Domino's over site accessibility, CNBC, www.cnbc.com/2019/10/07/dominos-supreme-court.html (archived at https://perma.cc/ZX56-A2VQ)
16. Beyoncé's Parkwood Entertainment sued over website accessibility, *The Guardian*, www.theguardian.com/music/2019/jan/04/beyonce-parkwood-entertainment-sued-over-website-accessibility (archived at https://perma.cc/WN7T-Z7Z8)
17. Rihanna's Fenty Beauty sued for ignoring accessibility for blind customers, Disability Insider, https://disabilityinsider.com/2019/07/05/accessibility/rihannas-fenty-beauty-sued-for-ignoring-accessibility-for-blind-customers/ (archived at https://perma.cc/BDY7-YJDP)
18. Williams v. Fenty Beauty LLC, Accessibility.com, www.accessibility.com/digital-lawsuits/pamela-fenty-2020-06-15 (archived at https://perma.cc/P3S3-GBUF)
19. Barnes & Noble class action claims website not accessible to blind, visually impaired users, Top Class Actions, https://topclassactions.com/disability-class-action-lawsuit/barnes-noble-class-action-claims-website-not-accessible-to-blind-visually-impaired-users/ (archived at https://perma.cc/9WBE-HYFF)

20 Hasbro class action claims fan site not accessible to blind, visually impaired visitors, Top Class Actions, https://topclassactions.com/disability-class-action-lawsuit/hasbro-class-action-claims-fan-site-not-accessible-to-blind-visually-impaired-visitors/ (archived at https://perma.cc/N7UK-77TV)

21 Coles to make online shopping site more accessible following disability discrimination case, *The Sydney Morning Herald*, www.smh.com.au/national/coles-to-make-online-shopping-site-more-accessible-following-disability-discrimination-case-20150218-13ig1g.html (archived at https://perma.cc/9BKE-B3RB)

22 Coles Group ranks number one in access and inclusion for Aussies with disabilities, Coles Group, www.colesgroup.com.au/media-releases/?page=coles-group-ranks-number-one-in-access-and-inclusion-for-aussies-with-disabilities (archived at https://perma.cc/SR7Y-TMLG)

23 Jargon, W3C, www.w3.org/WAI/GL/wiki/Jargon (archived at https://perma.cc/KX6H-PPEZ)

24 History of the Web Content Accessibility Guidelines (WCAG), Bureau of Internet Accessibility, www.boia.org/blog/history-of-the-web-content-accessibility-guidelines-wcag (archived at https://perma.cc/KEP3-9UMR)

25 Accessibility for Ontarians with Disabilities Act, 2005, Government of Ontario, www.ontario.ca/laws/regulation/110191 (archived at https://perma.cc/M3AP-Y8S4)

26 Fact sheet: New rule on the accessibility of web content and mobile apps provided by state and local governments, US Department of Justice – Civil Rights Division, www.ada.gov/resources/2024-03-08-web-rule/ (archived at https://perma.cc/R9U3-NFEQ)

27 Accessibility principles, W3C, www.w3.org/WAI/fundamentals/accessibility-principles/ (archived at https://perma.cc/TX8M-XV6Y)

28 Accessibility principles, W3C, www.w3.org/WAI/fundamentals/accessibility-principles/ (archived at https://perma.cc/TX8M-XV6Y)

29 Accessibility principles, W3C, www.w3.org/WAI/fundamentals/accessibility-principles/ (archived at https://perma.cc/TX8M-XV6Y)

30 Accessibility principles, W3C, www.w3.org/WAI/fundamentals/accessibility-principles/ (archived at https://perma.cc/TX8M-XV6Y)

31 Accessibility principles, W3C, www.w3.org/WAI/fundamentals/accessibility-principles/ (archived at https://perma.cc/TX8M-XV6Y)

32 WCAG levels, My accessible website, https://myaccessible.website/blog/wcaglevels/wcag-levels-a-aa-aaa-difference (archived at https://perma.cc/V3TH-BPWK)

33 Understanding WCAG 2.2, GOV.UK. www.gov.uk/service-manual/helping-people-to-use-your-service/understanding-wcag (archived at https://perma.cc/WK3M-FFFF). Fact sheet: New rule on the accessibility of web content and mobile apps provided by state and local governments, US Department of Justice – Civil Rights Division, www.ada.gov/resources/2024-03-08-web-rule/

(archived at https://perma.cc/96Q5-QLYP). European Accessibility Act compliance, WCAG, www.wcag.com/compliance/european-accessibility-act/ (archived at https://perma.cc/PH4D-BF6E)

34 WCAG levels, My accessible website, https://myaccessible.website/blog/wcaglevels/wcag-levels-a-aa-aaa-difference (archived at https://perma.cc/V3TH-BPWK)

35 WCAG levels, My accessible website, https://myaccessible.website/blog/wcaglevels/wcag-levels-a-aa-aaa-difference (archived at https://perma.cc/V3TH-BPWK)

36 ISO 14289-2:2024. (PDF/UA-2) Document management applications – Electronic document file format enhancement for accessibility – Part 2: Use of ISO 32000-2 (PDF/US-2)

37 PDF Accessibility Checker, PAC, https://pac.pdf-accessibility.org/en (archived at https://perma.cc/P65K-ZFBW)

38 Captions/Subtitles, W3C, www.w3.org/WAI/media/av/captions/ (archived at https://perma.cc/9BN5-MB4W)

39 CNIB clear print guidelines, The CNIB Foundation, www.cnib.ca/sites/default/files/2020-08/Clear%20Print%20Guidelines%202020.pdf (archived at https://perma.cc/F8N4-CRXK)

40 Americans with Disabilities Act of 1990, As Amended, US Department of Justice – Civil Rights Division, www.ada.gov/law-and-regs/ada/ (archived at https://perma.cc/Z6EY-9KCU)

41 Americans with Disabilities Act of 1990, As Amended, US Department of Justice – Civil Rights Division, www.ada.gov/law-and-regs/ada/ (archived at https://perma.cc/Z6EY-9KCU)

42 Americans with Disabilities Act Title III Regulations, US Department of Justice – Civil Rights Division, www.ada.gov/law-and-regs/regulations/title-iii-regulations/ (archived at https://perma.cc/N282-RGAX)

43 Americans with Disabilities Act Title II Regulations, US Department of Justice – Civil Rights Division, www.ada.gov/law-and-regs/regulations/title-ii-2010-regulations/ (archived at https://perma.cc/RB8F-88CV)

44 Fact sheet: New rule on the accessibility of web content and mobile apps provided by state and local governments, US Department of Justice – Civil Rights Division, www.ada.gov/resources/2024-03-08-web-rule/ (archived at https://perma.cc/3P6D-M9DA)

45 2023 ADA web accessibility lawsuit statistics: Full report, ADA site compliance, https://adasitecompliance.com/2023-ada-web-accessibility-lawsuit-statistics-full-report/ (archived at https://perma.cc/LPW9-L2FJ)

46 CDC data shows over 70 million U.S. adults reported having a disability, Centers for Disease Control and Prevention, www.cdc.gov/media/releases/2024/s0716-Adult-disability.html (archived at https://perma.cc/L5FF-RSQX)

47 Summary of the Accessible Canada Act, Government of Canada, www.canada.ca/en/employment-social-development/programs/accessible-canada/act-summary.html (archived at https://perma.cc/27N3-4LA7)

48 Summary of the Accessible Canada Act, Government of Canada, www. canada.ca/en/employment-social-development/programs/accessible-canada/ act-summary.html (archived at https://perma.cc/27N3-4LA7)

49 Accessible Canada Act, Canada Just Laws, https://laws-lois.justice.gc.ca/eng/ acts/a-0.6/ (archived at https://perma.cc/67ZR-N4NX)

50 Guidance on the accessible Canada regulations, Government of Canada, www.canada.ca/en/employment-social-development/programs/accessible-canada-regulations-guidance.html (archived at https://perma.cc/AFN3-SWB6)

51 Accessible Canada Act, Canada Just Laws, https://laws-lois.justice.gc.ca/eng/ acts/a-0.6/ (archived at https://perma.cc/67ZR-N4NX)

52 Accessible Canada Act, Canada Just Laws, https://laws-lois.justice.gc.ca/eng/ acts/a-0.6/ (archived at https://perma.cc/67ZR-N4NX)

53 Accessibility for Ontarians with Disabilities Act, 2005, Government of Ontario, www.ontario.ca/laws/regulation/110191 (archived at https://perma. cc/M3AP-Y8S4)

54 Accessibility for Ontarians with Disabilities Act, 2005, Government of Ontario, www.ontario.ca/laws/regulation/110191 (archived at https://perma. cc/M3AP-Y8S4)

55 Accessibility for Ontarians with Disabilities Act, 2005, Government of Ontario, Amount of administrative penalty 83. (1), www.ontario.ca/laws/ regulation/110191 (archived at https://perma.cc/M3AP-Y8S4)

56 The Accessibility for Manitobans Act, Accessibility Manitoba, https:// accessibilitymb.ca/accessibility/the-accessibility-for-manitobans-act.html (archived at https://perma.cc/AU4U-F92Z)

57 The Accessibility for Manitobans Act, Accessibility Manitoba, https:// accessibilitymb.ca/accessibility/the-accessibility-for-manitobans-act.html (archived at https://perma.cc/AU4U-F92Z)

58 Accessible British Columbia Act, BC Laws, www.bclaws.gov.bc.ca/civix/ document/id/complete/statreg/21019 (archived at https://perma.cc/Z2VA-7QVA)

59 Act to secure handicapped persons in the exercise of their rights with a view to achieving social, school and workplace integration, Légis Québec, www. legisquebec.gouv.qc.ca/en/document/cs/e-20.1 (archived at https://perma. cc/3GAH-2TEB)

60 Newfoundland and Labrador Accessibility Act, Government of Newfoundland and Labrador, www.assembly.nl.ca/Legislation/sr/statutes/a01-001.htm (archived at https://perma.cc/VMM2-78JH)

61 European Accessibility Act full timeline (with deadlines), Accessibly, https:// accessiblyapp.com/blog/eaa-timeline/ (archived at https://perma.cc/N6WM-X4WL)

62 Understanding the European Accessibility Act, NetGuru, www.netguru.com/ blog/european-accessibility-act (archived at https://perma.cc/Z3B5-LK2D)

63 Understanding the European Accessibility Act, NetGuru, www.netguru.com/ blog/european-accessibility-act (archived at https://perma.cc/Z3B5-LK2D)

64 Directive (EU) 2019/882 of the European Parliament and of the Council, European Union, https://eur-lex.europa.eu/legal-content/EN/TXT/?uri=CELEX%3A32019L0882 (archived at https://perma.cc/Y9PM-9VXB)

65 Understanding the European Accessibility Act, NetGuru, www.netguru.com/blog/european-accessibility-act (archived at https://perma.cc/Z3B5-LK2D)

66 Web Accessibility Directive: Frequently Asked Questions, EU Web Accessibility Directive, https://web-directive.eu/#toc1 (archived at https://perma.cc/NK5L-298S)

67 Understanding the European Accessibility Act, NetGuru, www.netguru.com/blog/european-accessibility-act (archived at https://perma.cc/Z3B5-LK2D)

68 The Equality Act 2010, GOV.UK, www.gov.uk/government/publications/equality-act-guidance/disability-equality-act-2010-guidance-on-matters-to-be-taken-into-account-in-determining-questions-relating-to-the-definition-of-disability-html#introduction (archived at https://perma.cc/C9KV-SSEY)

69 Understanding WCAG 2.2, GOV.UK, www.gov.uk/service-manual/helping-people-to-use-your-service/understanding-wcag#meeting-government-accessibility-requirements (archived at https://perma.cc/H6PF-QYCE)

70 Disability discrimination, Australian Human Rights Commission, https://humanrights.gov.au/sites/default/files/GPGB_disability_discrimination.pdf (archived at https://perma.cc/N3MS-HHKR)

71 Disability Discrimination Act 1992, Government of Australia, www.legislation.gov.au/C2004A04426/2018-04-12/text (archived at https://perma.cc/GYD2-AG5F)

72 Japan's (JIS X 8341) Website accessibility requirements and guidelines, Skynet Technologies, www.skynettechnologies.com/blog/japan-website-accessibility-jis-x-8341 (archived at https://perma.cc/V98D-LASN)

73 Accessibility of public services and information provided by public bodies, National Disability Authority, https://nda.ie/monitoring/monitoring/accessibility-of-public-services-and-information-provided-by-public-bodies (archived at https://perma.cc/3YFF-EBMJ)

74 FTC order requires online marketer to pay $1 million for deceptive claims that its AI product could make websites compliant with accessibility guidelines, Federal Trade Commission, www.ftc.gov/news-events/news/press-releases/2025/01/ftc-order-requires-online-marketer-pay-1-million-deceptive-claims-its-ai-product-could-make-websites (archived at https://perma.cc/QLL6-HAMD)

75 FTC order requires online marketer to pay $1 million for deceptive claims that its AI product could make websites compliant with accessibility guidelines, Federal Trade Commission, www.ftc.gov/news-events/news/press-releases/2025/01/ftc-order-requires-online-marketer-pay-1-million-deceptive-claims-its-ai-product-could-make-websites (archived at https://perma.cc/U7MH-YWMP)

76 Plain language is for everyone, even experts, Neilsen Norman Group, www.nngroup.com/articles/plain-language-experts/ (archived at https://perma.cc/WK9S-7TXM)

03

Creating a strategic cultural shift towards accessibility

What does it take to really embed accessibility into the fabric of your organization? It isn't 'someone else's problem'. It's not something that can be the sole responsibility of a 'head of accessibility' or 'the digital team'. Much more than a set of guidelines or tools, it's about building a culture that prioritizes inclusion at every level. In this chapter, we're exploring how to move beyond isolated efforts and create a holistic, strategic approach that transforms the way your team communicates and connects.

At its core, we're talking about making sure everyone can find and use the information and tools they need to do their jobs, use your services or buy your products without barriers. An accessible culture helps people feel seen, valued and included. It's about making decisions that demonstrate your organization's commitment to equity and respect, from the language you use in your messaging to the platforms and tools you choose. But building this culture requires intention. It means creating an environment where accessibility is integrated into daily workflows, championed by leaders and embraced by every team member as part of their role.

This chapter will guide you through practical steps to inspire and sustain this shift. We'll discuss how to create policies that align with your organization's values, train your team to think inclusively, and empower internal advocates to lead the charge. We'll also explore how to measure progress to ensure compliance and see how accessibility can enhance your brand's reputation, build trust and open doors to new opportunities.

Organizations that embrace accessibility as a fundamental part of their culture don't just meet expectations; they set new standards. They create environments where innovation and inclusivity thrive, and every message resonates with the people it's meant to reach. By the end of this chapter, you'll have the tools and inspiration to begin shifting your organization's culture in a meaningful, lasting and impactful way.

Defining a culture of accessibility

Accessibility isn't a one-off initiative; it's a mindset that informs every decision an organization makes. It means approaching everything, from internal processes to external communications, with user needs and inclusivity at the forefront. It's about creating an environment where everyone, regardless of their abilities, can participate fully, equitably and with dignity.

This culture goes beyond isolated efforts like adding alt text to images or ensuring a website meets WCAG standards. While these are important steps, they're just the starting point. When accessibility becomes part of an organization's DNA, it shifts the way teams think about their audiences, employees, and even their broader role in society.

Instead of asking, 'What's the bare minimum we need to do to comply with the law?' organizations start asking, 'How can we design meaningful and inclusive experiences for everyone?'

But creating this culture doesn't happen overnight. It requires intention, education, and an openness to unlearn old habits and embrace new ways of thinking. Mistakes will be made along the way, but those mistakes provide valuable learning opportunities. A culture of accessibility grows when organizations foster an environment where inclusivity is not just encouraged but expected.

The benefits of an accessible and inclusive culture

Organizations that prioritize accessibility reap significant benefits, both tangible and intangible. An inclusive culture creates ripple effects that positively impact everything from reputation to employee engagement to audience reach.

Enhanced reputation

We're living in a socially conscious marketplace; brands are scrutinized for their products and values. When organizations prioritize accessibility, they send a clear message: We value everyone, and we're committed to making a difference. This commitment builds trust and loyalty, strengthening customer, client and stakeholder relationships.

REAL-WORLD EXAMPLE
Microsoft's commitment to accessibility through technology

A great example is Microsoft, which has woven accessibility into its corporate ethos. From accessible software features to public campaigns celebrating inclusivity, Microsoft has built a reputation as a brand that truly cares about creating equitable experiences.[1]

Microsoft has consistently demonstrated leadership in accessibility, and its ongoing collaboration with partners and policymakers exemplifies how technology can drive meaningful change. In July 2024, Microsoft highlighted its work to advance accessibility as a fundamental right, emphasizing innovation and partnerships to break down barriers.

Key initiatives include developing AI-driven tools that enhance assistive technologies, such as Seeing AI and the Accessibility Insights suite, and advocating for global policy changes that prioritize digital inclusion.[2] Microsoft also works with partners like the Valuable 500 to align business strategies with accessibility goals, ensuring that inclusivity is at the heart of corporate decision-making.[3]

The company's efforts show that accessibility isn't just a technical feature – it's a foundational value that drives innovation, improves lives and sets new standards for collaboration. Microsoft's commitment serves as a compelling example of how integrating accessibility into technology and policy can create a more inclusive world for all.

As one of the world's leaders in business software, Microsoft has repeatedly demonstrated that accessibility makes smart business sense. Organizations that follow this example not only gain public trust but also position themselves as leaders in their industry.

Increased employee morale

When employees see their organization embracing accessibility, it fosters pride and a sense of purpose. As mentioned earlier, a culture of inclusion ensures that all employees, regardless of their abilities, feel valued and supported. For team members with disabilities, this can mean providing tools and accommodations that enable them to thrive. For other employees, it can instil pride in being part of an organization that aligns with their values.

Inclusive cultures also lead to better collaboration and innovation. When everyone feels they belong, they're more likely to share ideas, take creative risks, and work together to solve problems.

Broader audience reach

Globally, over 22 per cent of the population live with some form of disability,[4] representing one of the world's largest untapped markets. Add their friends, families and allies to the mix, and the numbers grow exponentially. Organizations that make accessibility a priority can engage with this vast audience, reaching people that competitors may overlook.[5]

For example, consider the power of video captions (we'll go more in-depth on this in Chapter 8). Initially designed for people who are D/deaf or hard of hearing, captions have become a mainstream tool that benefits everyone, from commuters watching videos without sound to non-native speakers learning a new language. By creating accessible content, organizations can reach more people and ensure their messages resonate with a diverse audience.

Accessibility as a reflection of organizational values

At its core, accessibility reflects an organization's commitment to respect, equity and social responsibility. It's a public declaration that every individual's right to engage, communicate and participate is valued.

This commitment means removing barriers and creating equal opportunities for everyone, while also amplifying diverse voices and perspectives. When organizations embed these principles into their culture, they're doing more than meeting legal standards – they're helping to build a more inclusive society.[6]

This doesn't just benefit the people being included but also the entire organization. A culture of accessibility fosters innovation by encouraging teams to think creatively about how to make experiences better for everyone. It also builds goodwill, making employees and audiences alike feel connected to the organization's mission.[7]

The shift from compliance to culture

One of the most significant shifts organizations can make is moving from a compliance mindset to a cultural mindset. Compliance is about meeting the minimum standards set by laws and regulations, while culture is about going beyond those standards to create something truly meaningful.

A compliance-first mindset might ask: Does this website meet WCAG standards?

A culture-first mindset asks: Is this website easy to use for everyone, including people with disabilities?

The difference may seem subtle, but it's profound. Compliance is reactive; culture is proactive. Compliance is about avoiding risks; culture is about embracing opportunities. Organizations that prioritize culture over compliance are the ones that set the standard for accessibility in their industries.

Building a path forward

Building an inclusive culture requires a shift in perspective, but it also requires action. It's about integrating accessibility into daily workflows, creating policies that reflect your values, and providing teams with the training and tools they need to succeed. It's about creating digital and physical spaces where everyone feels they belong.

And perhaps most importantly, it's about leading with empathy. This is a journey, not a destination, and every step forward is a step towards building a more inclusive world. Whether you're a small non-profit or a global corporation, the path to accessibility starts with a commitment to inclusion and a willingness to learn.

By changing your organization's culture and values, you're not just improving your communications – you're creating an environment where innovation, equity and connection can thrive. Organizations that embrace this mindset don't just meet expectations; they exceed them, setting the standard for others to follow.

Building the foundations for change

Creating this culture change requires more than good intentions; it demands a solid foundation built on leadership commitment, clear policies and an understanding of best practices. By establishing these foundational elements, organizations can ensure that accessibility becomes a core part of their identity rather than an afterthought. This section delves into three critical components of building that foundation: securing leadership buy-in, developing robust policies, and leveraging the standards and frameworks discussed in Chapter 2.

Leadership buy-in

Cultural transformation begins at the top. Leadership buy-in is critical to embedding accessibility into an organization's ethos. Without the commitment of executives and decision-makers, efforts risk being seen as optional, peripheral, or merely 'nice to have'. To move the needle, leaders need to champion accessibility as a strategic priority that aligns with the organization's mission and goals.[8]

Making the business case[9]

One of the most effective ways to secure leadership buy-in is to present a compelling business case. Highlight how accessibility benefits the organization in measurable ways, like:

- Reputation management: Demonstrate how accessibility builds trust and loyalty, showing that the organization values equity and inclusion. Point to successful case studies of brands that gained a competitive edge through accessibility efforts.[10]
- Audience reach: Emphasize the sheer size of the market. With over 1.6 billion people globally living with disabilities, accessible practices open doors to untapped audiences and foster broader engagement.[11]
- Compliance and risk mitigation: Stress the financial and reputational risks of non-compliance with laws and standards. Highlight the potential for legal challenges, fines and public backlash, and position accessibility as a proactive solution.[12]

Storytelling as a tool

Leaders are often moved by stories that connect accessibility to real people. As communicators, we know the power of storytelling to influence our audiences. Studies show that a good narrative has a bigger impact than facts alone.[13] Share testimonials from customers, employees or stakeholders who've experienced the positive impact of inclusive practices. Personalizing the issue helps leaders see accessibility not as an abstract concept but as a tangible way to make a difference.

Engaging leaders directly

Encourage leaders to participate in accessibility training or events like Global Accessibility Awareness Day. Experiencing barriers at first hand, whether by navigating a website using a screen reader or attempting to follow a video without captions, can help leaders understand the urgency and importance of these efforts. Their personal involvement sends a powerful message to the rest of the organization.

> ### A NOTE ON DISABILITY-RELATED SIMULATIONS
>
> Disability-related simulations, like blindfolding participants to mimic sight loss or using wheelchairs to experience mobility challenges, may seem like effective ways to promote empathy. However, research highlights significant drawbacks. These simulations can unintentionally reinforce negative stereotypes, portraying disabilities as insurmountable obstacles or creating a sense of helplessness.
>
> Instead of relying on simulations, organizations can prioritize authentic learning experiences. Engage directly with people with disabilities to hear their stories, gain insights and understand diverse perspectives. Disability-led workshops, open dialogue and real-life experiences offer a more accurate and respectful way to foster awareness and inclusivity, ensuring that education is rooted in empowerment, not assumptions.[14]

Developing effective policies

Policies are the roadmap that guides your organization towards accessibility and, in turn, inclusion. While leadership sets the tone, policies provide the structure and accountability needed to sustain change. A strong accessibility policy isn't just a document; it's a living framework that evolves with the organization.

Key elements of an accessibility policy

Specific and actionable guidelines Outline clear, practical steps for accessibility across various areas, such as digital content, physical spaces and employee training. For instance, the policy might require all videos to include captions and transcripts or mandate that event spaces meet specific standards.

Alignment with organizational values Tie the policy to the organization's mission and goals. For example, if innovation is a core value, frame accessibility as a way to drive creative solutions and foster inclusive design.

Accountability measures Specify who is responsible for implementing and monitoring accessibility efforts. This could include assigning roles, creating committees or setting up reporting mechanisms for barriers or concerns.

Drafting and implementing the policy

When developing an accessibility policy, involve a diverse group of stakeholders. Include voices from across the organization, like HR, marketing, IT and employees with disabilities, to ensure the policy addresses a range of needs and perspectives. Once the policy is drafted, communicate it widely and provide training to help employees understand their roles in its implementation.

Embedding policies into organizational practices

Policies should not exist in isolation. To be effective, they need to be integrated into the fabric of the organization. For example:

- Hiring practices: Ensure job postings are accessible and include language encouraging candidates with disabilities to apply.
- Procurement: Require vendors and partners to meet accessibility standards.
- Performance metrics: Incorporate accessibility goals into performance evaluations and departmental KPIs.

Learning from Chapter 2: Standards, guidelines and laws

In Chapter 2, we explored legal frameworks and standards including the Web Content Accessibility Guidelines (WCAG), the Americans with Disabilities Act and the Accessibility for Ontarians with Disabilities Act. These standards provide the foundation for policies, ensuring organizations meet compliance requirements while building inclusivity.

Using legislation as a starting point

While accessibility laws and standards set the baseline, they should be seen as the floor, not the ceiling. Use these frameworks as a foundation to build policies that reflect your organization's unique context. For example:

- Tailoring WCAG: If your organization heavily relies on video content, focus on WCAG guidelines related to captions and audio descriptions.
- Beyond legal compliance: Consider how your policies can go beyond compliance to address broader equity and inclusion goals, like creating a culture of belonging or promoting universal design.

Connecting standards to culture

Compliance with standards like WCAG or ADA isn't just about avoiding fines; it's about aligning with equity, respect and inclusion values. Use these standards to inform not just what you do but how you do it.

For instance, a commitment to WCAG's Operable principle (ensuring content can be navigated by everyone) might inspire your team to rethink user interfaces to make them more intuitive for all users.[15]

EXAMPLES OF POLICY IN ACTION

Corporate example

A global tech company might integrate WCAG compliance into its product development cycle, ensuring accessibility is prioritized from the design stage rather than retrofitted later.

Non-profit example

A non-profit focused on community events could create a policy requiring all venues to meet physical accessibility standards and provide sign language interpreters for key events.

Building the foundation for a sustainable future

Leadership buy-in, clear policies and a strong connection to accessibility standards are the cornerstones of lasting cultural transformation. By securing leadership commitment, creating actionable policies, and using legislation as a guide, organizations can lay the groundwork for meaningful change. These foundational elements ensure compliance and signal a deep commitment to equity, respect and inclusion – values that resonate with employees, stakeholders and audiences alike.

Creating an accessibility action plan

Turning accessibility from a concept into a daily practice requires a structured, actionable approach. An action plan serves as your blueprint, guiding your organization's efforts to build inclusion into every facet of its operations. From setting measurable goals to aligning with broader organizational objectives, a well-crafted plan ensures that accessibility isn't just an afterthought but a core element of your strategy. Let's explore the steps you need to take when creating an accessibility action plan that's both practical and impactful.

Setting clear objectives

Every successful plan begins with clearly defined goals. Objectives should be realistic, measurable and directly tied to actionable steps. Vague intentions like 'improve accessibility' lack the focus needed to drive meaningful change. Instead, aim for SMART objectives (Specific, Measurable, Achievable, Relevant and Time-bound).[16]

A SMART ACCESSIBILITY OBJECTIVE

Specific: Clearly state what you want to achieve. Instead of saying 'Make content accessible', specify 'Ensure all new videos include captions'.

Measurable: Attach a metric to gauge progress. 'Caption 100 per cent of videos published after January 1' is measurable.

Achievable: Set goals that are realistic given your organization's resources. For example, 'Ensure all PDF resources meet accessibility standards by year-end' may be achievable with the right tools and training.

Relevant: Tie objectives to your organization's mission. For a university, for instance, 'Make all course materials accessible to students with disabilities' aligns with the goal of equitable education.

Time-bound: Establish a clear deadline to maintain accountability, such as 'Conduct accessibility training for all staff by March 31'.

Setting SMART objectives not only keeps your efforts focused but also creates a sense of urgency and accountability. These goals act as milestones, providing clarity and motivation to everyone involved.

Conducting an accessibility audit

Before making meaningful changes, you need to understand where your organization currently stands. This is where an accessibility audit becomes invaluable. Think of it as a health check for your organization's inclusivity efforts, identifying gaps and areas for improvement.

What to audit

1 Digital platforms: Test your website, apps and social media channels for WCAG compliance. This includes evaluating elements like colour contrast, keyboard navigation and alt text usage.[17]
2 Internal communications: Review employee handbooks, training materials and intranet platforms to ensure they're accessible for all.
3 Customer touchpoints: Examine external-facing content such as emails, brochures and videos to identify accessibility barriers.
4 Event accessibility: Assess past events to see if accommodations like captions, sign language interpreters and accessible venues were provided.

How to audit[18] [19]

- Automated tools: Use tools like WAVE, Siteimprove or Google Lighthouse for quick insights into digital accessibility.
- *Manual testing:* Combine automated reports with manual checks, like navigating your website with a keyboard or using screen readers like NVDA or VoiceOver.
- *Engage experts:* Hire accessibility consultants or work with disability advocacy groups to gain a professional assessment of your content and practices.

The audit serves as your baseline. By documenting findings, you can identify patterns, prioritize tasks and create a roadmap for improvement. For instance, if your audit reveals that none of your videos have captions, this becomes a priority item in your action plan.

Mapping accessibility to organizational goals

As we keep repeating, it's more than compliance; it's about creating a meaningful connection between inclusion and your organization's broader goals. When accessibility is aligned with mission-critical objectives, it becomes an integral part of your strategy rather than a separate initiative.

Aligning accessibility with core objectives

- *Innovation and creativity:* Accessibility often leads to innovative design solutions. For example, optimizing a website for screen readers might also improve usability for mobile users, benefiting everyone.
- *Customer loyalty:* Consumers value brands that prioritize inclusion. Accessible practices signal that your organization cares about all its customers, building trust and loyalty. For instance, adding alt text to images on your e-commerce site makes shopping easier for customers with disabilities and enhances the experience for everyone.
- *Employee retention:* Accessibility fosters a more inclusive workplace, which can boost morale and reduce turnover. Employees who feel supported and valued are more likely to stay engaged and contribute to the organization's success.
- *Reputation and brand trust:* By demonstrating a commitment to accessibility, you position your organization as a leader in inclusivity. This not only enhances your brand image but also attracts socially conscious consumers and partners.
- *Compliance and risk management:* While accessibility brings numerous benefits, it's also a legal requirement in many regions. Aligning accessibility efforts with compliance goals helps you avoid fines and litigation while also creating a culture of proactive inclusion.

> **PRACTICAL EXAMPLES**
>
> - If your organization's mission focuses on education, ensuring that all course materials are accessible supports the goal of providing equitable learning opportunities.
> - For a retail brand, creating an accessible online shopping experience ties directly to the objective of improving customer satisfaction and driving sales.
> - A non-profit that prioritizes community engagement might map accessibility to its mission by ensuring that all events are inclusive and welcoming to diverse audiences.

Mapping accessibility to these goals creates a clear narrative for why it matters. It becomes easier to justify resource allocation, secure leadership buy-in and motivate teams when they see how accessibility contributes to the organization's overall success.

Next steps in your action plan

Once your objectives are set, your audit is complete, and accessibility is tied to organizational goals, it's time to create a detailed roadmap. Break down your plan into actionable steps, such as:

- training staff on accessible communication practices
- developing templates for documents, emails and presentations
- setting deadlines for improvements, like ensuring all videos posted after a certain date include captions
- regularly revisiting your accessibility goals to track progress and adjust as needed

Creating an action plan is all about embedding the inclusion of people with disabilities into the fabric of your organization. By setting SMART objectives, conducting thorough audits, and aligning accessibility with your core goals, you're laying the groundwork for meaningful change.

This plan isn't static; it's a living document that evolves as your organization grows and as accessibility standards advance. Regularly revisit your objectives, engage your team and celebrate progress to maintain momentum.

The result? A workplace, brand and culture where accessibility isn't just a task; it's a value that resonates with employees, customers and stakeholders alike. By making accessibility part of your strategy, you're not only meeting today's expectations but also building a foundation for tomorrow's opportunities.

Embedding accessibility in daily workflows

Accessibility should never be an afterthought. By embedding it into daily workflows, you create an environment where inclusive practices are second nature. This approach not only makes your communications and operations more effective but also helps build a culture of respect and equity.

Making accessibility a team effort

One of the most common misconceptions about accessibility is that it's the responsibility of a single department, whether it's marketing, IT or HR. In reality, it requires a collaborative, organization-wide effort. Each team plays

FIGURE 3.1 Accessibility is everyone's responsibility

SOURCE Matisse Hamel-Nelis

a critical role, and empowering every team member to contribute creates a shared sense of ownership and accountability.

Breaking down responsibilities across teams

Marketing and communications: Ensure all external and internal content, whether social media posts, videos or newsletters, is accessible to all audiences. This includes writing clear copy, adding alt text to images and captioning videos.

Human resources: Prioritize accessible hiring practices, such as offering alternative formats for job applications and ensuring interview processes accommodate people with disabilities.

IT and web development: Build and maintain digital tools, platforms and websites that are accessible, compliant with WCAG guidelines, and usable by individuals relying on assistive technologies.

Event teams: Organize inclusive events, whether in-person or virtual, by including accommodations like captioning, ASL interpreters and accessible venues.

Leadership: Champion accessibility by making it a core value, allocating resources and holding teams accountable.

By defining specific roles and responsibilities, you ensure that accessibility isn't just one person's job but a collective commitment. Regular team discussions, cross-departmental collaborations and shared accountability are key to embedding these principles into your organizational culture.

Accessible communication practices

Clear communication ensures your message reaches everyone. From emails to social media posts, there are practical steps you can take to integrate accessibility into all communication channels.

Emails
Emails are often the primary mode of communication in organizations, so they must be accessible to all recipients. Use plain language to ensure clarity and avoid jargon. Format emails with a clear hierarchy, using headings and bullet points for better readability. If your email includes visual elements, such as charts or images, add alt text to describe their content.[20]

Documents
Whether it's a proposal, report, or internal memo, documents should always be created with accessibility in mind. Use built-in heading styles in Microsoft Word or Google Docs to create a logical structure that screen readers can easily navigate. Avoid relying on colour alone to convey meaning and ensure sufficient contrast between text and background.[21] We'll go more in-depth in Chapter 6.

Social media
As covered in Chapter 7, accessible social media content is a must. Add alt text to all images, provide captions for videos, and use Camel or Pascal Case for hashtags (e.g. #AccessibleCommunications) to make them screen-reader friendly. Plain language and clear calls to action also improve engagement and accessibility.

Presentations
When creating slide decks, ensure that each slide has a clear title and logical structure. Use high-contrast colour schemes and readable font sizes, and avoid cluttering slides with excessive text. If your presentation includes multimedia elements like videos, always provide captions or transcripts. More on this in Chapter 6.

Audio and video content
Videos and podcasts are powerful communication tools, but they exclude many viewers and listeners without proper accommodations. Always

caption videos and provide transcripts for audio content. For visually complex videos, consider adding audio descriptions to convey visual information. Chapter 8 will focus on how to make these content pieces accessible.

Tools and resources

One of the biggest barriers to embedding accessibility in daily workflows is a lack of knowledge or tools. Fortunately, a growing number of resources are available to simplify the process. These tools can make applying accessibility more approachable for your team and help standardize practices across your organization. You'll also find checklists and reminders at the end of this book.

Templates and standards

- Develop or improve templates for documents, emails and presentations. For example, pre-built templates with correct heading levels, alt text placeholders and accessible colour schemes can save time and reduce errors.
- Create style guides that include accessibility requirements. For example, your style guide might specify font types and sizes, preferred file formats and instructions for adding captions and alt text.

Training modules

Invest in training programmes to build your team's accessibility skills. These could include:

- workshops on creating accessible documents, presentations and digital content
- webinars focused on specific tools, such as screen readers or accessibility checkers
- certifications, such as those offered by the International Association of Accessibility Professionals (IAAP)

Feedback loops

Accessibility tools are only part of the solution. Encourage ongoing feedback from employees, customers and stakeholders who rely on assistive technologies. Their insights can reveal gaps in your approach and help refine your processes.

Making accessibility routine

Embedding these principles into daily workflows is about creating habits. Encourage your team to approach every task, from drafting an email to designing a social media campaign, with accessibility in mind. Here are some strategies to make this approach routine:

- *Incorporate accessibility into onboarding:* Introduce best practices as part of new employee training to set expectations from the start.
- *Create accessibility champions:* Identify individuals in each department who can advocate for accessibility and provide ongoing support to their teams.
- *Schedule regular reviews:* Periodically audit your communication materials and workflows to ensure they remain accessible as standards and technologies evolve.
- *Celebrate successes:* Recognize and reward efforts to improve accessibility, whether it's a marketing team producing an inclusive campaign or an IT team developing an app that works for everyone.

The long-term impact

When accessibility becomes a natural part of daily workflows, the impact is profound. You're not just meeting legal requirements or reaching new audiences; you're building a culture of inclusivity that resonates with employees, customers and stakeholders. These communication practices ensure that everyone can engage with your organization's message, strengthening trust and building loyalty.

By making it a team effort, standardizing accessible communication practices, and leveraging the right tools and resources, your organization can lead the way in creating a more inclusive world, one task, one document and one conversation at a time.

Training and awareness: Building accessibility knowledge and confidence

Education plays a vital role in building an inclusive culture. Training and awareness efforts are essential for equipping your team with the knowledge, tools and confidence they need to create accessible experiences in their daily work. However, effective training isn't just about delivering information; it's about inspiring action, cultivating a growth mindset, and addressing misconceptions that might act as barriers to progress.

Training programmes for teams

Effective training ensures that accessibility becomes second nature. Whether it's through hands-on workshops, e-learning modules, or real-world examples, tailored training programmes empower teams to embed these principles into their workflows with confidence and precision.

Customizing by the role

Accessibility training isn't one-size-fits-all. To make it impactful, training sessions should be tailored to the unique responsibilities and challenges of different teams within your organization:

- ***Content creators:*** Focus on writing inclusive copy, adding alt text to images, using user-centred design principles and structuring documents for readability.
- ***Developers:*** Train on coding practices that align with WCAG standards, such as keyboard navigation, semantic HTML and ARIA (Accessible Rich Internet Applications) roles.
- ***Designers:*** Provide guidelines for creating high-contrast visuals, using readable fonts and ensuring the accessibility of visual elements like infographics.
- ***Marketing teams:*** Cover social media accessibility, captioning for videos and strategies for crafting inclusive campaigns.
- ***Human resources:*** Train on accessible hiring practices, such as creating inclusive job postings, offering accommodations during interviews and providing barrier-free onboarding materials.

Delivery method

Offering flexibility in training delivery ensures accessibility and engagement for your team. Some effective methods include:

- ***Workshops:*** Host in-person or virtual sessions with interactive elements like group exercises or case studies. For example, you could task attendees with creating accessible versions of existing materials.
- ***E-learning modules:*** Develop self-paced courses that team members can complete at their convenience. Incorporate videos, quizzes and downloadable resources to make the content engaging.

Real-world examples: Use practical, organization-specific scenarios to demonstrate how these principles can be applied. For example, show how alt text can transform a product image on social media, or how captions enhance the accessibility of a promotional video.

Guest speakers: Invite accessibility experts or advocates to share their experiences and provide insights into the real-world impact of inclusive practices.

Measuring training effectiveness

Training programmes are only as good as their outcomes. Evaluate their effectiveness by:

- collecting feedback through surveys or follow-up discussions
- assessing improvements, such as a reduction in errors flagged by accessibility checkers or an increase in the number of captioned videos produced
- tracking participation rates and ensuring training reaches all relevant teams

Encourage a growth mindset

Accessibility is an evolving field, and mistakes are inevitable. What sets successful organizations apart is their willingness to learn, adapt and improve. By fostering a growth mindset, you create an environment where accessibility becomes a journey of continuous improvement rather than a fixed goal.

Normalize mistakes

Mistakes are a natural part of learning, especially in a field as nuanced as accessibility. For instance, a team member might accidentally write vague alt text or design a poor-contrast web page. Instead of focusing on blame, frame these moments as learning opportunities. Encourage team members to:

- share their experiences with the group to foster collective learning
- seek constructive feedback from colleagues or accessibility experts
- reflect on what went wrong and how to do better next time

By normalizing mistakes, you create a culture where team members feel safe experimenting with new accessibility practices without fear of judgement.

Celebrating progress

Recognize and celebrate progress, no matter how small. Did someone add captions to their first video? Highlight their effort in a team meeting or newsletter. Did a designer create an accessible template? Share it with the broader team as an example of great practice. Positive reinforcement not only boosts morale but also motivates others to prioritize accessibility in their work.

Addressing common misconceptions

Misconceptions about accessibility are widespread and can act as significant barriers to adoption. Addressing these myths head-on is critical to fostering organizational buy-in and commitment.

KEY POINTS

Myth 1: Accessibility is expensive

One of the most persistent misconceptions is that accessibility is prohibitively costly. While some initiatives, like retrofitting a website, can be resource-intensive, many practices are inexpensive or even free. For instance:

- Adding alt text to images or using plain language in your copy costs nothing but has a significant impact.
- Accessibility checkers, like those in Microsoft Word, are built into tools your team likely already uses.
- Free resources, such as colour contrast analysers and WCAG guidelines, provide actionable advice at no cost.

Instead of framing accessibility as a cost, position it as an investment. Accessible content reaches more people, enhances brand reputation and mitigates the risk of legal challenges, all of which contribute to long-term value.

Myth 2: Accessibility only benefits a small group

Another common myth is that accessibility only helps people with disabilities. While it's true these practices are critical for this audience, the benefits extend far beyond:

- Captions on videos help not only individuals who are D/deaf or hard of hearing but also viewers watching in noisy environments or non-native speakers of the language.

- Plain language makes content easier to understand for people with cognitive disabilities, but it also benefits anyone seeking clear, concise information.
- Keyboard navigation supports users with motor disabilities and improves usability for power users or those using non-standard input devices.

Myth 3: Accessibility is too complex

Some people perceive accessibility as overly technical or difficult to implement. While certain aspects, like coding for WCAG compliance, require specialized knowledge, many practices are straightforward:

- Writing alt text for images is a skill anyone can learn with a little practice.
- Using built-in accessibility checkers can be as simple as running a spell check.
- Designing high-contrast visuals involves basic colour theory and free online tools.

Breaking down accessibility into manageable steps helps demystify the process and empowers team members to take action.

Training and awareness are the bedrock of a successful accessibility initiative. By equipping your team with the knowledge and confidence they need, encouraging a growth mindset and dispelling common misconceptions, you lay the groundwork for lasting change. Remember, this is not a one-time effort; it's a continuous journey that benefits everyone, from your audience to your organization. Through education and support, you can ensure your team is ready to lead the way in creating a more inclusive world.

Measuring and sustaining progress: Keeping accessibility front and centre

Creating a culture of accessibility is an ongoing commitment that requires consistent evaluation and improvement. To truly embed these principles into your organization's practices, it's crucial to measure your progress, regularly update your strategies, and actively engage with feedback from those you serve. This process ensures that accessibility remains a living, evolving part of your organization rather than a one-time initiative.

Accessibility metrics that matter

To evaluate the success of your efforts, you need clear and actionable metrics. Key performance indicators (KPIs) help you understand what's working, where gaps exist, and how you can improve.

Defining KPIs

Every organization will have different metrics depending on its goals and audience. Some common KPIs to consider include:

- *Website usability scores*: Use tools like Google Lighthouse, Siteimprove or WebAIM's WAVE to measure the accessibility of your website. Look for improvements in areas like keyboard navigation, alt text coverage and colour contrast.
- *Audience engagement metrics*: Track video watch times, social media interactions and newsletter open rates. Accessible content often results in higher engagement, as it is usable by a broader audience.
- *Customer satisfaction ratings*: Gather feedback through surveys or reviews to gauge how accessible your services are perceived to be. Include questions such as, 'Did you find our website easy to navigate?' or 'Were our videos captioned to your satisfaction?'
- *Compliance rates*: Regularly review your adherence to accessibility standards like WCAG or local legislation. Aim for consistent improvement in compliance scores.

Measuring impact beyond the numbers

While metrics are valuable, don't overlook qualitative insights. For instance:

- positive testimonials from customers who appreciate your inclusive practices
- anecdotal evidence from employees who feel more confident creating accessible content
- recognition or awards for accessibility initiatives

Regular reviews and updates

Accessibility isn't static. As technology advances and standards evolve, so must your practices. Regular reviews and updates ensure that your organization stays ahead of the curve.

Schedule regular audits

Set a schedule for periodic accessibility audits, whether quarterly, biannually or annually. These audits should cover all areas of your organization's communication and operations, including:

Web content: Test your website and digital platforms for compliance with the latest WCAG guidelines. Ensure that new features or updates don't introduce barriers.

Documents and multimedia: Review PDFs, presentations, videos and other content to ensure they remain accessible as your materials evolve.

Internal processes: Evaluate whether accessibility is consistently integrated into workflows, from content creation to employee onboarding.

Keeping up with changing standards

Accessibility standards and technologies are constantly advancing. Stay informed by:

- monitoring updates to WCAG, PDF/UA and other guidelines
- attending relevant webinars, conferences or training sessions
- following industry leaders and organizations that share insights on accessibility trends, like the International Association of Accessibility Professionals (IAAP) or local advocacy groups

Documenting progress

Keep a record of your accessibility initiatives and their outcomes. This not only helps you track improvement over time but also demonstrates accountability to stakeholders. For example:

- Maintain logs of accessibility audits, including identified issues and their resolutions.
- Create annual reports highlighting achievements, challenges and next steps in your journey.

Feedback loops

Accessibility efforts are most effective when informed by the experiences of those who benefit from them. Establishing feedback loops allows you to identify blind spots, refine your practices and continuously improve.

Engaging employees

Your employees are on the front lines of accessibility implementation. Create opportunities for them to share insights, challenges and suggestions, like:

- regular team meetings or forums to discuss accessibility-related successes and obstacles
- anonymous surveys that encourage honest feedback on what's working and what needs improvement
- an open-door policy for raising concerns or sharing ideas about accessibility

Listening to customers

Your customers' experiences are invaluable in shaping your efforts. Consider the following strategies:

- Add a feedback form to your website or app with questions specific to accessibility, such as, 'Did you find this content easy to access?' or 'How can we improve your experience?'
- Monitor customer service channels for accessibility-related inquiries or complaints. Respond promptly and use the feedback to make adjustments.
- Host focus groups or user testing sessions with individuals who rely on assistive technologies to navigate your content or services.

Collaborating with stakeholders

Broaden your feedback network by involving stakeholders like partners, community organizations, or industry peers. They can provide valuable perspectives on trends, challenges and opportunities.

Turning feedback into action

Collecting feedback is only the first step. The real impact comes from using those insights to drive meaningful change. Here's how:

Prioritize issues: Focus on the feedback that aligns with your organizational goals and has the greatest impact on accessibility.

Communicate changes: Let your audience know how their feedback has influenced your practices. For example, if customers request more accessible PDFs, share an update when you implement this improvement.

Iterate continuously: View accessibility as an ongoing process. As you address one issue, look for new ways to enhance your practices and exceed expectations.

By defining clear metrics, committing to regular reviews, and actively listening to feedback, your organization can ensure that accessibility remains a priority, not an afterthought.

When accessibility becomes a core part of your organization's values, it transforms how you engage with audiences, employees and stakeholders. It builds trust, enhances reputation, and opens doors to new opportunities.

> KEY TAKEAWAYS
>
> This chapter explored the journey from compliance to creating a culture of accessibility, showcasing how organizations can move beyond basic requirements to integrate inclusivity into their DNA fully. By shifting the narrative from a checklist mentality to a proactive cultural mindset, we've seen how accessibility can become a foundation for meaningful connections, innovation and trust.
>
> *Defining accessibility as a core value*
>
> We began by understanding that accessibility isn't just a technical requirement – it's a reflection of an organization's values. When accessibility becomes a foundational principle, it informs every decision, from the tools you use to the way you communicate. By asking, 'How can we design meaningful and inclusive experiences for everyone?' organizations can reframe accessibility as an opportunity rather than an obligation. This mindset shift ensures equity and respect and drives collaboration and creativity across teams.
>
> *Building the foundations for change*
>
> Leadership buy-in and well-crafted policies are the cornerstones of cultural transformation. As we discussed, leadership needs to champion accessibility as a strategic priority, aligning it with broader organizational goals like innovation, reputation management and customer loyalty. Robust policies act as roadmaps, outlining actionable steps and ensuring department accountability. Drawing on the legal frameworks explored in Chapter 2, organizations can use compliance as a foundation to go above and beyond for their employees, customers and stakeholders.

Creating an accessibility action plan

We emphasized the importance of setting SMART objectives – specific, measurable, achievable, relevant and time-bound – to guide accessibility initiatives. Through audits and alignment with organizational goals, action plans become practical tools for embedding inclusion into everyday operations. For instance, efforts that support innovation, improve customer loyalty or enhance employee morale can serve as compelling drivers for change.

Embedding accessibility in workflows

True cultural transformation happens when accessibility becomes second nature in daily tasks. From creating accessible emails and documents to captioning videos and designing inclusive events, every touchpoint presents an opportunity to reinforce inclusivity. By making accessibility a shared responsibility across teams, supported by resources, templates and tools, organizations can ensure consistency and build a culture of collaboration.

The role of training and awareness

A culture of accessibility starts with education. Training programmes tailored to specific roles, whether for designers, developers or marketers, ensure everyone has the skills and confidence to prioritize inclusion. Dispelling common myths – like the misconception that accessibility is costly or only benefits a small group – helps foster buy-in. Encouraging a growth mindset creates an environment where mistakes are seen as opportunities to learn and grow.

Measuring and sustaining progress

Finally, we discussed the importance of measuring accessibility efforts through key performance indicators (KPIs) like usability scores, engagement metrics and compliance rates. Regular audits, coupled with feedback loops that engage employees, customers and stakeholders, ensure accessibility remains a living, evolving priority. Organizations can maintain momentum and adapt to changing standards and expectations by celebrating progress and addressing challenges.

Looking ahead

Creating this culture is a journey that requires commitment, intention and collaboration. As this chapter has shown, the benefits of accessibility extend far beyond compliance. They include stronger connections with audiences, improved employee morale, enhanced innovation and a reputation for leading with empathy and inclusivity.

In Part 2, we'll turn our attention to creating actionable strategies and tools for making accessible communications a reality.

References

1 Raising the bar on accessibility, Microsoft, www.microsoft.com/en-us/accessibility (archived at https://perma.cc/84N2-DPAA)
2 6 ways generative AI helps improve accessibility for all with Azure, Microsoft, https://azure.microsoft.com/en-us/blog/6-ways-generative-ai-helps-improve-accessibility-for-all-with-azure/ (archived at https://perma.cc/PLU2-52YP)
3 How Microsoft is working with partners and policymakers to advance accessibility as a fundamental right through technology, Microsoft, https://blogs.microsoft.com/on-the-issues/2024/07/26/how-microsoft-is-working-with-partners-and-policymakers-to-advance-accessibility-as-a-fundamental-right-through-technology/ (archived at https://perma.cc/KQN5-K4W6)
4 Unlocking the value of the disability market with new 2024 report, The Return on Disability Group, Inc., www.newswire.ca/news-releases/unlocking-the-value-of-the-disability-market-with-new-2024-report-886192337.html (archived at https://perma.cc/56UH-FYXD)
5 Driving disability inclusion is more than a moral imperative – it's a business one, World Economic Forum, www.weforum.org/stories/2023/12/driving-disability-inclusion-is-more-than-a-moral-imperative-it-s-a-business-one/ (archived at https://perma.cc/F2YN-WKF6)
6 Five good ideas for disrupting ableism in the workplace, Maytree, https://maytree.com/five-good-ideas/five-good-ideas-for-disrupting-ableism-in-the-workplace/ (archived at https://perma.cc/XBK8-RCVJ)
7 Leading with accessibility: The secret to thriving teams and happy clients, GHJ Advisors, www.ghjadvisors.com/ghj-insights/leading-with-accessibility-the-secret-to-thriving-teams-and-happy-clients (archived at https://perma.cc/LWW7-2YYE)
8 The business case for accessibility: How accessibility-awareness strengthens your company's bottom line, Paths to Equal Opportunity, https://navigator.wlu.ca/content/documents/fileItemController/business_case_for_accessibility.pdf (archived at https://perma.cc/LXB3-84QK)
9 Making the business case for accessibility, Recite Me, https://reciteme.com/news/business-case-for-accessibility/ (archived at https://perma.cc/5NM3-78SN)

10   Inclusive marketing: Building a loyal customer base through accessible digital and physical experiences, Boston University School of Hospitality Administration, www.bu.edu/bhr/2022/06/14/inclusive-marketing-building-a-loyal-customer-base-through-accessible-digital-and-physical-experiences/ (archived at https://perma.cc/Z79D-RPJZ)
11   Unlocking the value of the disability market with new 2024 report, The Return on Disability Group, Inc., www.newswire.ca/news-releases/unlocking-the-value-of-the-disability-market-with-new-2024-report-886192337.html (archived at https://perma.cc/8S3U-XNYZ)
12   The essential role of accessibility audits in achieving compliance, Accessibility Partners, https://accessibilitypartners.ca/the-essential-role-of-accessibility-audits-in-achieving-compliance/ (archived at https://perma.cc/E6NA-F78N)
13   C Grall, R Tamborini, R Weber and R Schmälzle. Stories collectively engage listeners' brains: Enhanced intersubject correlations during reception of personal narratives, *Journal of Communication*, 71 (2), 332–55, https://doi.org/10.1093/joc/jqab004 (archived at https://perma.cc/R9NA-9V5T)
14   What are alternatives to disability-related simulations to promote disability awareness? University of Washington, www.washington.edu/doit/what-are-alternatives-disability-related-simulations-promote-disability-awareness (archived at https://perma.cc/VJ57-84PD)
15   WCAG 2.1 Principles explained: Operability, Bureau of Internet Accessibility, www.boia.org/blog/wcag-2.1-principles-explained-operability (archived at https://perma.cc/Z7MP-NUT7)
16   How to write SMART goals, Atlassian, www.atlassian.com/blog/productivity/how-to-write-smart-goals (archived at https://perma.cc/8THT-QGDT)
17   A definitive guide on how to perform a web accessibility audit, DigitalA11Y, www.digitala11y.com/a-definitive-guide-on-how-to-perform-a-web-accessibility-audit/ (archived at https://perma.cc/Z5X9-49UW)
18   A definitive guide on how to perform a web accessibility audit, DigitalA11Y, www.digitala11y.com/a-definitive-guide-on-how-to-perform-a-web-accessibility-audit/ (archived at https://perma.cc/7TYS-P5EZ)
19   What is an accessibility audit? Level Access, www.levelaccess.com/blog/accessibility-audit/ (archived at https://perma.cc/CN5K-3ZGU)
20   Making accessible emails, Government of Canada, https://a11y.canada.ca/en/making-accessible-emails/ (archived at https://perma.cc/PP6Z-HL5H)
21   Accessible documents, Government of Canada, https://bati-itao.github.io/resources/accessible-documents-en.html (archived at https://perma.cc/KH37-DAYE)

PART TWO

Putting it together: A practical guide on embedding accessibility into your workflow

When we think of accessibility, we often imagine physical or technical accommodations, like ramps or screen readers. But language, expressing ideas, communicating values and sharing information are equally crucial in building inclusive experiences. And, making your communications clear and understandable benefits everyone.

In this part of the book, we'll address the nuts and bolts of accessible communication across various channels. Whether you're writing an article, document or presentation, crafting social media posts, producing a video, hosting a podcast or creating a web page, there's a chapter for you.

Creating accessible web content isn't just about ticking boxes; it's about ensuring everyone can access and benefit from what you make. It helps you reach more people, avoid unintentional exclusion, and provide a better experience for everyone, regardless of their ability.

Accessibility is easier with the right toolkit. Each upcoming chapter is packed with hands-on strategies, tips and actionable insights that will help you create content that works for everyone. We'll also introduce essential tools for creating and refining accessible multimedia, from transcription software to captioning services and audio editing tools. Think of each channel as a unique opportunity to connect inclusively, where specific tactics make your content universally available.

This part includes:

- creating content with plain and inclusive language
- accessible web 101
- getting started with accessible documents
- accessible social media
- accessible videos and podcasts

From writing a presentation that can be understood by your executive team to designing videos and podcasts that captivate a wider audience, you'll discover the keys to making each channel a gateway for inclusivity.

In the next chapters, we'll take your communication skills to the next level and unlock the true potential of your message. Accessibility isn't just an enhancement – it's a game-changer. Let's make every word, image and video count!

04

Creating content with plain and inclusive language in mind

Welcome to one of the most powerful tools in your toolkit: plain and inclusive language. When we think of accessibility, we often imagine physical or technical accommodations, like ramps or screen readers. But language, expressing ideas, communicating values and sharing information are equally crucial in building inclusive, accessible content.

Words matter, as do the way they're presented. And not all numbers are equal, either. In this chapter, we'll explore how plain and inclusive language is essential for effective communication and why it benefits not only people with disabilities but everyone who interacts with your content.

Writing accessible content involves knowing who you are writing for, as well as understanding how they'll use that information.

We're going to talk about the importance of using the right words for our audiences. We're going to consider accessible numbers, too.

In this chapter, we'll explore:

- more about what plain language means
- the difference between plain language and easy language
- how even experts prefer reading plain language
- what inclusive language means
- why it's not 'dumbing down' – and why that term is also not great – it's about making it faster for everyone to find what they need
- accessible numbers and dyscalculia
- accessible formats and dyslexia
- writing that meets your users where they are
- inclusive language choices

Why plain and inclusive language matters

Plain and inclusive language may seem simple, but it can significantly impact how well your audience connects with your message. Using clear, straightforward language can remove unnecessary barriers to understanding, making your content easier to engage with for people from all backgrounds, including those with cognitive disabilities, non-native speakers and individuals unfamiliar with complex terminology. Plain language isn't just about simplifying – it's about making your message more direct and memorable.

Similarly, inclusive language is key to making everyone feel welcome, respected and represented. Think about a time when you've read or heard language that felt like it didn't quite fit. Maybe it felt outdated, exclusive, or even offensive. Inclusive language is an intentional choice to create content that respects all identities, experiences and backgrounds. We'll look at why both of these approaches are indispensable to accessible communication.

Literacy, numeracy, dyslexia and dyscalculia

Low literacy and low numeracy are also important considerations for communicators. Some people – even those you work with – may have difficulties with words and numbers.

Low literacy refers to difficulty in reading, writing and understanding written information in daily life. It can affect a person's ability to communicate effectively, complete everyday tasks, and fully engage in society.[1][2]

People with low literacy may struggle with:

- reading instructions, emails, or important documents
- understanding medication labels and health information
- filling out job applications, forms, or contracts
- comprehending news articles, financial statements, or legal notices
- writing clearly and effectively for work or personal communication

Some people have dyslexia, which is a neurological difference. It's thought that up to 10 per cent of the global population is affected.[3] As well as presenting literacy difficulties, it can also make it harder to read long or complex sentences. Dyslexia can affect memory and processing skills.[4]

Low numeracy refers to difficulty in understanding and using mathematical concepts in everyday life. It affects a person's ability to work with numbers, perform calculations and interpret numerical information, which can impact decision-making, financial literacy and problem-solving.[5][6]

An estimated 25 per cent of people have difficulties with learning and using maths.[7] People with low numeracy may struggle with:

- understanding percentages, fractions and ratios
- reading charts, graphs and tables
- managing personal finances, budgeting, or calculating change
- measuring quantities in cooking, construction, or other tasks
- interpreting statistics or risk-related information (e.g. understanding medical or financial data)

Some people have dyscalculia. Dyscalculia is a cognitive difficulty in understanding and working with numbers. It's not widely known about but is estimated to affect between 3 and 7 per cent of people worldwide.[8]

Whether someone has dyslexia, dyscalculia or low literacy or numeracy, there are steps we can take to make sure content is easier to process.

Key concepts in plain and inclusive language

In this chapter, we'll break down the essential principles of plain and inclusive language, offering strategies and insights to help you communicate in a way that's accessible and engaging for everyone. From an overview of what we mean by 'plain' and 'inclusive' language, we'll move on to the core principles that make each approach so effective.

Here's what you can expect:

Understanding plain language principles: What does writing in 'plain language' mean, and how can it improve comprehension and engagement? We'll look at some foundational principles – conciseness, clarity and active voice – that help you craft messages that are easy to understand. Plain language doesn't mean oversimplifying; it means removing the unnecessary complexity that can turn readers away.

Defining inclusive language: Inclusive language isn't just about avoiding offensive terms. It's about intentionally choosing words that respect and embrace diversity. We'll explore what inclusive language looks like in practice and why it's essential for creating a welcoming experience for all readers. From person-first language to gender-neutral terms, there are numerous ways to make your language feel more inclusive.

Writing communications that meet your users where they are today: There are also particular scenarios that communications professionals may have to consider when writing their content that would affect your choice of language and tone.

Why these approaches work together: Plain language and inclusive language intersect in many ways – clear writing helps everyone access information, while inclusive language ensures everyone feels represented. We'll discuss how adopting both approaches helps ensure your audience feels respected and your message is accessible to everyone.

Techniques for writing in plain language

How do we actually apply plain language principles? In this section, we'll dive into practical writing strategies in a clear, direct and engaging way. You'll learn tips and techniques to help you strip away unnecessary complexity and jargon, making your content more accessible without losing any of its impact.

Some of the techniques we'll cover include:

- **Breaking down complex ideas**: Learn how to communicate complex ideas in a simple, digestible format.
- **Avoiding redundancies**: Explore ways to cut out the fluff and get straight to the point.
- **Using familiar words**: We'll discuss why familiar language helps readers connect with your message and improves comprehension.
- **Checking readability levels**: Get insights on using readability tools to ensure your content meets accessibility standards.

You'll come away with practical steps to enhance the clarity of your writing, making it easier for readers of all backgrounds to understand and engage with your content.

Techniques for writing with inclusive language in mind

What does it mean to write with inclusivity in mind? This section will explore ways to make your content more welcoming by using respectful, diverse and representative language. What we **won't** be doing is specifying an acceptable list of words and phrases; language evolves, and context matters. Here, you will find insights into:

- **Person-first language**: We'll discuss why it's essential to prioritize people over labels and how small language shifts can make a big difference.
- **Gender-neutral language**: Learn how to avoid gender assumptions in your writing and embrace gender-neutral terms.

- **Avoiding ableist language:** Discover why some words and phrases, often used casually, can be exclusive or harmful to people with disabilities.
- **Cultural sensitivity:** We'll look at how certain words and phrases may have different meanings across cultures and how to approach language choices thoughtfully.

The broader impact of plain and inclusive language

Finally, we'll discuss the broader implications of using plain and inclusive language within organizations and society at large. This section will touch on the ethical, legal and business reasons for adopting accessible language practices. You'll see how plain and inclusive language can enhance customer service, strengthen brand loyalty, and foster more meaningful connections with diverse audiences.

Inclusive language also helps organizations attract a broader talent pool and build trust with clients, employees and stakeholders. It's not just about the words you choose – it's about the values those words represent. We'll examine case studies and research that illustrate the tangible benefits of these practices, showing how accessible language can be a powerful tool for positive change.

Plain communication isn't just about changing a few words here and there – it's about transforming the way we communicate to create a more inclusive and accessible world. By the end, you'll have the tools and understanding needed to make your content more approachable, respectful and effective for a diverse audience.

Plain language is the language users understand the **first time they read it**, presented in a logical structure.[9] It's about choosing the right words that express your meaning, using the vocabulary your audience understands, with a simple sentence structure. Plain language is more than the words themselves; it's about making sure people can find the information in the first place, and that it's structured in a usable way.

Relearning how to write more accessibly

It can be surprising to consider communicating in this way. Focusing on plain language can feel like an 'unlearning' of the ways we've been rewarded for writing in the past. In our early years, we're encouraged to extend our vocabulary by using additional adjectives and making sentences more complex to prove we are able to construct more complex sentences.

As we go through the formal education process, we're evaluated on writing a minimum-length essay. Academic writing praises use and presentation of complex ideas, writing about ideas in a theoretical and passive way, and we're usually encouraged to write things using formal terminology. Our essays tend to be marked by people with more subject-matter expertise than we have, and the purpose of those essays is often to convey an understanding of that new subject in question.

However, when we get to business communications, research shows that even experts prefer reading information in plain language.[10] While many of our stakeholders are wedded to their technical terms that they're convinced everybody understands, that's just not the case. No one is reading your content in perfect conditions. Very few people have uninterrupted time to sit back and give 100 per cent of their attention to your information, however engaged and interested they are.

The majority of our communications are not scientific writing for a scientific audience – and even if they are, there are ways to make that easier to understand, too. Plain language helps people find the right information to continue with their task at hand – whether that's digesting news or a new policy, filling out a form, or selecting the right product that meets their needs.

The curse of knowledge

As the late science journalist Tim Radford pointed out in his Manifesto for the Simple Scribe,[11] it's important not to underestimate the intelligence of your readers – while remembering that they might not know as much as you do. When working with a subject that we're familiar with, it can be easy to forget how much we know about – and how much others may not be familiar with the subject matter. This 'curse of knowledge' is a cognitive bias, where we assume that other people know as much as we do about a subject. Whether that's us as communicators, or working with stakeholders who are subject matter experts, it can be easy to forget just how much we've learnt already through that writing process.

Consider the 1990 study,[12] in which Stanford University graduate student Elizabeth Newton devised a game where she assigned people to one of two roles: 'tapper' or 'listener'.[13] Each tapper was asked to pick a well-known song, such as 'Happy Birthday', and tap out the rhythm for the listener to guess. Tappers considerably overestimated the listener's ability to hear the tune – as they were privy to that key information to start with.

Plain language principles

Plain language uses words your user understands the first time they read it.

Use the language your audience understands and needs to know

As with all effective communication, knowing your audience is key. Taking time to understand who it is you're writing for and what their needs are will help make your message more compelling.

Understanding what your users need

You could consider creating a user story for your content to help identify what it is your audience really needs from that information.

The format goes:

- as a (person who is likely to read this content)
- I need to (understand, learn about, find out how to…)
- so that (I can take the appropriate next step)

For example:

- as an employee of this organization
- I need to understand this change in our annual leave process
- so I can make the right request

Now you're considering what your users need to know, it's important to use the terms they're most familiar with to help with readability. This also helps people find the right information too – plain language is better for search engine optimization (SEO)![14]

Selecting the right words for the message

There are lots of ways to learn more about what our audience needs. Using search data, analytics and tools like Google Trends can help identify the appropriate terminology. However, there's no real replacement for testing your communications with users to see if they're able to understand the information presented to them. This isn't (just) about using A/B testing to determine which headline is most effective to meet *your* business objective, it's about making sure the information you're presenting is understandable and meets the needs of your users.

> **USABILITY TESTING TIPS**
>
> *Don't ask your HR team or accessibility network for a list of disabled users.* Accessibility needs are a protected characteristic and it's not appropriate to share personal, sensitive data in this way. Also, the burden should not be resting on disabled colleagues to provide insights on top of their regular roles. There are organizations which can help recruit users for testing.
>
> *Ask for feedback.* Be open to feedback – and make those changes where possible. You could post about your journey on your company intranet or external blog, working out loud to show how you're improving your content.
>
> *Take some time to sit with your users and observe them.* It may not be appropriate or reasonable to do this with every piece of communication, but you can learn a surprising amount by sitting with your readers. Whether it's layout or language, people don't behave as expected and it's time well spent!
>
> *Writing can always be improved!* If you don't have time or budget for user testing with your audience, at least get a second pair of eyes – which is sometimes known as a 2i process. Whether it's someone who has user-centred content expertise, or with no subject matter experience, are they able to help pinpoint improvements?

Using the active voice – and when to use passive

It's usually accepted that the use of the active voice is preferable when thinking about plain language. Active voice makes it clear. As outlined in the WCAG 2 supplementary guidance, using a simple tense and voice is an accessible design pattern which 'benefits many people such as people with language impairments, dyslexia, or a memory impairment'.[15]

Active voice makes it clear who is supposed to take action. For example, 'It must be done' is passive voice and does not say who must act. 'You must do it' is active voice and clearly states who has the action.

Putting the aim of the sentence at the beginning can also make English sentences easier to follow. Local language experts may have additional linguistic advice that helps make content easy to understand.

In some circumstances, the passive voice may be acceptable – using it can help soften a negative message or make the user the hero of a story, as Oluwatoyin Adeoye argues.[16]

Avoid complex words when there are clearer options

There are lots of words that we end up leaning on to make our communications sound 'official', but there are usually simpler options that help improve the clarity of our message. There are cases where the more complex forms are specifically accurate, but most of the time words like these can be swapped out for a simpler option. The Plain English campaign has an A–Z of such words if you're looking for alternatives;[17] you may find that your editing software also suggests these for you now. There's more information about those digital tools later in this chapter.

TABLE 4.1 Complex vs clear words

Instead of this	Use this
Utilize	Use
Commence	Start
Ensure	Make sure
Obtain	Get
Assistance	Help
Terminate	End
Prior to	Before
Provide	Give
Require	Need
Leverage	Use

Spell out or explain technical terms and acronyms

Plain language can still use specific terminology. There's a time and a place for technical terms – and sometimes using a simpler word loses meaning. When writing for a general audience, make sure any specific terms, concepts or acronyms are explained the first time they're introduced. If it's a longer article or report, you might want to spell it out again later in the content, too.

How does domain expertise affect language choice?

When considering the most accessible approach to your writing, your audience's preferences may vary. As highlighted in a study by Hoa Loranger and

Kate Moran for NNGroup, experienced users may deem that content is not for them if things are oversimplified right at the start. However, experts still prefer simpler sentence structure and scannable content – so wider principles of plain language still apply.

What about signposting people to a glossary instead?

Maintaining a glossary can be a helpful reference for people new to a subject or industry and can be useful as a reference point for readers with dyslexia and other cognitive disabilities. However, referring to a separate page, rather than explaining the term in context, can also disrupt the user journey. This may mean that your reader doesn't make it to the end of your information as they've gone elsewhere for an explanation. If there are industry terms that you know are broadly understood by the majority of your audience, it can be better to provide a link out to additional information.

Avoid clichés and business jargon to achieve clarity

Jargon doesn't have to be technical to be confusing. Using clichés and unclear phrasing doesn't translate well for an international audience and may lead to misunderstandings, as well as being perceived as annoying for your readers, too. No one really wants to 'ideate and circle back regarding the strategic leveraging of optimal lexicographical selections as per best-in-class initiatives'. (Remember, words are important – we need to think carefully about choosing the right words for our audience!)

WHAT HAPPENS WHEN YOU USE 'OFFICIAL' TERMS

You may have seen examples where the terms people use don't match official names. Sometimes there may be a conflict with your brand's style guidelines – there might be the preferred term to refer to a product or service your organization offers. If you must use a specific term, providing an alternative alongside it can help – for example, if a policy name or product has changed, provide the old name alongside it to help users get the information they need. Otherwise, you may end up with workarounds that evolve to help users find the information they need – like with this hospital sign, which has X-ray, the term used by both patients and staff, hastily taped onto the professional signage.

FIGURE 4.1 X-ray, not imaging; when official terms don't match user needs you end up with patchy workarounds

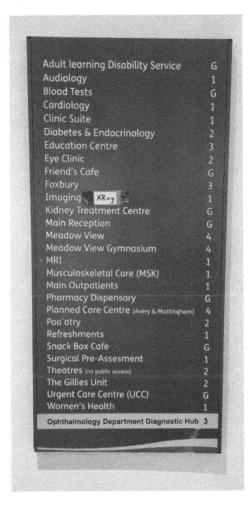

SOURCE Lisa Riemers

Well-structured shorter sentences and paragraphs

Shorter sentences are easier for everyone to read and understand, particularly when reading on a screen. There's no set rule (and indeed, guidance on this subject varies, depending on your format) but:

- GOV.UK guidance suggests[18] a sentence structure of 25 words or less.

- The Plain English campaign looks for 'a good average sentence length of 15–20 words'[19] to achieve its Crystal Mark accreditation.
- According to the Content Design London Readability Guidelines,[20] when writing for the web aim for an average sentence length of 15 words.

To keep your writing clear and succinct:

- *Aim to have no more than one idea in every paragraph.* If you need to, break your paragraphs down into smaller chunks of information.
- *Use bullet points to break up lists of information.* They're often easier to read and follow than a long complex sentence with commas.
- *Provide sub-headings to help readers scan information.* All users, even domain experts, find it easier to read information that has been clearly broken down.

Shorter content is not always better

While shorter sentences are easier to read, size doesn't always matter when considering overall content length. Writing should say as much as you need to say – and no more! Research shows that when trying to understand complex legal information, 78 per cent of responders preferred a longer version that explained what 'default judgement' meant over a shorter version of text that was very clear, yet did not explain that term.[21]

THE MAJORITY OF PEOPLE PREFER A LONGER EXPLANATION IF IT MAKES SENSE

When asked in a survey:

- 22 per cent — If you don't respond, the court will issue a default judgement.
- 78 per cent — If you don't respond, the court will issue a default judgement. That means you'll lose, and the court will give the plaintiff what he is asking for.

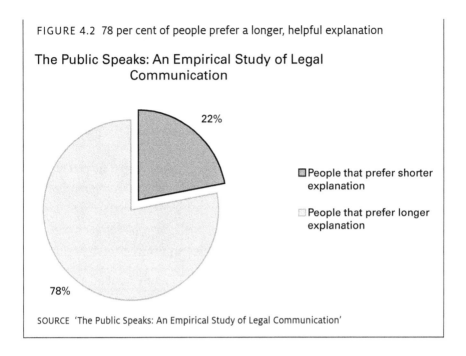

FIGURE 4.2 78 per cent of people prefer a longer, helpful explanation

SOURCE 'The Public Speaks: An Empirical Study of Legal Communication'

Consider your channel

Different communications channels have different word limits, restrictions and conventions. According to NNGroup, when writing for the web, aim for around 50 per cent of the overall words compared with a printed publication.[22]

When designing posters, reports and social media assets, think of the space available to you – and make sure you don't try and cram too many words in.

Experts prefer plain language

Clear legal information helps professionals be more productive. Christopher R Trudeau and Christine Cawthorne's study into people's understanding of legal information in the workplace found that professionals overwhelmingly preferred the plain language option.[23] The study found that a surprising number of people have to deal with legal information regularly throughout their working day.

'Overall, the vast majority of people prefer clear writing to traditional, hard-to-read writing when given the choice. Specifically, after averaging the results for all choice-of-language questions, 85.6 per cent of responders preferred the clearer version to the traditional version.'

An enormous majority of respondents also preferred plain language options over business jargon.

'In a group of 679 people, 632 (93 per cent) preferred the phrase "wasting time" compared to "round the houses".'

Trudeau and Cawthorne also found that 'a clear design helps facilitate easy finding and clear writing increases understanding. And doing both of these will increase productivity.'

Even lawyers don't like legalese – clear content is rated more highly

A Massachusetts Institute of Technology (MIT) study[24] found that 'while lawyers can interpret and recall information from legal documents better than non-lawyers, it's still easier for them to understand the same documents when translated into "plain English"'.

The study also found that documents written in plain language were more highly rated, perceived to be 'higher quality than the original documents, and more likely to be agreed to by themselves and their clients'.

An important development in this area is the ongoing work on an ISO standard for Legal Plain Language (ISO/DIS: 24495-2 – Plain Language Part 2: Legal Communication),[25] which aims to establish global guidelines for making legal documents clearer, more accessible and easier to understand. This standard, in draft in early 2025, seeks to address the barriers created by overly complex legal writing by promoting best practices for clarity, structure and readability. Once adopted, it will provide organizations, legal professionals and policymakers with a framework to ensure that contracts, policies and other legal texts are not just legally sound, but also comprehensible to the people who rely on them.

This aligns with findings from the MIT study, reinforcing that plain language doesn't just improve understanding, it enhances trust, engagement and decision-making for all stakeholders.

Get your facts straight when writing for domain experts

NNGroup ran a usability study which confirms domain experts prefer clear writing that provides succinct facts. According to the study by Hoa Loranger and Kate Moran, professionals are looking for scannable facts that they're able to cross-check themselves:[26]

- Provide proof – lead with data and facts.
- Front-load your content – summarize the key points, and provide more detail for those interested in finding out more.
- Cite your sources – and use recent data where possible.

Loranger and Moran also emphasized the importance of knowing your audience, as experts will quickly make a judgement call on whether that content is written for them.

Understanding the ISO Plain Language standard

Underpinning all of these principles is the ISO (International Organization for Standardization) Plain Language standard. ISO standards are globally agreed by experts in their respective fields. According to standard ISO 24495–1:2023(E)[27] 'Plain language ensures readers can find what they need, understand it and use it… [it] focuses on how successfully readers can use the document rather than on mechanical measures such as readability formulas.'

It has a similar-sounding approach to those POUR WCAG principles, with a slightly less memorable acrostic of RFUU: plain language must be relevant, findable, understandable and usable. As Gael Spivak points out in her blog post about the ISO Plain Language standard, plain language means that:

- readers get what they need (**relevant**)
- readers can easily find what they need (**findable**)
- readers can easily understand what they find (**understandable**)
- readers can easily use the information (**usable**)[28]

The ISO standard isn't just about the language – it also considers the structure, format and reading order of information to make sure that it's clear. It does not present a list of approved words and is not intended to be a style guide; rather it supplements existing style guides that organizations may already be working towards.

Access to ISO standards is not free but they do provide internationally agreed standards, and you may want to consider buying a copy for your organization's use.

> **PLAIN LANGUAGE CAN BE BEAUTIFUL**
>
> - **B**e clear and unambiguous.
> - **E**dit to remove unnecessary words and jargon.
> - **A**void clichés and idioms.
> - **U**se the language your audience understands the first time they hear it.
> - **T**ry to keep sentences short – and less than 25 words.
> - **I**nclude visuals to support text, with descriptive alternative text.
> - **F**ront-load your communications so important information is at the beginning.
> - **U**se clear, meaningful headings and break longer sentences up with bullets.
> - **L**ink text should be meaningful; avoid 'click here'.

How to write about statistics and numbers

Numbers, as with words, should be written and formatted clearly and consistently. When considering your information, do you need to present all of those numbers, with all of those decimal places?[29]

The following guidance is based on information from the UK's Office of National Statistics,[30] Digital.gov US guidelines[31] and the Government of Canada's content style guide,[32] to help present numbers in a consistent, accessible way.

Using words and numerals

- Write all numbers 10 and over as numerals, up to 999,999.
- Write numbers zero to nine as words unless they are technical, precise or relate to statistics.

Exceptions for using numerals

- dates (2 July 2025 or July 2, 2025 – always spell out the month name to avoid regional confusion)
- figure or table references (Figure 1)
- statistical data
- when a range crosses 10 (e.g. 9 to 12 respondents)

Exceptions for using words

- proper names (First Baptist Church)
- titles (Three Men in a Boat)
- figurative expressions (one day)

Ordinal numbers

- Write out first through ninth as words.
- For 10 and above, use numerals with 'th' in regular text size (10th, 50th, 150th), not superscript.

Phone numbers

- When writing out phone numbers, consider your audience.
- For content that is targeted at, or may be of interest to, international users, remove the leading zero from the number and replace it with your country's international dialling code.
- Do not include the zero you have removed in brackets; this is particularly important for accessibility as it can affect how some assistive technologies read the number. Do not use 00 instead of the plus symbol (+) as it does not work from all countries.
- This is in line with the UN's International Telecommunication Union standards, which are recognized worldwide.

Hyphens and special characters

Some symbols and special characters can make your content confusing and difficult to read, especially for users who have accessibility needs.[33] Some users depend upon assistive technologies that read out every character and symbol.

When considering special characters:

- don't use a hyphen (-) to indicate a range of numbers – use 'to' instead
- use 'and' instead of the ampersand symbol (&, sometimes called the 'and sign')

- don't use the plus and minus symbols (+ and -), unless in a dataset or table
- avoid using an exclamation mark (!), unless quoting directly.
- using a forward slash symbol (/) can be ambiguous – do not use one to replace words like *and* or *or*

Readability levels, formulas and caveats

You may have heard of readability scores – those numbers that tools like Flesch-Kincaid or the Gunning Fog Index assign to your writing. These scores are meant to estimate how easy or difficult a piece of text is to read, based on things like sentence length and word complexity. However, in the world of user-centred design and accessible communication, many experts consider these algorithms to be outdated and not always useful.

It's easy to focus on hitting a specific readability score, thinking that a lower grade level automatically makes your writing better. But these numbers don't always tell the full story. As usability experts Caroline Jarrett and Janice 'Ginny' Redish point out, readability scores aren't always 'reliable, valid, or helpful'.[34] In other words, just because a tool gives you a certain score doesn't mean your writing is clear or well-structured for your audience. A readability score might tell you that your text is 'easy to read', but it doesn't consider whether it really makes sense or if it's meeting your audience's needs.

That's not to say that readability tools are useless. In fact, they can be helpful when used as a guide rather than a rule. They can highlight areas where your writing may be too dense, overly complex, or difficult to follow. But these tools should never replace human judgement. No algorithm understands your audience better than you do.

One important thing to keep in mind is that some readability tools require you to upload your text online. This could pose a security risk if you're working with sensitive, proprietary, or personally identifiable information. Before using any tool, check your organization's IT policies on acceptable use and data protection. If you're unsure whether you can use a particular tool, consult your IT team.

Hemingway app

Hemingway is a free (with paid-for options) browser-based tool that checks writing for common errors. From highlighting lengthy sentences to suggesting simpler words, it can be a great way to get a digital second pair of eyes. The paid-for options can also be used to suggest fixes and tone.

Grammarly

Grammarly is a subscription-based tool that provides a similar service to Hemingway. It's an AI-powered writing assistant that helps users create clear, concise and accessible content by analysing tone, readability and complexity. Its clarity and conciseness features suggest ways to simplify complex sentences, replace jargon with plain language, and improve overall comprehension. Grammarly also assesses reading levels, helping writers tailor their content to suit their audience, whether it's a general readership or a more specialized group.

Microsoft Word's built-in tools

Microsoft Word now has a pretty strong built-in editor that checks your content for grammar, readability and tone. It highlights areas of concern for you to check and may provide suggestions to improve your content. This is in addition to the Accessibility checker, which also checks for colour contrast, alt text and document structure – there's more information about that in Chapter 6.

General AI tools like Claude, ChatGPT and Google Gemini

We're starting to see value in using AI tools that are built on large language models (LLM). Not all tools are created equal, and by the time you read this the various market leaders will likely have evolved beyond recognition. However, using an LLM as a second pair of digital eyes can be a way to highlight where your information doesn't flow as logically as it might, or make some suggestions to write things in a simpler and more plain language way. When using generative AI, however, it's vital to make sure you check all of your outputs. A feature (or bug) with them is that the words appear plausible – but may not be factually accurate. Sometimes, a response that isn't correct can also help you understand where your source content was unclear, as it's been misinterpreted by the model!

The difference between plain language and easy reading

When we started writing this book and talking to friends who know about accessibility, we quickly realized that many people confuse Easy Read with plain language. While they share a common goal – making information easier to understand – they are not the same. Both styles aim to simplify communication, but Easy Read is typically far less complex than plain language and often includes supporting images.

One way to think about these different approaches is to imagine them on a spectrum of readability. At one end, you have Easy Read, designed for individuals with learning disabilities, cognitive challenges, or lower literacy levels. In the middle, you have plain language, which simplifies complex information while still being engaging and professional. At the far end, you have technical or academic language, which is highly detailed and specialized but often difficult for a general audience to process.

What is Easy Read?[35]

Easy Read is a highly simplified form of writing that breaks down complex ideas into short, direct sentences. It typically:

- uses short words and simple sentence structures
- avoids jargon, abbreviations, or abstract concepts
- includes supporting images or icons to reinforce meaning
- structures information clearly, often with large text and ample white space

Easy Read is primarily designed for people with intellectual or cognitive disabilities. Still, it can also be helpful for others, including people learning a new language, individuals with lower literacy levels, or those struggling with reading comprehension.

However, because Easy Read simplifies information so much, it may be too basic for a general audience. Some nuances or important details might be lost in the effort to make the content easier to understand.

What is plain language?

Plain language is a more flexible approach that makes information clearer without oversimplifying it. It is designed for a wide range of readers, including professionals, the general public, and those who may not have expertise in a given topic. Effective plain language writing:

- removes unnecessary complexity while keeping the meaning intact
- uses shorter sentences and familiar words but does not eliminate all technical terms
- ensures that the writing is engaging, structured and easy to follow
- focuses on clarity, readability and accessibility without sacrificing essential details

Plain language is useful in government communications, legal documents, healthcare information and corporate messaging – anywhere clarity is key.

Finding the right balance

Choosing between Easy Read and plain language depends on your audience. If you are communicating with people who have learning disabilities or cognitive challenges, Easy Read may be the best option. If you are writing for a broad audience, plain language is likely to be the better choice.

For international communication, incorporating elements of Easy Read, like simplified sentence structures, clear formatting and images, can help make content more accessible, especially for readers who speak English as a second language. Additionally, providing information in multiple languages ensures that everyone, regardless of their background, can understand and engage with your content.

Ultimately, good communication is about making information as clear, inclusive and useful as possible, whether that means using Easy Read, plain language, or a combination of both.

Writing that meets your users where they are

Some disabilities are situational. Whether your users are stressed, tired, busy juggling multiple priorities or distracted by their environment, plain language helps make content that gets the point across succinctly.

There are also particular situations and scenarios you may have to consider when writing content that would affect your choice of language and tone.

Cognitive ability and the burden of cognitive load

The term 'cognitive load' was originally used to describe the mental effort required to learn new information. Whether someone is neurotypical or has a cognitive disability, there are lots of factors that affect our capacity to process information. People's cognitive abilities are dynamic, and an individual can be impacted on a temporary or permanent basis.[36] If the cognitive load is too high, it can leave our audience feeling overwhelmed, annoyed, or simply unable to process the words in front of them. As communicators there are circumstances to take into consideration, some of which could be considered situational disabilities but all of which can affect our audience's ability to understand.

Understanding the impact of stress

Many of us experience stress in our everyday lives to some extent. The level of stress our readers are experiencing affects the way they are able to process information. It's rare that our colleagues complain about being too quiet, or too relaxed. When communicating with people experiencing workplace stresses, like restructures, whistleblowing, or grievances, their ability to process information may be impaired.

Our customers are not generally sitting around and waiting for our emails, either. Getting some downtime to read through detailed information without interruption is rare – and when considering our audiences, they may also be experiencing stressful situations.

If our content is helping people navigate those situations – for example, moving house, or navigating sickness policies – it is even more important to make it as clear as possible.

Burnout has a significant impact on cognitive ability

At extreme levels of sustained stress, if someone is experiencing a condition called burnout, it can substantially impact their ability to process information. A study into accessibility and cybersecurity behaviour found that users experiencing burnout are more susceptible to detecting a phishing email or security warning.[37] Reduced cognitive abilities can impact the way our audience reads our information – let's work to reduce that cognitive load to start with.

Grief, trauma and bereavement

When we consider communications for people who may have experienced trauma, grief or bereavement we need to be mindful of their unique needs and emotional state. As Jax Wechsler points out in *Designed With Care*, trauma can have a real cognitive impact and can affect a reader's ability to concentrate. This may also include the ability to read and process information and recall details. Wechsler goes on to explain that the impact of past trauma can have a very real effect on the present and can continue to influence how people perceive information.[38]

Users may not have any experience or prior knowledge of the subject matter, as outlined by Joanne Schofield on the Co-Op Digital blog. There are a number of specific scenarios that might be new for people, with a number of terms and processes they might not have dealt with, like probate.[39] In addition to cognitive load, it's vital to consider user needs and their perspective when choosing the right language. It's important to avoid those clichés and platitudes like 'time is a great healer' while remembering that everyone processes grief differently.[40]

Marginalized audiences

When considering diverse audiences, the greater stress and mental burden that marginalized populations experience can leave less working memory available for reading and learning. As Iva Cheung points out, using plain language isn't just a communications choice, it can be a political decision. A stance that makes it easier for everyone to understand the information available to them.[41]

Inclusive language: Words matter

Language shapes how we see the world, connect with others and express ideas. But words aren't static.[42] They evolve over time, reflecting cultural, identity and lived-experience shifts. That means inclusive language isn't a one-time lesson; it's an ongoing commitment to learning, adapting and ensuring our words reflect respect, accuracy and inclusion.

As communicators, we are responsible for staying on top of language changes. What was once considered appropriate may now be outdated or even offensive. Instead of seeing this as an impossible task, we should view it as an opportunity to listen, learn and do better. Inclusive language isn't about political correctness; it's about recognizing the dignity of every person and ensuring our communication reflects that.

Why inclusive language matters

The words we choose shape perceptions and create either inclusive or exclusive spaces.

It builds trust and credibility
When organizations use inclusive language, they demonstrate respect for diverse communities. It strengthens employee, customer and stakeholder relationships by ensuring people feel acknowledged and valued. Trust is built when individuals see themselves reflected in communications that prioritize inclusivity.

It prevents harm and exclusion
Certain phrases can unintentionally reinforce stereotypes or marginalize people. Thoughtful word choices help avoid alienating audiences and instead create welcoming environments. For instance, replacing gendered terms like 'chairman' with 'chair' ensures that leadership roles feel open to all.

It enhances communication
Clear, inclusive language ensures that messages are easily understood by diverse audiences, including people with disabilities, non-native speakers and those from different cultural backgrounds. The language that avoids jargon, uses plain wording, and respects diverse identities leads to stronger engagement and connection.

Key principles of inclusive language

Person-first and identity-first language
Person-first language emphasizes the individual before the descriptor (e.g. 'a person with a disability' rather than 'a disabled person'). Identity-first language, on the other hand, acknowledges that some people embrace their identity as central to who they are (e.g. 'Deaf person' rather than 'person with deafness').[43]

    Best practice: When in doubt, ask people how they prefer to be identified. Some communities prefer person-first language, while others (like many in the disability community) prefer identity-first language.

Avoid ableist, ageist and gendered language
Everyday phrases often contain biases that go unnoticed. The words we choose can either foster inclusivity or unintentionally reinforce biases. Many everyday phrases contain ableist, ageist, or gendered language, often without us realizing.[44]

Ableist language

Ableist language refers to words and phrases that reinforce negative stereotypes about disabilities. Common expressions like 'crazy', 'lame', 'tone-deaf', or 'blind to an issue' can be harmful by associating disabilities with negative connotations. Instead, opt for precise, descriptive words that accurately express what you mean.[45]

> Instead of: 'That idea is insane.'
>
> Try: 'That idea is surprising/unexpected.'
>
> Instead of: 'He turned a blind eye to the issue.'
>
> Try: 'He ignored the issue.'

Ageist language

Ageist language contributes to stereotypes about older adults, making assumptions about their abilities or cognitive function. Terms like 'elderly' or 'senile' can be dismissive or demeaning. Instead, use people-first language and be specific when needed.[46]

> Instead of: 'The elderly struggle with technology.'
>
> Try: 'Older adults may have varying levels of experience with technology.'
>
> Instead of: 'She's getting senile.'
>
> Try: 'She has dementia.'

Gendered language

Many traditional terms assume a male default, which excludes or minimizes gender diversity. Avoid using 'chairman', 'fireman', 'guys' when addressing mixed-gender groups. Instead, use neutral alternatives.[47]

> Instead of: 'Hey guys, let's get started.'
>
> Try: 'Hey everyone, let's get started.'
>
> Instead of: 'The chairman approved the policy.'
>
> Try: 'The chair approved the policy.'

By being intentional with language, we can create more inclusive spaces where everyone feels seen and respected.

Being mindful of culture and racially inclusive language

Language plays a significant role in shaping perceptions and reinforcing societal norms. Using culturally and racially inclusive language means being intentional about the words we choose to avoid harm, foster respect and ensure accurate representation.

Avoid terms with harmful histories

Many commonly used phrases have roots in oppressive histories. For example, 'grandfathered in' originates from racist voting laws that disenfranchised Black Americans after the Civil War, while 'powwow' holds deep cultural and ceremonial significance for Indigenous communities. Using such terms outside of their proper context can diminish their meaning and contribute to systemic exclusion. Instead, opt for alternatives like 'exempt from new rules' instead of 'grandfathered in'.

Be specific about identities

Grouping diverse communities under broad labels like 'Asians' or 'Latinos' erases unique identities and lived experiences. Instead, specify South Asian, East Asian, Mexican or Puerto Rican when applicable. This approach ensures accurate representation and acknowledges the diversity within racial and ethnic groups.[48]

Follow evolving language norms

Capitalization matters when referring to racial and ethnic identities. Capitalizing 'Indigenous', 'Black' and 'Latino' signals respect and recognition of their distinct cultures and histories. This practice aligns with style guides from organizations like the Associated Press[49] and reflects evolving norms in inclusive communication.

Recognizing the importance of pronouns and gender identity

One of the simplest yet most impactful ways to show respect is by using the correct pronouns. Misgendering someone, whether intentional or not, can cause harm and contribute to a culture of exclusion. Using gender-neutral language and recognizing diverse gender identities helps create a more inclusive environment.

What are pronouns?

Pronouns are words we use in everyday language to refer to ourselves or others. They can be an important way to express your gender identity. 'I', 'me', 'she/her', 'he/him' and 'they/them' are some examples of pronouns.[50]

Why pronouns matter

Pronouns are a fundamental part of identity. Referring to someone with the wrong pronouns can invalidate their identity and make them feel unseen. Whether in workplace communications, customer interactions, or social settings, using inclusive language demonstrates respect and ensures everyone feels valued.[51]

> **Best practices for gender-inclusive language**
>
> ***Ask instead of assuming:*** If unsure, politely ask someone's pronouns instead of making assumptions based on their name or appearance.
>
> ***Use 'they/them' as a singular pronoun:*** When someone's gender is unknown or unspecified, using 'they' ensures inclusivity.
>
> ***Choose gender-neutral alternatives***: Replace gendered terms like 'husband' or 'wife' with 'partner' when speaking generally.

Practical tips for implementing inclusive language

As language evolves, so must our approach to communication. Implementing inclusive language requires intentional effort, regular reflection and a commitment to continuous learning. Here are key strategies to help integrate inclusive language into your communications effectively.

Stay educated: Keep up with evolving language

Language is dynamic. Words and phrases that were once acceptable may no longer align with current cultural and societal understandings. Staying informed about inclusive language trends ensures that your communications remain respectful and relevant.

Ways to stay educated

- Follow reputable sources such as the American Psychological Association (APA), the Center for Inclusive Design and Innovation (CIDI) and advocacy organizations that focus on inclusive language.

- Read language guides like the APA Inclusive Language Guidelines to stay up to date with best practices.
- Engage with communities directly impacted by exclusionary language, so listen to their perspectives and learn from their lived experiences.
- Attend training sessions on inclusive communication, DEI (Diversity, Equity and Inclusion) and accessibility.

By staying informed, you demonstrate a commitment to using language that respects all identities and lived experiences.

Audit your content: Identify and eliminate outdated language

To ensure inclusivity, it's essential to regularly review your written and verbal communications. This includes digital content, internal documents, social media, presentations and marketing materials.

Steps to conduct a content audit

1 Review all written materials (e.g. website content, reports, newsletters) for outdated or exclusionary language.
2 Analyse internal and external messaging to ensure it reflects inclusivity and respects diverse audiences.
3 Identify terms that reinforce stereotypes or marginalize communities, replacing them with more appropriate language.

Seek feedback: Invite diverse voices to review communications

One of the most effective ways to ensure inclusive language is by involving people from diverse backgrounds in the review process. This includes colleagues, employees, community members and external experts.

Ways to gather feedback

- Create an internal review group composed of individuals from diverse perspectives.
- Conduct surveys or focus groups to assess whether audiences find language choices inclusive and respectful.
- Collaborate with DEI or accessibility specialists to provide insight on inclusive communication practices.

- Encourage anonymous feedback to allow individuals to voice concerns about language without fear of judgement.

> A university communications team might seek input from student accessibility groups before publishing campus-wide messaging to ensure it resonates with all students.

Use style guides: Standardize inclusive language practices

Having a structured approach to inclusive language helps maintain consistency across all communications. Style guides offer valuable frameworks to ensure messaging aligns with best practices.

Key style guides and resources

- APA Inclusive Language Guidelines: Covers best practices for writing about race, ethnicity, disability, gender and age.[52]
- *The Conscious Style Guide*: A resource that provides updates on inclusive language trends.[53]
- Organization-specific policies: Many institutions and businesses develop their own inclusive language guidelines tailored to their audiences and industries.

Be open to learning and growth

Recognizing that language evolves and being open to change is crucial. Mistakes will happen, but what matters is the willingness to learn and do better.

Key mindsets for growth

- Acknowledge feedback gracefully. If someone points out that a term is outdated or offensive, listen and make adjustments.
- Adapt as language changes. Words that are appropriate today may not be in the future. Stay flexible and willing to update materials accordingly.
- Lead by example. Encourage colleagues, teams and organizations to adopt inclusive language practices and provide guidance when necessary.

Small changes, big impact

Implementing inclusive language isn't just about avoiding offensive terms. It's actually about creating belonging, respect and equity. Inclusive language creates meaningful connections, enhances credibility and demonstrates a commitment to fairness and equity. As we continue to evolve in our communication practices, remember that every word holds power, and it's up to us to use it responsibly.

> **PLAIN LANGUAGE AND INCLUSIVE LANGUAGE INTERSECT IN MANY WAYS**
>
> In this chapter we discussed the importance of plain and inclusive language, as well as the importance of understanding our audience's situation.
> In summary:
>
> - Clear writing helps everyone access information, while inclusive language ensures everyone feels represented.
> - Language matters – the words we choose shape perceptions and create either inclusive or exclusive spaces.
> - Plain language makes things easier for everyone – and even experts prefer it!
> - Using plain language can feel like a relearning of how to write but it helps us write more clearly for our audience.
> - The curse of knowledge is a cognitive bias that makes us forget how much we know compared to what our audience might understand.
> - The ISO Plain Language standard is a globally agreed standard for plain language.
>
> *The principles of plain language*
> When considering plain language we should:
>
> - Use the language our audience understands – it's better for findability and SEO as well as accessibility.
> - Avoid complex words when there are clearer options.
> - Spell out or explain technical terms and acronyms.
> - Avoid clichés and business jargon to achieve clarity.
> - Use well-structured shorter sentences and paragraphs to enhance readability.

- Tell users what they need to know – shorter content is not always better.
- Use the active voice in most cases, though there are times when the passive voice may be preferable.

We also covered:

- how to write about statistics and numbers
- readability levels, formulas and caveats, including tools like the Hemingway app, Grammarly, Microsoft's built-in checkers and AI tools
- the difference between plain language and easy reading

We considered the factors which affect how our audience understands our information and meet them where they are. Cognitive ability and cognitive load can all be affected by stress, grief, trauma and bereavement. Marginalized audiences can be additionally impacted by their lived experiences.

The benefits of inclusive language

Using inclusive language:

- builds trust and credibility
- prevents harm and exclusion
- enhances communication

Key principles of inclusive language

Key principles of inclusive language include:

- using person-first and identity-first language to emphasize the individual
- avoiding ableist, ageist and gendered language, which reinforce bias
- being mindful of culture and racially inclusive language to avoid harm, foster respect and ensure accurate representation
- recognizing the importance of pronouns and gender identity to create a more inclusive environment

Practical tips for implementing inclusive language

- Stay educated: As language evolves, we should be open to learning new ways of using language to make sure our messaging stays relevant.
- Audit your content: Identify and eliminate outdated language to ensure inclusivity.

- Seek feedback: Invite diverse voices to review and improve our communications.
- Use style guides: Standardizing inclusive language practices makes it easier to stay relevant and consistent.

Small changes can have a big impact

Language is important – and even small changes can have a massive impact on our audience.

References

1. Challenges of low literacy, Literacy Pittsburgh, www.literacypittsburgh.org/the-challenge/ (archived at https://perma.cc/9BE6-Z62S)
2. P Easton, V A Entwistle and B Williams. Health in the 'hidden population' of people with low literacy: A systematic review of the literature, *BMC Public Health,* 10, 459, https://doi.org/10.1186/1471-2458-10-459 (archived at https://perma.cc/9FDU-9HP4)
3. Dyslexia, The British Dyslexia Association, www.bdadyslexia.org.uk/dyslexia (archived at https://perma.cc/A53E-WG6H)
4. About Dyslexia: Things to consider, The British Dyslexia Association, www.bdadyslexia.org.uk/dyslexia/about-dyslexia/things-to-consider (archived at https://perma.cc/56EA-57ED)
5. Low numeracy is associated with poor financial well-being around the world, National Library of Medicine, https://pmc.ncbi.nlm.nih.gov/articles/PMC8608299/ (archived at https://perma.cc/654A-SH7Y)
6. Designing for people with dyscalculia and low numeracy, Design in government, https://designnotes.blog.gov.uk/2022/11/28/designing-for-people-with-dyscalculia-and-low-numeracy/ (archived at https://perma.cc/SWC4-RJ9D)
7. About dyscalculia, The British Dyslexia Association, www.bdadyslexia.org.uk/dyscalculia/how-can-i-identify-dyscalculia (archived at https://perma.cc/WHL9-RKG2)
8. Dyscalculia, Cleveland Clinic, https://my.clevelandclinic.org/health/diseases/23949-dyscalculia (archived at https://perma.cc/8FJV-T9KR)
9. What is plain language? Plain Language Association International, https://plainlanguagenetwork.org/plain-language/what-is-plain-language/ (archived at https://perma.cc/3AEP-T9TP)
10. Plain language is for everyone, even experts, Neilsen Norman Group, www.nngroup.com/articles/plain-language-experts/ (archived at https://perma.cc/9V2A-WFHX)

11 Manifesto for the simple scribe – my 25 commandments for journalists, The Guardian, www.theguardian.com/science/blog/2011/jan/19/manifesto-simple-scribe-commandments-journalists (archived at https://perma.cc/3JVL-9CFC)

12 The rocky road from actions to intentions, Stanford University ProQuest Dissertations & Theses, www.proquest.com/openview/b740253d9b78599786f59d6b6055cc3b/1?pq-origsite=gscholar&cbl=18750&diss=y (archived at https://perma.cc/E8QU-B2AV)

13 The curse of knowledge, Harvard Business Review, https://hbr.org/2006/12/the-curse-of-knowledge (archived at https://perma.cc/2HYG-75KJ)

14 SEO and usability, Neilsen Norman Group, www.nngroup.com/articles/seo-and-usability/ (archived at https://perma.cc/Z5DJ-KY9D)

15 Cognitive accessibility design pattern: Use a simple tense and voice, Supplemental guidance to WCAG 2, W3C Web Accessibility Initiative, www.w3.org/WAI/WCAG2/supplemental/patterns/o3p02-simple-tense/ (archived at https://perma.cc/4CCS-DLWD)

16 Passive voice in UX writing: what really matters? UX Content Collective, https://uxcontent.com/passive-voice-isnt-the-problem-misuse-is (archived at https://perma.cc/U8YE-GMBZ)

17 The A-Z of alternative words, Plain English Campaign, https://cdn.website-editor.net/s/08adc49f98924cb8b7dddec4cafb071e/files/uploaded/A_to_Z_of_alternative_words_.pdf

18 Sentence length: why 25 words is our limit, GOV.UK, https://insidegovuk.blog.gov.uk/2014/08/04/sentence-length-why-25-words-is-our-limit/ (archived at https://perma.cc/XZ22-UX28)

19 Frequently asked questions about the Crystal Mark, The Plain English Campaign, www.plainenglish.co.uk/services/crystal-mark/frequently-asked-questions.html

20 Content Design London – Readability guidelines, https://readabilityguidelines.co.uk/clear-language/simple-sentences/ (archived at https://perma.cc/E6ZL-9RGT)

21 C R Trudeau. The public speaks: An empirical study of legal communication, *Scribes Journal of Legal Writing,* 14, 121, https://ssrn.com/abstract=1843415 (archived at https://perma.cc/Y53W-NMYV) or http://dx.doi.org/10.2139/ssrn.1843415 (archived at https://perma.cc/Y53W-NMYV)

22 Plain language is for everyone, even experts, Neilsen Norman Group, www.nngroup.com/articles/plain-language-experts/ (archived at https://perma.cc/G8JJ-BGSH)

23 C Trudeau and C Cawthorne. The public speaks, again: An international study of legal communication, *University of Arkansas at Little Rock Law Review,* 40 (2), https://lawrepository.ualr.edu/lawreview/vol40/iss2/3 (archived at https://perma.cc/CN3T-7TZU)

24   E Martínez, F Mollica and E Gibson, Poor writing, not specialized concepts, drives processing difficulty in legal language, Cognition, 224, https://doi.org/10.1016/j.cognition.2022.105070 (archived at https://perma.cc/497L-T68Q)

25   ISO/PRF 24495-2 Plain language Part 2: Legal communication, ISO, www.iso.org/standard/85774.html (archived at https://perma.cc/N3PJ-56YY)

26   Writing digital copy for domain experts, Neilsen Norman Group, www.nngroup.com/articles/writing-domain-experts/ (archived at https://perma.cc/9SQK-D336)

27   ISO 24495-1:2023 Plain language Part 1: Governing principles and guidelines, ISO, www.iso.org/standard/78907.html (archived at https://perma.cc/D475-X4JM)

28   The ISO plain language standard: For most languages and cultures, and for all sectors, Editors Canada, www.noslangues-ourlanguages.gc.ca/en/blogue-blog/iso-langage-simple-plain-language-eng (archived at https://perma.cc/ACW7-VAD8)

29   Designing for people with dyscalculia and low numeracy, Design in government, https://designnotes.blog.gov.uk/2022/11/28/designing-for-people-with-dyscalculia-and-low-numeracy/ (archived at https://perma.cc/AME8-C7BR)

30   Numbers should be written and formatted in a clear and consistent way. We always use numerals when presenting statistics; however, there are some instances where we do use words for clarity and readability. Writing numbers, Office of National Statistics Service Manual, https://service-manual.ons.gov.uk/content/numbers/writing-numbers (archived at https://perma.cc/6BW6-QJF4)

31   Digital.gov style guide, https://digital.gov/style-guide/#numbers-symbols-dates-time-and-places-2 (archived at https://perma.cc/D6KH-9549)

32   4.6 Numbers, Canada.ca, https://design.canada.ca/style-guide/#wp4-6 (archived at https://perma.cc/FEN2-KWXY)

33   Formatting and punctuation, Office for National Statistics Service Manual, https://service-manual.ons.gov.uk/content/formatting-and-punctuation/symbols-and-special-characters (archived at https://perma.cc/7RS3-KS2X)

34   Readability formulas: 7 reasons to avoid them and what to do instead, UX Matters, www.uxmatters.com/mt/archives/2019/07/readability-formulas-7-reasons-to-avoid-them-and-what-to-do-instead.php, (archived at https://perma.cc/7387-5MR3)

35   What is Easy Read? Scope Australia, www.scopeaust.org.au/news/what-is-easy-read (archived at https://perma.cc/3M22-BVA4)

36   L Palmer. The relationship between stress fatigue and cognitive functioning, *College Student J.*, 47 (2), 312–25

37   B Naqvi, J Kävrestad and A K M N Islam. Inclusive and accessible cybersecurity: Challenges and future directions, *Computer*, 57 (6), 73–81, doi: 10.1109/MC.2024.3376827 (archived at https://perma.cc/F4LJ-WHKC)

38   J Wechsler (2024) Chapter 1 What is trauma? In R Edwards (ed.) *Designed with Care: Creating Trauma-informed content,* independently published, UK

39 Improving customer experience with content design: How we joined up services in different business areas, https://digitalblog.coop.co.uk/2022/05/23/improving-customer-experience-with-content-design-how-we-joined-up-services-in-different-business-areas/ (archived at https://perma.cc/VRD9-NY23)

40 Support around death: Do's and don'ts of communication with those who are bereaved, Cruse Bereavement Care Scotland, www.sad.scot.nhs.uk/bereavement/communication-with-those-who-are-bereaved/ (archived at https://perma.cc/DGE7-T3PY)

41 Plain language to minimize cognitive load: A social justice perspective, IEEE Xplore, https://ieeexplore.ieee.org/document/8110648 (archived at https://perma.cc/7WQT-S2FL)

42 How language shapes our reality, Medium, https://quantumdesignteam.medium.com/how-language-shapes-our-reality-cf7401218db2 (archived at https://perma.cc/Q785-SDC2)

43 Disability language style guide, National Center of Disability and Journalism, https://ncdj.org/style-guide/ (archived at https://perma.cc/KSA2-Q29H)

44 The harmful ableist language you unknowingly use, BBC, www.bbc.com/worklife/article/20210330-the-harmful-ableist-language-you-unknowingly-use (archived at https://perma.cc/4RB7-H28S)

45 Types of ableist language and what to say instead, Very Well Mind, www.verywellmind.com/types-of-ableist-language-and-what-to-say-instead-5201561 (archived at https://perma.cc/532P-7JGZ)

46 Ageism: Where it comes from and what it does, Research Gate, www.researchgate.net/publication/351854063_Ageism_Where_It_Comes_From_and_What_It_Does (archived at https://perma.cc/MW8V-8TXD)

47 NATO Gender-inclusive language manual, NATO, www.nato.int/nato_static_fl2014/assets/pictures/images_mfu/2021/5/pdf/210514-GIL-Manual_en.pdf (archived at https://perma.cc/73DH-8WR9)

48 The Asian American Journalists' Association style guide, AAJA style guide, www.aajastyleguide.org/ (archived at https://perma.cc/5272-Q4N8)

49 AP stylebook online, www.ap.org/solutions/platforms/ap-stylebook/ (archived at https://perma.cc/9RDY-JCW8)

50 A beginner's guide to pronouns and using pronouns in the workplace, Stonewall, www.stonewall.org.uk/resources/workplace-trans-inclusion-hub/a-beginners-guide-to-pronouns-and-using-pronouns-in-the-workplace (archived at https://perma.cc/78T8-VZAP)

51 Why sharing gender pronouns is important in the workplace, Culture Amp, www.cultureamp.com/blog/gender-pronouns-in-workplace (archived at https://perma.cc/U5XG-3GLV)

52 Inclusive language guide, American Psychological Association, www.apa.org/about/apa/equity-diversity-inclusion/language-guidelines (archived at https://perma.cc/TC9T-X7Q2)

53 Conscious Style Guide, https://consciousstyleguide.com/ (archived at https://perma.cc/5C2K-SAPC)

05

Writing for and creating an accessible web presence: The basics

When we talk about web accessibility, it's easy to focus on compliance. Things like meeting WCAG standards, following legal guidelines and checking off requirements. But it isn't just about rules; it's about creating an inclusive, user-friendly web experience for everyone. We're talking about making sure that every person, regardless of ability, can engage with content, navigate websites, and interact with digital platforms seamlessly.

The reality is that web accessibility benefits everyone, not just people with disabilities. A well-structured, easy-to-read website helps users with limited bandwidth, those using mobile devices in bright sunlight, and even fast-moving professionals skimming content on the go. Captions on videos help users who are D/deaf or hard of hearing, but they also support people watching in noisy environments. Good contrast and clear typography benefit those with low vision but also improve readability for tired eyes after a long workday.

Yet, too many organizations treat it as an afterthought, and that's a mistake, not just ethically but strategically. A poor web experience can mean lost revenue, legal consequences and frustrated users who will quickly leave a site that isn't intuitive or usable. Businesses that prioritize accessibility gain a competitive edge, building stronger relationships with their audiences and fostering trust.

This chapter will explore web usability, engagement and experience. We'll explain how user-centred design benefits everyone, why businesses and organizations should prioritize it, and the real-world impact of getting it right or wrong. At the end of the day, the web is for all of us, and it's up to us to make sure it stays that way.

Writing for the web: How people read differently online

How people read online vastly differs from how they consume print materials. Unlike books, newspapers or even PDFs, web users don't always read word for word – they scan, skim and jump around to find the information they need as quickly as possible. Because of this, web content must be structured in a way that ensures clarity, engagement and accessibility.

Understanding how users interact with online content can help communicators write in ways that improve readability, usability and inclusivity. We will explore how online reading behaviour differs from print, why shorter, clearer content is crucial, and how to structure digital content for a better user experience.

F-patterns, Z-patterns and mobile behaviour

When people read books or newspapers, they typically move in a linear fashion from left to right, top to bottom. But when reading online, users tend to scan the page rather than read every word. Research on eye-tracking behaviour has shown that readers follow specific patterns when engaging with digital content.

The F-pattern: How users scan text-heavy content

Studies by the Nielsen Norman Group reveal that users scan online content in an F-shape, meaning they focus first on the top headline and the first few sentences, then skim down the left side of the page while reading occasional words along the way.[1] This means that:

- The first few lines of any web page or section are the most crucial – users decide whether to stay or leave within seconds.
- Long paragraphs get skipped because users aren't reading in-depth.
- Readers are more likely to notice bolded, bulleted, or visually distinct text. However, screen readers may process visual elements differently.

USE FORMATTING ELEMENTS WISELY

- Only bold **2 to 3 words** at a time.
- Avoid italics as they're harder to read.

- Don't underline words for emphasis as users may confuse them for hyperlinks.
- Use the built-in formatting options in your content management system or email software for headings, bullets and numbered lists.

The Z-pattern: How users scan visual layouts

People tend to follow a Z-pattern on pages with more graphics, buttons or images. They scan across the top (like a banner or navigation bar), move diagonally down to the next key point, and then scan across again. This behaviour is more common on landing pages or promotional content, where designers strategically place CTAs (calls to action) along this path.[2]

Mobile reading behaviour: Scrolling, tapping and pinching[3]

With over half of the global web traffic coming from mobile devices,[4] writing for accessibility must account for mobile reading behaviours:

- Smaller screens mean less text is visible at once, so concise paragraphs and clear headings are essential.
- Scrolling behaviour is different – users move quickly through content but will stop if something catches their eye.
- Clickable elements need to be well-spaced to prevent accidental taps.

Right-to-left websites

Right-to-left (RTL) websites, used primarily for languages like Arabic, Hebrew and Persian, require unique design considerations to ensure readability and usability. Unlike left-to-right (LTR) layouts, RTL interfaces follow a mirrored reading pattern, meaning navigation menus, images and interactive elements should be aligned accordingly. However, accessibility challenges often arise when developers fail to optimize text alignment, spacing and UI elements, leading to confusing or inconsistent layouts.[5]

Ensuring proper bidirectional support is crucial. When multilingual content appears on the same page, elements like numbers, punctuation and embedded LTR text (such as English product names or URLs) should flow naturally without disrupting readability. Additionally, clear visual hierarchy and ample white space help users scan and comprehend content more efficiently. By designing with RTL accessibility in mind, communicators can provide an inclusive experience for diverse audiences, ensuring that content is translated and structured for seamless engagement.[6]

Shorter sentences, concise paragraphs and plain language for readability

Because online users scan rather than read deeply, shorter sentences and concise paragraphs significantly improve readability and accessibility. Plain language, as we talked about in Chapter 4, ensures that content is clear to a broad audience, including those with cognitive disabilities, non-native English speakers and people using screen readers.[7]

Keep sentences short and direct[8]

Long, complex sentences require more cognitive effort and slow down reading speeds. When writing for the web:

- Aim for an average sentence length of 15–20 words.
- Break up long ideas into multiple sentences instead of using commas to connect clauses.
- Use active voice instead of passive voice to make content clearer.

> **EXAMPLE**
>
> **Bad**: 'The implementation of new accessibility guidelines should be considered by website designers in order to improve overall user experience.'
>
> **Good**: 'Website designers should follow new accessibility guidelines to improve user experience.'

Use concise paragraphs[9]

Dense text is intimidating online, and large blocks of text can cause readers to disengage. Instead of writing paragraphs that resemble print-style writing:

- Keep paragraphs to 2–3 sentences at most.
- Introduce one idea per paragraph.
- Break complex concepts into multiple sections with subheadings.

Prioritize plain language[10]

Like we mentioned in Chapter 4, plain language isn't about oversimplifying; it's about making content clear, direct and accessible to everyone.

- Use common, everyday words instead of jargon.
- Replace technical terms with simpler explanations.
- Avoid corporate or bureaucratic language. People respond better to conversational, reader-friendly content.[11]

> **EXAMPLE**
>
> **Bad**: 'We are in the process of assessing our compliance with accessibility legislation.'
>
> **Good**: 'We are checking if we meet accessibility rules.'

Descriptive headers and clear subheadings for better navigation

Headers and subheadings do more than break up text, as they help screen readers, search engines, and all users navigate content easily.

Use descriptive, informative headers[12]

Instead of vague headers, make sure they provide a clear idea of what follows.

> **EXAMPLE**
>
> **Bad**: 'More details'
>
> **Good**: 'How to apply for funding'

Organize content with subheadings[13]

Subheadings help users scan and find information quickly. They should:

- Use H2 for main sections and H3 for subtopics to create a structured hierarchy.
- Avoid using all caps, which can be harder to read for some users.
- Be concise but descriptive so users know what to expect.

Bullet points and numbered lists for easier skimming[14]

Lists improve readability by breaking information into digestible chunks. Bullet points are useful for summarizing key points, while numbered lists help when sequence matters.

When to use bullet points

Use bullet points for:

- key features or benefits

- quick summaries
- pros and cons

EXAMPLE

Bad: 'Our programme offers resources for accessibility training, workshops, expert guidance and policy updates.'

Good: 'Our programme offers:

- accessibility training
- workshops on inclusive design
- expert guidance
- policy updates'

When to use numbered lists
Use numbered lists when steps need to be followed in order.

EXAMPLE

How to add alt text to an image:

1. Open your document or web page editor.
2. Click on the image.
3. Select 'Edit Alt Text'.
4. Write a clear, descriptive explanation of the image.
5. Save your changes.

Writing for web accessibility isn't just about making content easier to read; it's about making sure everyone can engage with your content, regardless of ability. By understanding how people read online, using clear language, and structuring content in a way that supports scanning and navigation, communicators can create digital experiences that are more inclusive, user-friendly and engaging.

Remember: good accessibility is good communication. Clear, concise content is more effective, inclusive and impactful for all users.

Hyperlinks: Making navigation clear and meaningful

Hyperlinks are the foundation of digital navigation, guiding users through websites, documents and online resources. But not all links are created equal – some can be confusing, misleading, or even completely inaccessible to users with disabilities.[15]

For many, clicking a link is effortless. However, hyperlinks must be designed with clarity and structure in mind for those using screen readers, voice commands, or alternative input devices. A poorly labelled link can create a frustrating experience, making it difficult for users to determine where a link will take them or whether it's relevant to their needs.

By following these best practices, communicators can ensure that every hyperlink is clear, descriptive and easy to navigate for all users.

Avoiding vague links like 'Click here' or 'Read more' – Why context matters

Too often, hyperlinks use vague, generic phrases like 'Click here', 'Read more', or 'Learn more'. While they may seem harmless, these phrases lack meaningful context, particularly for people using screen readers.[16]

Imagine navigating a web page using a screen reader, allowing users to quickly skip from link to link to assess the page's content. If every link simply says 'Click here', the user has no way of knowing where each one leads. They're left with a list of links that all sound the same, making navigation frustrating and inefficient.[17]

> **EXAMPLE**
>
> **Bad**: 'For more details on accessible design, click here.'
>
> **Good**: 'Learn more about accessible design best practices.'
>
> The second example provides clear context by embedding the link in a descriptive phrase, telling users exactly what to expect when they click.

Why vague links are problematic:

- They lack meaning when read out of context.
- They do not provide SEO value, making them harder to index in search engines.

- They slow down navigation for users relying on assistive technology.

Instead, hyperlinks should always provide enough information to make sense on their own.

Writing descriptive hyperlinks that tell users what to expect

A good hyperlink acts as a preview of what's on the other side. Users should know exactly what they'll find before they click.[18]

BEST PRACTICES FOR DESCRIPTIVE LINKS

1. Use keywords and relevant phrases: Instead of linking a vague phrase, embed the hyperlink in descriptive, keyword-rich text.

   Bad: 'To learn about accessibility, click here.'

   Good: 'Read our guide on web accessibility best practices.'

2. Make links self-explanatory: Ensure that the linked text alone conveys its purpose, even if it's read out of context.

   Bad: 'Download report.'

   Good: 'Download the 2025 Digital Accessibility Report.'

3. Avoid linking full URLs in body text: Long URLs are difficult to read aloud and can be cumbersome for assistive technology users.

   Bad: 'Visit www.example.com/2025-accessibility-guide.html to read more.'

   Good: 'Explore our 2025 Accessibility Guide for in-depth insights.'

4. Be mindful of length.

   Too short: 'Here'

   Too long: 'For a comprehensive overview of inclusive design best practices that can help organizations improve digital accessibility, click here.'

   Just right: 'Read our inclusive design best practices.'

5. Differentiate links within body content: If multiple links appear in a paragraph, ensure they don't sound identical. Better still is to provide multiple links in a list to make it easier for everyone.

   Bad: 'Learn about accessibility here, usability here and compliance here.'

   Better: 'Explore accessibility fundamentals, usability principles and compliance requirements.'

Best: 'Explore:
- accessibility fundamentals
- usability principles
- compliance requirements'

6 Avoid hiding email addresses behind text. Accidentally clicking on a mail-to link can disrupt the user experience for everyone, particularly if it opens a mail client unexpectedly.

Bad: 'To get in touch, contact us.'

Good: 'Contact the team on hello@ouraddress.com'

Best practices for link placement, colour contrast and underlining[19]

Accessibility goes beyond just the words in a hyperlink; it also involves visual presentation and placement.

Place links strategically

- Position important links early in content to ensure they are noticeable.
- Avoid burying links deep in long paragraphs.
- Separate links for different topics, rather than cramming multiple links into one sentence.

EXAMPLE

Bad: 'If you're interested in web accessibility, check out our guide here, or if you'd like to learn more about compliance, click this link.'

Good: 'Want to improve digital accessibility? Explore our web accessibility guide. Need compliance insights? Read our compliance checklist.'

Ensure strong colour contrast

- Links must have enough contrast against the background to be legible for users with low vision or colour blindness.
- Avoid using colour alone to differentiate links. Many colour-blind users can't distinguish between links and regular text without additional formatting.

> **EXAMPLE**
>
> **Bad:** A light grey hyperlink on a white background. Use tools like WebAIM's Contrast Checker to test colour contrast.
>
> **Good:** A dark blue hyperlink on a white background.

Always underline links

- Underlining is the universal signal for a hyperlink.
- Do not rely on colour alone to differentiate links from regular text.
- Avoid removing underlines with cascading style sheets (CSS) unless you add another indicator (such as bolding or a hover effect).

How assistive technologies interpret links and why structure matters

Screen readers navigate pages by jumping from link to link, allowing users to hear a list of all available links on a page. If those links lack context, users may have difficulty determining where they lead.[20] Not all screen readers work in the same way but there are some general principles to follow.

How screen readers handle links

- Screen readers announce links in isolation from surrounding text.
- They can skip generic words like 'click here', making vague links useless.
- Some screen readers allow users to pull up a list of all links on a page, meaning links should make sense out of context.

Improving link structure for assistive technology

- Use concise, informative text for every link.
- Avoid duplicating identical link text (e.g. multiple 'Read more' links).
- Ensure links are logically structured within the content.

Note: Try to avoid a link to open in a new tab, unless you are explicitly telling users it will be taking them to a new tab.

Hyperlinks are more than functional elements; they shape the way people navigate and engage with digital content. Clear, accessible links enhance usability, comprehension and inclusivity for everyone.[21]

By avoiding vague language, using descriptive text, ensuring strong contrast and structuring links with accessibility in mind, communicators can create a seamless digital experience for all users, regardless of how they interact with content.[22]

At the end of the day, good hyperlinking is good communication. Whether your audience is clicking, tapping or listening, your links should always be clear, informative and easy to use.

Visual accessibility: How to make images meaningful for everyone

Images are an integral part of digital communication. They add depth to storytelling, enhance comprehension, and make content more engaging. But without proper accessibility considerations, they can also create barriers for people who rely on screen readers, have low vision, or process information differently.

That's why providing multiple layers of description, image titles, alt text, captions and detailed descriptions is essential. These elements ensure that all users, regardless of ability, can access and understand visual content in meaningful ways.

Why images need multiple layers of description

Images are not one-size-fits-all when it comes to accessibility. Different users interact with visual content in various ways, and a single descriptive layer isn't always enough.[23] For example:

- A screen reader user may rely entirely on alt text to understand an image.
- Someone with low vision might magnify an image but still need a caption to grasp finer details.
- A user with a cognitive disability might benefit from a clear, written description alongside an image.
- A person browsing a page in a noisy environment may not be able to rely on audio narration and instead look to text-based context for understanding.

By offering multiple layers of description, content creators ensure that all users receive the information they need in the way that works best for them.

Let's break down the key components of effective image accessibility.

Writing effective alt text

Alternative text (alt text) is the first and most fundamental layer of image accessibility. It provides a concise, meaningful description of an image so that screen readers can relay its content to users who can't see it.[24] But writing effective alt text is both an art and a science.

Be concise yet descriptive

Alt text should provide just enough detail to convey the image's purpose without unnecessary fluff. A good rule of thumb is to keep it under 125 characters, as most screen readers cut off at that point.

> EXAMPLE
>
> **Good:** 'A woman in a wheelchair using a ramp outside a coffee shop.'
>
> **Bad:** 'A woman outside a shop.'

Some users like to understand more information about an image. Use of alt text depends on the intention of the image in the first place, but to provide more information, make sure you front-load the key information.

> EXAMPLE
>
> **Good:** A woman in a wheelchair using a ramp on her way into a café. She has curly brown hair and is wearing a red jacket and jeans.
>
> **Bad:** 'A woman with curly brown hair, wearing a red jacket and jeans, propelling herself in a wheelchair up a concrete ramp leading into a café with a glass door.'

Don't state the obvious

Avoid redundant phrases like 'Image of...' or 'Photo of...' Screen readers already announce that it's an image before reading the alt text.

Convey purpose, not just content

If an image serves a functional purpose (e.g. a button, an icon), describe the function rather than the appearance.

> **EXAMPLE**
>
> **Good** (for a search icon): 'Search the site.'
>
> **Bad** (for a search icon): 'Magnifying glass icon.'

Skip decorative images

If an image is purely decorative and adds no meaningful content, mark it as decorative in the HTML (alt=""). This prevents screen readers from announcing unnecessary details.[25] As highlighted in the W3C guidelines, what makes an image truly decorative is entirely subjective. As Eric Bailey argues, 'Image placement on the modern web is highly intentional.'[26] What one person considers adds a 'vibe' or feeling for a page may get in the way of others finding the information – but that feeling may provide valuable context and help set the tone of the content.

> **TIP**
>
> Images *may* be decorative when they are:
>
> - visual styling such as borders, spacers and corners
> - supplementary to link text to improve its appearance or increase the clickable area
> - illustrative of adjacent text but not contributing information ('eye candy')
> - identified and described by surrounding text[27]

The role of captions in image accessibility

Captions serve a different role from alt text. While alt text is primarily for screen reader users, captions are visible to everyone and provide additional clarity.[28]

Why captions matter

- They enhance comprehension by summarizing or explaining the visual.
- They are particularly useful for complex images, like infographics or maps.
- They benefit all users, including those in noisy environments who may rely on text rather than audio cues.

> **BEST PRACTICES FOR WRITING CAPTIONS**
>
> Make them informative but not redundant. If the surrounding text already describes the image, the caption should provide extra value.
>
> **Example**: A caption accompanying an image of a protest could add context like, 'Protesters in Toronto rally for disability rights in front of City Hall.'
>
> Align captions with the image's role. If an image is meant to evoke emotion or set a tone, the caption can reflect that.
>
> **Example**: A caption for an image of a dog adoption event might read, 'Dozens of excited rescue dogs meet their future families at this weekend's adoption fair.'
>
> Make captions scannable. Use clear, short sentences so users can quickly grasp the content.

Extended descriptions: When alt text and captions aren't enough

Sometimes, an image is too detailed or complex to be described effectively in a single caption or alt text.[29] This is especially true for:

- infographics
- charts and graphs
- maps
- highly detailed illustrations

In these cases, a longer description is needed, often placed within the body text or linked to a separate page.

> **BEST PRACTICES FOR EXTENDED IMAGE DESCRIPTIONS**
>
> **Provide a summary before the details**. Instead of immediately launching into every aspect of a graph, start with the key takeaway.
>
> **Example**: 'This chart shows that mobile internet usage has increased by 40 per cent in the past five years.'
>
> **Break up long descriptions**. Use bullet points or paragraphs to make content digestible.

> **Ensure the data is available in a non-visual format.** If an infographic presents statistics, include those numbers in a text-based list.
>
> **Link to an accessible version when needed.** If space is limited, provide a link to a full-text version of the infographic.

Bringing it all together: A holistic approach

Using a combination of alt text, captions and descriptions ensures that images are truly accessible to all users. Here's how these elements can work together. The following example is a graph which uses demo data to illustrate the rise of home working at a fictional company.

FIGURE 5.1 Home working trends

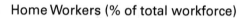
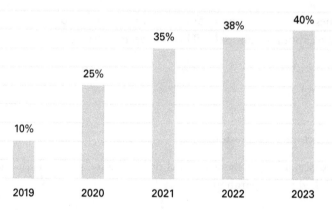

SOURCE Lisa Riemers

Caption: 'Remote work trends have surged, with a 30 per cent rise in adoption over the past four years.'

Extended description: 'From 10 per cent in 2019, jumping to 25 per cent during 2020 and rising to 40 per cent by 2023, this shows the impact of the pandemic on working practices. A section below the image provides a full breakdown of the data, including key figures and a discussion of the factors contributing to the trend.'

Communicators can ensure that their visuals are engaging, meaningful and inclusive by considering accessibility from multiple angles.

Ensuring web accessibility goes far beyond just adding alt text to images. Thoughtful captions, well-structured descriptions and a holistic approach to image accessibility can make the digital space more inclusive for everyone. As technology evolves, so will the ways we integrate images into content. The key is to remain intentional, ensuring that all users, regardless of ability, can fully engage with and benefit from the visuals we create.

So next time you add an image to your content, ask yourself: Is this accessible to everyone? If not, it's worth taking that extra step.

Visual design: Accessibility beyond alt text

When we think about web accessibility, alt text is often the first thing that comes to mind. While crucial for screen reader users, accessibility goes far beyond image descriptions. The way we design web content, from typography and spacing to colour contrast and responsiveness, plays a major role in ensuring readability and usability for all users.

Thoughtful visual design doesn't just benefit people with disabilities; it creates a better experience for everyone. When text is easy to read, navigation is seamless, and content adjusts smoothly across devices, it leads to higher engagement and better user retention.

This section explores the key principles of accessible visual design and how they enhance digital communication.

Choosing accessible fonts

The choice of font can make or break readability. While decorative and stylized fonts may look appealing, they often create barriers for users with dyslexia, visual or cognitive disabilities. Not all fonts are created equal, and some are more accessible than others. However, experts disagree on a definitive list of accessible fonts, as some readers have different needs.[30]

GOOD PRACTICES FOR FONT ACCESSIBILITY

Use sans-serif fonts. Fonts like Arial, Verdana, Tahoma and Open Sans are generally considered easier to read because they lack decorative strokes (serifs). Serif fonts like Times New Roman can be harder for some users to process, especially at smaller sizes.[31]

> - **Avoid overly decorative or script fonts.** Fancy, cursive or handwritten fonts may look elegant, but they reduce legibility, especially for users with dyslexia or low vision.[32]
> - **Stick to font sizes of at least 16 px.** A minimum of 16px (1 rem) is recommended for body text. Anything smaller can cause strain, especially for users on mobile devices or those with visual disabilities.[33]
> - **Prioritize letter spacing (kerning) and line spacing (leading)**
> - Kerning refers to the space between individual letters. Too little or too much space can make words difficult to recognize.
> - Leading is the vertical space between lines of text. A comfortable line height of 1.5 x the font size improves readability and prevents text from appearing too cramped.
> - **Limit the number of fonts per page.** Using too many fonts creates visual clutter and inconsistency. Stick to one or two fonts throughout a website to maintain a clean and accessible design.

Why line spacing, kerning and leading matter for readability

Spacing in typography plays a crucial role in making content readable for all users, especially those with cognitive or visual disabilities.

Line spacing (leading)

Poor leading: Too little space between lines makes the text feel cramped and hard to follow.

Recommended: A minimum line height of 1.5 x the font size improves readability and reduces eye strain.

Letter spacing (kerning)

Poor kerning: Letters that are too close together can make words difficult to distinguish.

Recommended: Adequate spacing between letters prevents misreading and helps users with dyslexia process words more easily.

Word and paragraph spacing

Avoid justified text alignment. It creates uneven gaps between words, making reading difficult for users with cognitive disabilities. Instead, use left-aligned text (or right-aligned for RTL websites) for better readability.

Use clear paragraph breaks. Long blocks of text can overwhelm users. Breaking content into short paragraphs (2–3 sentences each) makes it more digestible.

Responsive design: Ensuring accessibility across devices

Web users interact with content across various devices, like desktops, tablets and smartphones. A design that looks great on a large screen may break or become unreadable on smaller screens.

How to make your content responsive and accessible

1. Use a mobile-first approach. More users browse the web on their phones than on desktops. Design for smaller screens first, then scale up.
2. Ensure text resizes properly. Users should be able to zoom in on text without losing clarity or breaking the layout.
3. Avoid fixed-width elements. Use relative units like percentages instead of fixed pixel widths to allow content to adapt dynamically.
4. Make buttons and links touch-friendly. Use a minimum tap target size of 44x44 pixels for interactive elements. Ensure adequate spacing between links so users don't accidentally tap the wrong one.[34]
5. Check responsiveness with real users. Use tools like Google's Mobile-Friendly Test to evaluate how content adapts. Conduct user testing with assistive technology (e.g. screen readers on mobile devices).[35]

By designing with responsiveness and accessibility in mind, we ensure that content remains usable, readable and engaging across all platforms.

Accessible colour contrast considerations

How often have you visited a web page or seen content on social media that uses white text on a light blue sky, or a busy patterned background? When considering online content – whether web pages, emails, apps or social media assets, choosing an accessible colour palette is key. It can be tempting to select a muted colour palette to match a theme or vibe; however, when that design comes at the cost of readability, it makes it harder to read for everyone.

Not everyone experiences colour in the same way

While low-contrast colour schemes make it harder for those who are partially sighted or in poor lighting conditions, there are many reasons why people perceive colours differently. With 1 in 12 men and 1 in 200 women being colour-blind,[36] colour contrasts may not be as strong as you might think. It's not just red-green colour-blindness either; there are a number of conditions which may affect what colours people see.[37] Also, some users may prefer to use their devices in dark mode – does your email still work if the colours are inverted?

Don't rely on colour to convey important information

To make sure everyone can see your information, avoid using colour alone to convey instructions or critical details.

> **TIP**
>
> When displaying a report with a Red/Amber/Green rating, incorporate additional visual cues. You could:
>
> - use distinctive shapes
> - add different shading patterns
> - include the appropriate letter
>
> These strategies help colour-blind people and those reading black-and-white printouts read your information more effectively.

Select an accessible palette

Depending on the platform, you may have limited ability to affect the selection of colours available. However, there are steps you can take to use those colours more effectively online.

> **TIPS**
>
> Use built-in accessibility checkers, where available in your design tools, to set up nice, clear templates that set you up for future communications.
>
> Use a service like Whocanuse.com[38] to see how your chosen colours might be perceived.
>
> Consider a higher contrast selection, such as black text on an off-white background, which is generally good practice.
>
> **Note**: While high contrast is typically recommended, be aware that some users, including those with dyslexia, may find stark black on white challenging to read. Finding a balanced approach is key.[39]

Test with your audience

There's no one-size-fits-all approach and it's vital that you test your communications with your users. Perhaps your corporate devices provide particular limitations, or your audience is using your information in low-light conditions. People have different needs, even when they have similar disabilities.

Accessibility in visual design is about clarity, usability and inclusivity. By choosing readable fonts, ensuring proper spacing, maintaining strong colour contrast, and optimizing for mobile devices, communicators can enhance the user experience for all audiences.

Accessible design is about creating content that works for everyone, no matter how they access it. By integrating inclusive design principles, organizations can reach broader audiences, improve engagement and demonstrate a commitment to digital inclusion.

KEY TAKEAWAYS

Creating an accessible web presence is about improving usability and ensuring digital content is accessible to all users, regardless of ability. This chapter explored the fundamental principles of accessible web content and provided actionable strategies to enhance digital accessibility.

We began by discussing the importance of accessibility beyond legal requirements, emphasizing that an inclusive web benefits everyone, from people with disabilities to users navigating content on mobile devices or in challenging environments. Accessibility should be a core consideration from the start, not an afterthought.

Next, we examined how people read and interact with content online, highlighting key reading patterns like the F-pattern and Z-pattern. Understanding these behaviours allows communicators to structure content in a way that improves readability and engagement. We also explored how mobile users interact differently with web content and the importance of designing for right-to-left (RTL) languages.

To enhance web readability and usability, we covered best practices for writing short, clear and accessible content. This included the use of plain language, concise paragraphs and structured headings to support navigation. Bullet points, numbered lists and descriptive hyperlinks were also discussed as essential tools for improving content clarity and skim-ability.

Hyperlinks, as critical navigation elements, were examined in detail. We explored why vague links like 'Click here' create barriers and how to craft descriptive, meaningful hyperlinks that enhance both usability and SEO. Best practices for link placement, colour contrast and underlining were also addressed to ensure accessibility across different user needs.

We then turned our focus to visual accessibility, emphasizing the need for thoughtful image descriptions, effective alt text, and the importance of captions and extended descriptions. Making images meaningful for all users requires a layered approach, ensuring that content is accessible to screen reader users, individuals with low vision and those who process information differently.

Finally, we discussed accessibility in visual design beyond alt text. Typography, spacing and contrast are key factors that affect readability and usability. Choosing accessible fonts, ensuring proper line spacing and designing responsive layouts help create a seamless and inclusive digital experience across devices.

Looking ahead

An accessible web presence is a necessity, not a luxury. By integrating accessibility best practices into digital content, communicators can create more inclusive, engaging and user-friendly experiences for all. The strategies outlined in this chapter provide a foundation, but accessibility is an ongoing commitment that requires continuous learning, testing and adaptation.

As we move forward, the next chapter will delve into the importance of accessible document formats, exploring standards like PDF/UA and best practices for making PDFs and other digital documents accessible. Just as web accessibility enhances online experiences, document accessibility ensures that all users can equitably access important information.

References

1 F-shaped pattern of reading on the web: Misunderstood, but still relevant (even on mobile), Nielsen Norman Group, www.nngroup.com/articles/f-shaped-pattern-reading-web-content/ (archived at https://perma.cc/Q9FC-EBDK)
2 Visual hierarchy: Organizing content to follow natural eye movement patterns, Interaction Design Foundation, www.interaction-design.org/literature/article/visual-hierarchy-organizing-content-to-follow-natural-eye-movement-patterns (archived at https://perma.cc/YKJ8-4QEC)
3 Insights: Mobile accessibility, Fable, https://makeitfable.com/article/insights-mobile-accessibility/ (archived at https://perma.cc/MNA5-FJF6)

4 75+ mobile surfing stats on internet traffic from mobile devices (updated), Thrive Agency, https://thriveagency.com/news/75-mobile-surfing-stats-on-internet-traffic-from-mobile-devices-updated/ (archived at https://perma.cc/6U8L-HJ86)

5 Designing a robust right-to-left UI in Arabic, Hebrew and Farsi, Medium, https://uxdesign.cc/designing-a-robust-right-to-left-ui-in-arabic-hebrew-and-farsi-d1e662a09cfa (archived at https://perma.cc/5T94-824L)

6 Lost in translation: Tips for multilingual web accessibility, Ben Myers, https://benmyers.dev/blog/multilingual-web-accessibility/ (archived at https://perma.cc/9Q8E-QB24)

7 How users read on the web, Nielsen Norman Group, www.nngroup.com/articles/how-users-read-on-the-web/ (archived at https://perma.cc/FCD7-4A3Q)

8 Simple sentences, Content Design London – Readability Guidelines, https://readabilityguidelines.co.uk/clear-language/simple-sentences/ (archived at https://perma.cc/4V2E-CPHH)

9 Keep text succinct, W3C, www.w3.org/WAI/WCAG2/supplemental/patterns/o3p05-succinct-text/ (archived at https://perma.cc/4UVN-MWK4)

10 Avoid jargon, PlainLanguage.gov, www.plainlanguage.gov/guidelines/words/avoid-jargon/ (archived at https://perma.cc/Z9KD-72GU)

11 C R Trudeau. The public speaks: An empirical study of legal communication, Scribes Journal of Legal Writing, 14, 121, https://ssrn.com/abstract=1843415 or http://dx.doi.org/10.2139/ssrn.1843415 (archived at https://perma.cc/Z44H-AG97)

12 Digital accessibility 101: Descriptive links and headers, AudioEye, www.audioeye.com/post/digital-accessibility-descriptive-links-headers/ (archived at https://perma.cc/WD43-J8NP)

13 Headings, W3C, www.w3.org/WAI/tutorials/page-structure/headings/ (archived at https://perma.cc/7X2Y-LHRG)

14 Structure with headings and lists, eCampus Ontario, https://accessibility.ecampusontario.ca/accessibility/best-practices/headings-and-lists/ (archived at https://perma.cc/A5N2-6BYQ)

15 Navigation and hyperlinks, Niagara College Accessibility Hub, https://accessibilityhub.niagaracollege.ca/articles/websites/navigation-and-hyperlinks/ (archived at https://perma.cc/X3A5-647K)

16 Don't use 'click here', Medium, https://heyoka.medium.com/dont-use-click-here-f32f445d1021 (archived at https://perma.cc/Z9Y8-NYLR)

17 Hyperlinks in websites and documents, Accessibility for Ontarians with Disabilities Act, https://aoda.ca/hyperlinks-in-websites-and-documents/ (archived at https://perma.cc/S35H-YYJN)

18 Guidelines on designing better hyperlinks, Medium, https://medium.com/design-bridges/designing-better-links-for-websites-and-emails-a-guideline-5b8638ce675a (archived at https://perma.cc/MCG2-WZHL)

19 Enhancing accessibility: Link text best practices, Level Access, www.levelaccess.com/blog/enhancing-accessibility-link-text-best-practices/ (archived at https://perma.cc/523C-2HVQ)

20 Link purpose (in Context) (Level A), W3C, www.w3.org/WAI/WCAG22/Understanding/link-purpose-in-context.html (archived at https://perma.cc/68B2-N7HT)

21 7 crucial accessibility considerations for seamless digital interaction, A11Y Collective, www.a11y-collective.com/blog/accessibility-considerations/ (archived at https://perma.cc/8XJD-V2XV)

22 Master the art of accessible link text, WCAG, www.wcag.com/blog/writing-meaningful-link-text/ (archived at https://perma.cc/C6DL-G3YD)

23 Accessibility: Image Alt text best practices, Siteimprove, https://help.siteimprove.com/support/solutions/articles/80000863904-accessibility-image-alt-text-best-practices (archived at https://perma.cc/V9RB-DNNW)

24 What is alternative text? Image alt text with examples, TechSmith, www.techsmith.com/blog/how-to-create-alternative-text-for-images-for-accessibility-and-seo/ (archived at https://perma.cc/SPX7-G4XF)

25 Decorative images, W3C, www.w3.org/WAI/tutorials/images/decorative/ (archived at https://perma.cc/7RAV-4CBD)

26 Your image is probably not decorative, Smashing Magazine, www.smashingmagazine.com/2021/06/img-alt-attribute-alternate-description-decorative/ (archived at https://perma.cc/4K9R-VNNV)

27 Decorative images, W3C, www.w3.org/WAI/tutorials/images/decorative/ (archived at https://perma.cc/FPG6-7TU6)

28 Alt text, and captions, and titles, Oh my!, Kanopi Studios, https://kanopi.com/blog/alt-text-and-captions-and-titles-oh-my/ (archived at https://perma.cc/EEA2-Q82E)

29 Complex images, W3C, www.w3.org/WAI/tutorials/images/complex/ (archived at https://perma.cc/47XP-QBD6)

30 Accessible fonts and readability: the basics, Scope, https://business.scope.org.uk/font-accessibility-and-readability-the-basics/ (archived at https://perma.cc/V4UV-XZJH)

31 What is an accessible font? Accessibility Checker, www.accessibilitychecking.com/blog/fonts-accessibility/ (archived at https://perma.cc/5GYX-DAD3)

32 Choosing accessible fonts: Enhancing readability and inclusivity, DigitalA11Y, www.digitala11y.com/choosing-accessible-fonts-enhancing-readability-and-inclusivity/ (archived at https://perma.cc/KB3Q-EW5G)

33 How to pick the perfect font size: A guide to WCAG accessibility, A11Y Collective, www.a11y-collective.com/blog/wcag-minimum-font-size/ (archived at https://perma.cc/B3RV-RDQA)

34 Target size (minimum) (Level AA), W3C, www.w3.org/WAI/WCAG22/Understanding/target-size-minimum.html (archived at https://perma.cc/KUQ5-T3YY)

35 Mobile app accessibility testing checklist, BrowserStack, www.browserstack.com/guide/accessibility-testing-for-mobile-apps (archived at https://perma.cc/PZ8M-F2WUq)
36 About colour blindness, Colour Blind Awareness, www.colourblindawareness.org/colour-blindness/ (archived at https://perma.cc/PF5G-PXCG)
37 Visual disabilities, color-blindness, Web AIM, https://webaim.org/articles/visual/colorblind (archived at https://perma.cc/WA8N-KK5K)
38 Who can use this color combination? www.whocanuse.com/ (archived at https://perma.cc/MF49-DJXE)
39 How to write dyslexic friendly web content: colours and fonts, Scope, https://business.scope.org.uk/how-to-write-better-website-content-for-people-with-dyslexia/ (archived at https://perma.cc/QRD9-U328)

06

Getting started with accessible documents

Imagine sending out an important report, presentation or brochure that beautifully conveys your brand's message – only to realize that a portion of your audience cannot engage with it. Maybe the screen reader can't read the text, or the images lack descriptions. This oversight doesn't just limit your reach; it excludes individuals who rely on accessibility features to interact with digital content. Perhaps it's destined to be printed out and the local print equipment isn't up to standard – now that document is hard to interpret for everyone.

This chapter will explore the fundamentals of accessible document design, breaking down what makes a document usable for everyone and why it matters. We'll tackle everything from structuring content with headings to adding alt text to images, setting reading orders and using proper tools for testing. Whether you're a seasoned professional or just starting, you'll learn practical steps to create documents that resonate with diverse audiences.

But this chapter isn't just about compliance; it's about empowerment — documents open doors to knowledge, opportunity and connection. When you commit to accessibility, you're sending a clear message: your business values inclusivity and respects every individual's right to access information.

Together, we'll demystify the process, equip you with tools and best practices, and set you on a path towards creating documents that not only inform but include. Accessible communication starts here.

A quick overview: Types of documents and why accessibility matters

When it comes to professional communications, documents come in many forms, each with unique challenges and opportunities for accessibility.

Whether you're crafting a polished PDF report, designing a visually engaging presentation, or analysing data in a spreadsheet, understanding the needs of your audience is essential. This section provides a snapshot of the types of documents covered in this chapter and their roles in creating inclusive communication.

Text documents: Everyday essentials

Text documents are the backbone of daily communication, encompassing everything from internal memos to client proposals. Common pitfalls include improperly structured headings, missing alt text for images and ambiguous hyperlinks. Making text documents accessible ensures inclusivity and improves clarity and usability for all readers.

Presentations: Visual storytelling in action

Presentations are powerful tools for communicating ideas in team meetings, stakeholder briefings, or public events. However, slides often fall short of being accessible. Issues like low contrast, unstructured content, or lack of alt text for visuals can exclude audience members. The best presentations are structured with clear navigation, legible fonts and inclusive multimedia, ensuring everyone can engage with your message.

Spreadsheets: Navigating numbers with clarity

Spreadsheets play a critical role in organizing and analysing data, but their accessibility can be challenging. Complex layouts, merged cells and unlabelled data can make navigation difficult for screen readers. Use clear headers, meaningful labels and high-contrast visuals to make data more understandable and inclusive, even for those relying on assistive technologies.

PDFs: The versatile standard

PDFs are a cornerstone of professional communication due to their universal compatibility and polished appearance. PDFs are often the final, shareable version of a document, from annual reports to brochures. However, PDFs can become inaccessible to people who rely on screen readers or other assistive technologies without proper tagging, alternative text for visuals and logical reading orders.

Why covering these document types matters

These document types represent how professional communicators share information with internal and external audiences. Each has its own set of requirements. By addressing the specific challenges and best practices for each type, this chapter equips you with the tools to make your work more impactful and accessible to all.

Up next, we'll consider the specifics of creating accessible PDFs, presentations, text documents and spreadsheets, complete with actionable tips and examples to guide you every step of the way.

Text documents: Simplicity meets functionality

Text documents are the backbone of professional communication. These documents are critical in conveying information, whether they're reports, memos, proposals or instructional manuals. Ensuring that text documents are accessible is not just a best practice but an essential step towards fostering inclusivity. Text documents should cater to everyone, including those using assistive technologies like screen readers or magnifiers. This section delves into how to create text documents that are both simple and functional while meeting accessibility standards.

Building an accessible foundation

Accessible documents begin with a solid foundation, using structured content to give clarity for all users, including those who rely on assistive technologies.

Structuring content with headings, lists and proper spacing

- Headings: Use proper heading styles (e.g. Heading 1, Heading 2, etc) to create a logical structure. This helps screen readers navigate the document efficiently and allows all users to quickly find the information they need.[1]
- Lists: Use bulleted or numbered lists for sequences and grouped information. This improves readability and helps screen readers differentiate between items.[2]
- Spacing: Avoid cramming text. Use adequate line spacing (e.g. 1.5 or double spacing) and maintain clear margins to make your document easy to read.[3]

- Using plain language: Write in clear, straightforward language, avoiding jargon or overly complex terms. This benefits readers with cognitive disabilities or those unfamiliar with technical terminology.
- Inclusive language: Use gender-neutral terms (e.g. 'they' instead of 'he/she', unless you know the person's preferred pronouns) and avoid ableist or exclusionary language. For instance, say 'person who uses a wheelchair' rather than 'wheelchair-bound'.

SPACING: CREATING BREATHING ROOM FOR ACCESSIBILITY IN YOUR CONTENT

When it comes to designing accessible documents, proper spacing plays a crucial role in enhancing readability and reducing strain. For individuals with visual, cognitive or learning disabilities, like dyslexia, clear and spacious layouts make content significantly easier to process:

- Line spacing (leading): Adequate line spacing ensures that text doesn't feel cramped or overwhelming. A minimum of 1.5 or even double spacing provides enough room for the eyes to track from one line to the next without confusion. This is particularly important for individuals who use magnification tools, as closely packed text can become challenging to decipher when zoomed in.[4]
- Line length and column width: Very long and very short lines are harder to read. According to the Plain English Campaign, a line of body text should normally contain 60 to 72 characters, or about 10 to 12 words. Consider your column widths to give your words space to breathe.[5]
- Kerning (letter spacing): Kerning refers to the space between individual letters. For accessibility, slightly increased letter spacing can improve readability, especially for individuals with dyslexia or low vision. Avoid overly tight kerning, as it can cause letters to blur together, making words harder to distinguish. However, excessive spacing can disrupt the flow of reading, so aim for a balanced approach.[6]
- Margins and padding: Clear margins and sufficient white space around text blocks create a cleaner design, preventing visual clutter. Margins provide a natural boundary, guiding the reader's eye and making the content feel more approachable.[7]

Paying attention to spacing, kerning and leading ensures it's usable and welcoming for all readers, regardless of their abilities. These small adjustments can make a big difference in how your message is received and understood.

Accessibility features in word processing tools

Modern word processing tools like Microsoft Word and Google Docs offer built-in features to help you create accessible documents. These features, when used correctly, make the process straightforward and effective.

Adding alt text to images and meaningful hyperlinks

- Alt text for images: Add descriptive alt text to all images, charts and graphics. This ensures that users who rely on screen readers can understand the visual content. For example, as we covered in Chapter 5, instead of writing 'Image of a graph', describe the graph's purpose: 'Bar graph showing a 20 per cent increase in sales from Q1 to Q2.'[8]
- Meaningful hyperlinks: Use descriptive link text rather than generic phrases like 'click here' or 'read more'. For example, 'Download the accessibility guide' is more useful than 'Click here'.[9]

Using built-in accessibility checkers

- Microsoft Word: Word's Accessibility Checker highlights issues such as missing alt text, insufficient contrast or improper heading structures. It also provides recommendations for fixing these problems.
- Google Docs: Although Google Docs doesn't have a dedicated checker, you can use third-party add-ons like GrackleDocs to evaluate and improve your document's accessibility.

Common mistakes to avoid

Creating accessible documents requires attention to detail and an understanding of common pitfalls that can inadvertently create barriers.

Over-reliance on tables for layout

Tables are often misused to control the visual layout of a document, which can confuse screen readers. Tables should only be used for presenting tabular data. When you do use tables:[10]

- Include clear headers for rows and columns.
- Avoid merging cells, as this can disrupt the logical reading order.
- Present data which makes sense reading from left to right.
- Ensure the table has a concise caption describing its purpose.

Example of a good table and a bad table

TABLE 6.1 An example of an inaccessible table

Date	Dest.	Est HT	Est LT
08/03/25	Bow Creek	09:18	15:41
09/03/25	St Saviour	10:44	17:12
AGM			
11/03/25	Bow Creek	16:00	10:06

TABLE 6.2 A more accessible table

Date	Destination	High tide	Low tide
08 Mar 25	Bow Creek	09:18	15:41
09 Mar 25	St Saviour	10:44	17:12
10 Mar 25	AGM	n/a	n/a
11 Mar 25	Bow Creek	16:00	10:06

Missing document metadata (known as document properties) for screen readers

FIGURE 6.1 Document metadata in an MS Word file

SOURCE Matisse Hamel-Nelis, Lisa Riemers

Metadata, otherwise known as the document properties, provides crucial context for screen reader users. When it's missing or incomplete, the document may be less accessible. There are two levels of metadata – within the files themselves, and within the content management system (CMS) used to access a document if it's stored online. Within the CMS, displaying the file size and type helps users identify whether the file is what they're looking for, and if they've got the data to be able to download it. At document-level, this means that screen reader users will be able to get the context and know they're reading the right thing.[11]

Adding keywords and categories, particularly those that have been tested with users, will also help with findability for everyone.

Within the file itself, always include:

- Document title: Provide a descriptive title in the document properties (e.g. 'Annual Financial Report 2024').
- Language setting: Specify the primary language of the document to ensure screen readers pronounce words correctly.
- Author information: Include the document's creator for added context.

Practical tips for accessible text documents

- Avoid overuse of bold or italics: Too much bold or italicized text can make a document harder to read. Use these styles sparingly to emphasize key points. **Note:** Screen readers don't read out this type of formatting in this context. You'll want to ensure the wording emphasizes the importance of what is being highlighted.
- Stick to simple fonts: Choose sans-serif fonts like Arial or Calibri, which are easier to read on screens. Avoid decorative fonts, particularly for important information.
- Use colour wisely: A limited familiar palette is easier to read than using multiple colours of text. Don't rely on colour alone to convey meaning – pair colour with text or symbols. This ensures the message is clearer to everyone, including those who are colour-blind.

WHAT ABOUT FONTS DESIGNED FOR DYSLEXIA?

Did you know that some fonts are specifically created to assist readers with dyslexia? Fonts like OpenDyslexic[12] and Dyslexie[13] are designed with unique letter shapes and heavier bottoms to reduce letter-swapping and improve

> readability. These fonts aim to minimize visual confusion and make text more accessible for individuals with dyslexia.
>
> While not a universal solution, they can be a helpful tool when paired with other accessible design practices like ample spacing and clear layout.

Accessible text documents combine clear structure, inclusive language and thoughtful use of built-in tools to create content that serves all users effectively. By adhering to these practices and avoiding common mistakes, professional communicators can ensure their documents are not only functional but also inclusive, helping to bridge communication gaps and create equity.

Structuring slide decks for accessibility

Creating accessible slide decks means that everyone, regardless of ability, can engage with your presentation content. Accessible slides enhance usability for audiences who rely on assistive technologies and improve the clarity and effectiveness of your message for everyone.

Logical slide order and clear headings

A well-structured slide deck follows a logical flow that aligns with the presentation's narrative. This structure is essential for both comprehension and accessibility.

Slide order
Ensure slides are arranged sequentially to reflect the progression of your presentation. An illogical sequence can confuse everyone, particularly screen reader users who navigate slides in the order they appear.

Headings
Use clear, descriptive headings on each slide. These serve as navigation aids for screen readers, helping users quickly understand the slide's content and purpose. For example, instead of a generic title like 'Key Points', use 'Three Strategies for Engaging Customers'.[14]

Slide titles as navigation aids for screen readers

Slide titles are critical for making presentations accessible to screen reader users:

- Assign a unique and descriptive title to every slide. Titles like 'Challenges in Digital Accessibility' or 'Solutions for Inclusive Design' provide meaningful context.
- Avoid leaving slide titles blank or reusing the same title across multiple slides, as this can confuse screen reader users navigating through the deck.

Design considerations

Thoughtful design plays a significant role in ensuring your slides are accessible and visually appealing.

Use high-contrast colour schemes[15]

- Opt for high-contrast combinations, such as dark text on a light background or light text on a dark background, to enhance readability for viewers with low vision or colour blindness.
- Avoid using colour alone to convey meaning. For instance, instead of highlighting important points in red, use bold text or an icon alongside the colour to ensure accessibility.

Large, legible fonts

- Choose sans-serif fonts like Arial, Calibri or Verdana for readability.[16]
- Set font sizes to a minimum of 24 points for body text and 36 points for headings to ensure text is visible, even from a distance.[17]

Minimize animations and transitions

- Overuse of animations or transitions can distract viewers or cause discomfort for individuals with cognitive disabilities or vestibular disorders.[18]
- If animations are necessary, use simple effects and ensure they are not essential to understanding the content.

Ensuring multimedia accessibility

Multimedia elements such as videos and audio clips can enrich a presentation but require careful consideration to ensure accessibility.

Add captions and videos

- Include captions for all embedded videos to support viewers who are D/deaf or hard of hearing.
- Tools like YouTube's auto-captioning feature or professional transcription services can help generate accurate captions.

Provide transcripts for audio

- Offer written transcripts for any audio content, allowing users who cannot hear the audio to access the information.

Avoid auto-playing multimedia

- Ensure that multimedia does not auto-play when the slide loads, as this can disrupt screen reader users or catch viewers off guard.

Tools for accessibility

Modern presentation tools include built-in features to check and improve the accessibility of your slides.

Microsoft PowerPoint[19]

- Accessibility checker: Use PowerPoint's built-in Accessibility Checker to identify and fix issues such as missing alt text or insufficient contrast.
- Alt text: Add descriptive alt text to images, charts and graphics through the Format Picture or Format Object pane.
- Reading order pane: Verify the logical reading order of slide content to ensure screen readers interpret elements correctly.

Google Slides[20]

- Alt text: Right-click on images or objects to add alt text that describes their content and purpose.
- Manual contrast adjustments: While Google Slides doesn't have an automated accessibility checker, you can manually adjust colour contrast and font sizes for accessibility.

Apple Keynote[21]

- Keyboard navigation: Keynote supports keyboard navigation, which is essential for users who cannot use a mouse.

- Alt text: Add alt text to images via the Accessibility Description field in the Format pane.

Tips for inclusive presentations

- Accessible sharing: When sharing slide decks digitally, provide the file in an accessible PDF format with tags and logical structure. If presenting using Microsoft Teams, using the built-in 'Live' sharing functionality means that meeting participants are able to navigate through the presentation at their own speed, and zoom in if required.
- Inclusive delivery: During live presentations, describe visual elements aloud for audience members who may have low vision.
- Don't overcrowd your slides: Break complex ideas down into multiple slides if needed. Each slide should have one key objective or idea, with supporting information. If you have a technical diagram, consider breaking it down into stages.
- Practice and feedback: Test your slides with assistive technologies like screen readers and gather feedback from users with disabilities to improve accessibility.

Why accessible slide decks matter

Accessible slide decks benefit everyone, not just those with disabilities. They improve clarity, enhance usability and demonstrate your commitment to inclusion. Whether presenting in person or sharing slides online, designing for accessibility ensures your message reaches the widest possible audience. By applying these strategies and leveraging available tools, professional communicators can create impactful presentations that genuinely resonate.

Making spreadsheets accessible

Spreadsheets are indispensable tools for organizing and analysing data, but their functionality can present unique challenges for accessibility. For individuals relying on assistive technologies such as screen readers, navigating a poorly designed spreadsheet can be frustrating or even impossible. Ensuring your spreadsheets are accessible and meet compliance standards is important for inclusivity and usability for all users. This section provides a detailed guide on creating accessible spreadsheets by organizing data, enhancing visual accessibility, and leveraging built-in accessibility tools.

Organizing data for clarity

Proper organization is the foundation of an accessible spreadsheet. A well-structured spreadsheet not only improves readability but also makes navigation intuitive for assistive technologies.

Using clear headers for columns and rows[22]
- Clearly label all columns and rows to provide context for the data they contain. For example, instead of 'A1' and 'B1' use descriptive headers like 'Sales Region' and 'Q1 Revenue'.
- Use the 'Header Row' option in your spreadsheet tool (e.g. Microsoft Excel, Google Sheets) to designate headers, which allows screen readers to identify them and convey their purpose.

Avoiding blank cells that disrupt navigation[23]
- Avoid leaving blank rows or columns within your data table, as screen readers may misinterpret them as the end of the data set. If a cell must remain blank, use a placeholder like 'N/A' or 'No Data' for clarity.
- Consolidate data into contiguous blocks to make it easier for screen readers to process the content logically.

Logical layout and tab order[24]
- Arrange data in a logical sequence. Ensure that users can navigate through the spreadsheet from left to right and top to bottom without confusion.
- Test the tab order to ensure it follows the logical flow of information.

Visual accessibility

Visual design plays a critical role in ensuring that spreadsheets are usable for individuals with visual impairments or colour blindness.

Applying sufficient colour contrast
- Use high-contrast colour combinations (e.g. dark text on a light background) to ensure that text is readable. Tools like the TPGi Colour Contrast Analyser can help verify compliance with accessibility standards.

- Avoid using colour alone to convey information. For example, instead of marking cells red for negative values, add a symbol like a minus sign or use text labels like 'Negative'.

Avoiding excessive use of merged cells[25]

- Merged cells can disrupt navigation for screen readers, as they may misinterpret the structure. Instead, use centre alignment or creative formatting to achieve a similar visual effect without merging.
- If merging cells is unavoidable, ensure that screen reader users can still understand the relationship between the merged data and its corresponding headers.

Ensuring chart and graph accessibility

- Add descriptive titles and labels to charts and graphs to provide context. For example, instead of 'Chart 1', use 'Sales Growth by Quarter'.
- Use patterns or textures in charts to differentiate data series, rather than relying solely on colour.

Tips for interactive spreadsheets

Interactive spreadsheets with features like drop-down menus or input fields can enhance usability, but they also require additional attention to accessibility.

Labelling drop-down menus and input fields

- Provide clear labels for all interactive elements, such as drop-down menus or input fields, so users understand their purpose. For instance, instead of a generic 'Select an Option', use 'Select Your Sales Region'.
- Use data validation rules to ensure that inputs meet required formats or constraints, which can minimize errors and improve usability for all users.

Providing instructions

- Include instructions for interacting with the spreadsheet, either as a separate tab or in a visible cell. For example, explain how to use drop-down menus or what type of data should be entered in specific fields.

Protecting cells and sheets

- Lock cells that contain formulas or instructions to prevent accidental edits while allowing users to interact with input fields. Ensure this protection does not hinder screen reader navigation.

Testing accessibility in spreadsheets

Testing is a crucial step in ensuring that your spreadsheets meet accessibility standards and function well for all users. Accessibility tools built into spreadsheet software can identify common issues and provide guidance for improvements.

Microsoft Excel's accessibility checker[26]

Microsoft Excel includes a robust accessibility checker that scans for issues like missing headers, merged cells, or insufficient colour contrast. To use it:

1 Navigate to the 'Review' tab.
2 Select 'Check Accessibility'.
3 Review the results and follow the recommendations for fixes.

The checker also provides a severity rating for issues, helping you prioritize critical updates.

Google Sheets[27]

While Google Sheets doesn't have a built-in accessibility checker, third-party add-ons like Grackle Sheets can evaluate your spreadsheet for compliance and suggest improvements.

Manual testing

- Use a screen reader like NVDA or JAWS to navigate your spreadsheet. Test how effectively the screen reader conveys the data, labels and structure to ensure usability for individuals relying on assistive technologies.
- Check whether users can easily navigate through tabs, input fields and interactive elements without encountering barriers.

Accessible spreadsheets not only meet legal and ethical standards but also demonstrate a commitment to inclusivity. By organizing data thoughtfully, enhancing visual accessibility and leveraging built-in tools, you can create spreadsheets that serve diverse audiences effectively. As spreadsheets are often integral to decision-making, their accessibility has a direct impact on the inclusivity of processes and outcomes. Taking the extra steps to ensure they are usable by all is an investment in equity, professionalism and broader audience engagement.

Accessible graphs, charts and data visualizations: Turning numbers into inclusive stories

Graphs, charts and data visualizations are powerful tools for making complex information digestible. For professional communicators, they're indispensable for presentations, reports and social media. But if designed without accessibility in mind, these visuals can exclude significant portions of your audience. Accessible data visualizations ensure inclusivity and enhance clarity for all viewers, regardless of their abilities.

This section will explore how to design visuals that communicate effectively and inclusively, from adding alt text to selecting tools that make accessibility easier.

Designing visuals for all audiences

Accessible data visualizations begin with intentional design choices that make your content clear and engaging for everyone. While there are countless 'interesting' infographics, the best data visualizations offer information in a way that doesn't hide it from those who have visual or cognitive disabilities. This includes the flow, colours, fonts and sizing you choose to use.[28]

Adding descriptive titles and labels
Why does it matter?
Clear titles and labels provide essential context, helping viewers understand the purpose and message of the visualization at a glance.

Tip
Include a descriptive title that summarizes the takeaway (e.g. 'Sales Growth by Region, Q1 2023'). Label axes, data points and legends clearly, avoiding abbreviations or jargon where possible.

Ensuring legibility
Contrast and fonts
Use high-contrast colour schemes (e.g. dark text on a light background) and large, readable fonts. For presentations or printed materials, test the visibility from different distances or formats.

Simplify
Avoid overcrowding your chart with excessive data points or labels. Focus on the most critical information and remove visual clutter.[29]

Alt text and data narratives

Alt text is your audience's gateway to understanding a chart's story without relying on visuals. For individuals using screen readers, it's essential to go beyond simply describing the chart's appearance.

Writing meaningful alt text
Key components
Summarize the chart's main message rather than describing every visual element. For instance, instead of 'Bar chart with blue and red bars', write, 'Bar chart showing a 20 per cent increase in sales for Product A compared to Product B in 2023'.

Keep it concise
While it's important to provide context, avoid overwhelming users with overly detailed descriptions. Prioritize the takeaway.

Providing a data table
Why include a data table?
Some users prefer interacting with raw data rather than interpreting a visual. Including a linked or embedded table allows them to explore the numbers in a format that suits their needs.

Tip
Place the table near the chart for easy reference and ensure it has clear headers for screen readers to interpret accurately.

Best practices for colour use

Colour is a powerful tool for creating visually appealing charts, but relying solely on it can exclude individuals with colour blindness or partial sight.

Avoiding reliance on colour alone
Use multiple visual cues to differentiate data points. For example, pair colours with patterns, textures, or icons. Instead of a red bar for 'loss' and a green bar for 'profit', add diagonal stripes to the red bar and dots to the green bar.

Choosing accessible colour palettes
Use tools like the WebAIM Colour Contrast Checker or TPGi Colour Contrast Analyser to ensure your colour choices meet accessibility standards.

High contrast between text, data points and backgrounds improves readability for everyone.

Tools for creating accessible visuals

Creating accessible graphs and charts doesn't require starting from scratch. Many popular tools now include features specifically designed to support accessibility.

Excel
Excel is widely used for creating charts and includes built-in accessibility features:

- Enable the 'Accessibility Checker' to identify potential barriers.
- Use the 'Alt Text' option to describe the purpose of the chart.
- Leverage templates with simple, clean layouts.

Tableau[30]
Tableau is a powerful data visualization tool that supports accessibility through:

- screen-reader-friendly outputs when embedding visualizations online
- built-in options for alt text and captions
- interactive dashboards that allow users to explore data in multiple ways

Google Sheets
Google Sheets offers basic yet effective tools for creating accessible charts:

- Include alt text for visuals directly within the sheet.
- Ensure sufficient contrast between chart elements.
- Provide tabular data alongside visualizations.

Generative AI tools
Some generative AI tools like Claude can generate visualizations based on natural language suggestions. You don't need to understand how to code to create the vector-based outputs. Including accessibility considerations like alternative text, clear colour contrast and labelling your data in your prompt can provide an accessible graph or chart – although, as with all generative

AI outputs, you'll need to check that there haven't been any 'creative' amends or updates to your data.

Online tools for accessibility

Consider tools like Chartbuilder[31] or Datawrapper,[32] simplifying chart creation while maintaining accessibility features. These platforms often include tutorials and built-in checks to guide your design.

Accessible graphs and charts are about more than meeting compliance standards, they're about telling your story in a way that everyone can engage with. By focusing on clear design, thoughtful alt text and accessible tools, you ensure that your visualizations resonate with diverse audiences.

By following these guidelines, your data visualizations can become tools of empowerment, breaking down barriers and making complex information universally understandable.

VENNGAGE: AN ACCESSIBLE ALTERNATIVE TO CANVA

Venngage is a user-friendly infographic and visual content creation tool that offers features to support accessibility, making it a great choice for creating accessible graphs, charts and infographics:[33]

- Start with predesigned templates that prioritize clean layouts and readability, reducing the risk of cluttered or inaccessible designs.
- Add alternative text descriptions to your visuals to ensure users relying on screen readers can understand the content.
- Venngage provides curated colour palettes that meet contrast ratio guidelines, ensuring text and visuals are easy to read for individuals with visual or cognitive disabilities.
- Choose from a variety of accessible font styles and sizes to enhance readability. Venngage also allows you to adjust line spacing and text alignment for improved legibility.
- Export your creations as PDFs or PNGs while ensuring the output maintains accessibility features like alt text or clear layout structures.
- The easy-to-use interface reduces design complexity, enabling users to focus on accessibility while building visually compelling content.

Accessible PDFs: Designing for universal access

PDFs are incredibly versatile and widely used, but this flexibility can pose challenges when it comes to accessibility. A visually stunning PDF that isn't designed with user needs in mind risks excluding a significant portion of your audience – especially those who rely on assistive technologies like screen readers.

PDFs have become a universally used way to present information, but they create a lot of accessibility challenges, depending on the way they're produced. For example, made in Adobe InDesign, you're able to apply more best practices to make an accessible PDF vs if you scan a document which creates a PDF as an image.

In WebAIM's 2019 survey, 75 per cent of screen reader users said PDF documents are likely to pose significant accessibility issues.[34] PDFs can be time-consuming to fix and they're not always necessary. Sometimes stakeholders want to use a PDF so 'no one will change my content' when a Word document or PowerPoint presentation would work perfectly for internal documents. If information is for an external audience, an OpenDocument format (.ODT files)[35] means that users don't need a particular software licence to access the information. That's not a format that many communications professionals are used to using – and when done correctly, PDFs are just as accessible as an HTML-first web page. Also, there are times when a PDF is the more appropriate format, so let's consider how to make them accessible.

WHEN ARE PDFS THE MOST APPROPRIATE FORMAT?

- Annual reports or financial summaries.
- Static content like guides, manuals, or white papers.
- Documents requiring a high-quality print format.
- Materials distributed via email or for download.
- Archived or finalized documents that shouldn't be updated frequently.

What makes a PDF accessible?

Accessible PDFs aren't just a technical checkbox; they're a commitment to ensuring your content is usable for everyone. Let's explore the key elements of PDF accessibility, best practices for creation and essential tools for testing and validation.

Accessible PDFs ensure all users can easily navigate and understand their content, whether they're using a mouse, keyboard or assistive tools like screen readers. Here are the foundational elements that make a PDF accessible.

Tags and logical reading order[36]

Tags are the backbone of accessible PDFs, acting as the structure that screen readers use to interpret content. Tags define headings, paragraphs, lists and tables, creating a logical flow. Screen readers may present content in a confusing, disjointed order without proper tagging, frustrating users.

A well-structured PDF ensures:

- headings are hierarchical and logical (e.g. H1, H2, H3)
- lists are tagged as actual lists, not just styled text
- tables include headers and are logically structured for easy navigation

Embedded fonts and selectable text

Text in PDFs must be actual text – not an image of text. Scanned documents or PDFs created from images are inaccessible unless optical character recognition (OCR) is applied to convert the image-based text into real, selectable text.[37] Additionally, embedded fonts ensure the text is displayed consistently across all devices and platforms, even if the viewer hasn't installed the original font.

Best practices for PDF creation

Creating accessible PDFs starts with proper design and preparation, whether you're using a tool like Adobe Acrobat or converting a document from Word, PowerPoint, InDesign or another publishing software.

Start with accessibility in mind

- Use accessibility features in your source software to set up proper headings, alt text and logical structure.
- When exporting your document to a PDF format, ensure it is exported as a tagged PDF to retain all accessibility features embedded during creation. Most tools like Microsoft Word, Google Docs and Adobe InDesign offer options to create tagged PDFs during the export process. Be sure to check settings for features like 'Create Tagged PDF' or 'Enable Accessibility Features' to ensure all content remains accessible. Additionally, tagged PDFs improve reflow for mobile devices, allowing users to view the document more easily on smaller screens.

Add alt text to images and links

- Provide descriptive alt text for every image, explaining its purpose in the context of the document.
- Use meaningful link text that tells users where the link will take them (e.g. 'Download the report' instead of 'Click here').

Ensure colour contrast and font readability

- Use high-contrast colour schemes to ensure text is easily readable against the background.
- Choose clear, legible fonts and avoid using small font sizes, especially for body text.

WHEN SIZE REALLY MATTERS: BEST PRACTICES FOR ACCESSIBLE FONT SIZES

Font size is a crucial consideration for accessibility, as text that is too small can exclude individuals with visual or cognitive disabilities or those using small screens. Let's break down the recommended minimum font sizes for different formats, ensuring clarity and readability for all users.

For reports

A minimum font size of 12 points is recommended for body text, as this provides sufficient clarity for most users without requiring magnification tools. Headings should be larger, at least 16–18 points, to provide a clear hierarchy and improve navigation for screen readers.

For presenting at a conference

A minimum font size of 24 points for body text and 36–40 points for headings is ideal. This ensures that even the back rows can follow the presentation. Contrast is equally important, so pair text with a high-contrast background to maximize visibility.

For spreadsheets

A font size of 12 points is recommended for cell content to maintain readability, especially when the document is shared electronically or printed. For header rows and column titles, consider using 14 points or bold formatting to

> distinguish them clearly. Avoid reducing font sizes below 10 points, even for detailed notes or subtext, as smaller fonts can make the content difficult to read, particularly for users with low vision. Also, use alternating row shading or borders to separate data visually, enhancing clarity without solely relying on font adjustments.

Keep file sizes manageable
Large PDFs can be difficult to download and navigate. Optimize your files by compressing images and using efficient design practices to ensure smooth user experiences.

Testing and validation

Even the most thoughtfully created PDFs need thorough testing to ensure accessibility. Thankfully, several tools can help you verify your work.

PAC (PDF Accessibility Checker)[38]
PAC (PDF Accessibility Checker) is a robust, free tool specifically designed to test PDFs for accessibility. In early 2025, it stands as the industry standard for automated accessibility checks. PAC is highly regarded for its ability to thoroughly evaluate compliance with the PDF/UA (Universal Accessibility) standard, the recognized benchmark for ensuring PDF accessibility. This tool offers detailed, actionable reports that identify missing tags, improper reading order, untagged images and other common barriers affecting usability for individuals relying on assistive technologies.

PAC allows creators to address and resolve barriers effectively by pinpointing these issues for communicators to resolve. While automated tools like PAC are invaluable for quickly identifying potential problems, it's essential to pair their use with manual testing to achieve the highest level of accessibility. As the go-to tool in its category, PAC is an indispensable resource for communicators and organizations committed to inclusive design.

Adobe Acrobat Accessibility Checker[39]
Adobe Acrobat Pro includes a robust built-in accessibility checker that serves as a critical resource for evaluating your PDF for common issues. This tool provides a straightforward way to identify potential barriers that could

impede usability for individuals relying on assistive technologies. Key features include the ability to:

- highlight untagged elements or structural problems, such as missing or improperly nested tags
- validate the logical reading order of your content, ensuring it flows correctly for screen readers
- identify missing alt text for images and improperly labelled form fields, both of which are essential for user navigation and understanding

However, while the Adobe Acrobat Accessibility Checker is a valuable starting point, it's important to note that passing its checks does not guarantee full compliance with PDF/UA standards or true accessibility. The tool is designed to flag technical issues but cannot evaluate the usability of a document for diverse audiences. For instance, it cannot determine if alt text adequately conveys the purpose of an image or if the reading order logically aligns with the visual design.

Adobe Reader[40]

The free Adobe Reader software also provides a 'read aloud' function so you can check the reading order and flow of information, but it doesn't provide any additional information.

Browser-based read-aloud functionality

Web browsers like Edge and Chrome have built-in functionality that can read your web page or document out loud, help you identify some aspects of reading order, and do an initial check that your document behaves as you'd expect it to.

Manual testing: The essential step beyond automation

While automated tools like PAC and Adobe Acrobat are invaluable for identifying technical accessibility issues, they cannot replace the insight gained through testing conducted by real humans. Manual testing ensures that your PDF is not only technically compliant but also genuinely usable and accessible for people relying on assistive technologies.

Why manual testing matters

Automated tools focus on identifying technical barriers but lack the capacity to assess the user experience. For example, while they may flag missing alt text, they cannot determine if the existing alt text is meaningful or conveys the necessary context for an image. Similarly, they might confirm the presence of tags but cannot evaluate whether those tags accurately reflect the document's structure or logical reading order.

Key steps for manual testing

1 Use a screen reader to navigate the document.

Experience the PDF from the perspective of users who rely on screen readers, such as NVDA, JAWS, or VoiceOver. Pay attention to the following:

- Logical reading order: Verify that the screen reader reads content in the intended sequence, matching the visual layout of the document.
- Headings: Ensure that headings are appropriately tagged and provide a clear structure for navigating the document.
- Lists and tables: Check whether lists are announced correctly and tables include proper headers for easy interpretation.

As mentioned previously, you can also use a built-in browser reader, although they won't necessarily pick up all of these aspects.

2 Check links and navigation

Interactive elements like hyperlinks and navigation tools should be accessible and functional:

- Hyperlinks: Confirm that all links are tagged correctly and provide descriptive text, such as 'Read more about accessibility standards' rather than generic phrases like 'Click here'.
- Bookmarks: For longer documents, ensure links within your content are logically organized and allow users to jump to key sections easily.

3 Evaluate the alt text for images

Alt text descriptions are essential for conveying the purpose of images to screen reader users. During manual testing, ask yourself:

- Does the alt text accurately describe the image's purpose and content?
- Is the description concise yet meaningful?
- Are decorative images marked as 'artefacts' to prevent screen readers from announcing unnecessary content?

4 Test interactive elements

For PDFs with forms or interactive elements, ensure they are fully accessible:

- Form fields: Verify that all form fields are labelled clearly and announced correctly by screen readers.
- Keyboard navigation: Test whether users can navigate the entire document, including forms, links and interactive features, using only a keyboard.

5 Assess visual accessibility

While screen readers are a focus of manual testing, consider the visual aspects of your document:

- Colour contrast: Manually review colour contrast to ensure text is legible against its background.
- Font size and style: Check that fonts are easily readable and consistent throughout the document.

Making manual testing a regular practice

Manual testing should be an integral part of your workflow for creating accessible PDFs. Encourage team members to familiarize themselves with screen readers and basic accessibility principles. By understanding how users engage with your documents, you can design and refine content that meets both technical standards and real-world needs.

Incorporating manual testing into your accessibility process complements automated tools, providing the comprehensive approach needed to create truly inclusive and user-friendly PDFs.

Tools and resources for document accessibility: Simplifying the path to inclusion

Making your documents accessible doesn't have to be daunting, especially with the right tools and resources in your corner. Whether you're creating a report, a presentation, or a PDF, leveraging software, guidelines and online tools can simplify the process and ensure your content is inclusive and compliant. This section will guide you through the essential resources every professional communicator should know about to create accessible documents that resonate with diverse audiences.

Software to simplify the process

The first step to document accessibility is understanding which tools can make your workflow easier and more effective. These software options are built with accessibility in mind.

Adobe Acrobat

Adobe Acrobat is the gold standard for creating and editing accessible PDFs. Its robust suite of tools allows you to:

- add tags to ensure a logical reading order for screen readers
- check and repair issues with the built-in accessibility checker
- add alt text to images and meaningful links

Pro tip: Use Adobe's 'Make Accessible' wizard to streamline the process, especially if you're new to PDF accessibility. However, always make sure to run it through a PDF checker like PAC to ensure it meets PDF/UA compliance.

Microsoft Office Suite

Accessibility built-in: Whether you're using Word, Excel or PowerPoint, Microsoft Office offers a range of features to make your documents accessible:

- Use the built-in accessibility checker to identify and fix common issues.
- Add alt text to images, graphs and charts directly in your document.
- Leverage templates designed with accessibility in mind.

Excel for data: Create clear and accessible tables by using proper headers and avoiding merged cells.

Google Workspace

Collaboration meets accessibility: Google Docs, Sheets and Slides are fantastic for creating accessible content in collaborative environments.

Key features include:

- adding alt text to visuals
- screen-reader compatibility for navigating content
- real-time collaboration while maintaining accessibility standards

Pro tip: Use Google's accessibility add-ons for additional support, like screen reader compatibility and voice typing.

Online resources and testing tools

The internet is full of resources to help you master document accessibility. From checklists to tutorials and validation tools, these resources ensure you stay on track.

Checklists and tutorials
Accessible document checklists Look for guides provided by trusted organizations like WebAIM or government accessibility offices. These checklists provide step-by-step instructions for creating accessible documents, from headings to hyperlinks.

YouTube tutorials Channels focused on accessibility often feature walk-throughs for using tools like Adobe Acrobat or Microsoft Word to create accessible content.

Vendor resources Software providers like Adobe and Microsoft offer detailed guides and FAQs to support users in meeting accessibility standards.

You're not alone: Document accessibility vendors

Ensuring your documents meet accessibility standards can feel overwhelming, but the good news is you don't have to do it alone. A growing number of vendors specialize in document accessibility, offering expertise and tools to help organizations create inclusive materials.

Whether you're working on PDFs, presentations or spreadsheets, these professionals can guide you through remediation, compliance and optimization, saving you time while ensuring your content is accessible to everyone.

GrackleDocs
GrackleDocs offers a range of services and tools designed to ensure your documents meet the highest accessibility standards, empowering organizations to create inclusive, impactful content.[41]

What GrackleDocs offers:

- Grackle Service: This service provides accessibility specialists who will ensure your PDFs are fully compliant with accessibility standards like WCAG and PDF/UA.[42]

- Grackle Scan: Grackle Scan simplifies the task of managing inaccessible PDFs by automating scans across your websites and repositories. It delivers detailed reports, tracks progress over time and provides actionable insights to help you prioritize remediation. With real-time compliance checks for WCAG and PDF/UA standards, Grackle Scan ensures your documents stay accessible, saving time and reducing risks while fostering inclusivity.[43]
- Grackle PDF: Grackle PDF simplifies accessibility for complex documents, providing an advanced tool that ensures compliance with PDF/UA, WCAG and Section 508 standards. Start with a tagged PDF, identify accessibility issues and resolve them efficiently with just a few intuitive clicks, which we've found makes document remediation more straightforward.[44]
- Grackle Training: Empower your team with Grackle's digital accessibility training. Designed for individuals and teams of all experience levels, this training programme teaches the principles of accessible document creation and compliance with WCAG, PDF/UA and other standards. With hands-on learning, participants gain the confidence to apply accessibility best practices across their workflows.[45]

Accessibil-IT

Accessibil-IT is an accessibility solutions provider who specializes in making digital content inclusive for everyone. They offer expert services in document accessibility, including PDF and website remediation, ensuring compliance with standards like WCAG, PDF/UA and Section 508. With a commitment to innovation and inclusivity, Accessibil-IT empowers organizations to create barrier-free digital experiences, helping them reach broader audiences and meet accessibility requirements with confidence.[46]

Axes4

axes4 is a company dedicated to simplifying PDF accessibility. Their innovative tools and services help organizations create, test and remediate PDFs to meet global accessibility standards like PDF/UA and WCAG. axes4's user-friendly software solutions ensure your documents are inclusive, easy to navigate, and compliant with accessibility regulations.[47]

What axes4 offers:

- axesWord: Easily create accessible PDFs directly from Microsoft Word.[48]
- axesPDF: Efficiently remediate existing PDF documents to meet accessibility standards.[49]

- axesCheck: A powerful tool for validating and testing PDF/UA compliance.[50]
- axesTraining: Expert guidance to help your team master PDF accessibility and compliance.[51]

Allyant

Allyant provides solutions designed to make PDF documents accessible and compliant with global accessibility standards like WCAG and PDF/UA. Their comprehensive tools and services help organizations create, test and remediate accessible documents, ensuring inclusivity and compliance every step of the way.

What Allyant offers:

- PDF remediation Services: Expert remediation to ensure your existing PDFs meet accessibility standards.[52]
- CommonLook PDF: A powerful Adobe Acrobat plugin designed to simplify compliance with WCAG, PDF/UA, HHS and Section 508 accessibility standards. This robust tool enables users to efficiently test, remediate and verify documents, delivering faster and more accurate results than Adobe Acrobat alone.[53]
- CommonLook Office: CommonLook Office simplifies the creation of accessible PDF files directly from Microsoft Word and PowerPoint, surpassing the native PDF functionality of Microsoft Office. It goes beyond basic accessibility, quickly identifying and resolving issues while automating key tasks to save you time and effort. What makes CommonLook Office stand out is its built-in guidance for meeting various accessibility standards, including Section 508, HHS, WCAG and PDF/UA.[54]
- CommonLook PDF Validator: This Adobe Acrobat Pro plugin simplifies the process of ensuring accessibility compliance by identifying and highlighting issues within your PDFs. Beyond automated checks, it guides you through essential manual tests to achieve complete accessibility compliance. With support for standards like Section 508, WCAG, PDF/UA and HHS, you can confidently meet even the most rigorous guidelines.[55]

All of this to say

Accessible document creation doesn't happen in isolation – it's a blend of using the right tools, adhering to trusted guidelines and leveraging resources that simplify the process. The goal isn't just to meet legal requirements but to create materials that genuinely include and empower all readers.

Whether you're starting with a simple Word document or exporting a polished PDF, these tools and standards equip you to make every piece of content accessible, impactful and ready to reach the widest possible audience. It's not just good practice; it's good communication.

Real-world examples of accessible documents in action

Creating accessible documents isn't just about meeting legal requirements, it's about making sure your message reaches and resonates with everyone. These real-world examples show how accessible documents can enhance communication, foster inclusivity and set a standard for excellence.

Case Study 1: An inclusive annual report

The challenge

A nonprofit organization needed to publish its annual report online to share accomplishments, financial updates and upcoming goals with donors, board members and stakeholders. However, their previous reports excluded key audiences due to inaccessible PDF formats.

The solution

The communications team redesigned their report using accessibility best practices:

- Tags and logical reading order: They tagged headings, tables and text to ensure a logical flow for screen readers.
- Alt text for charts and images: Each graph and infographic included concise alt text describing key insights, ensuring visually impaired readers could access the data.
- High contrast and readable fonts: By using a clean design with bold headings and sans-serif fonts, they improved readability for all audiences.

The impact

Feedback from stakeholders highlighted how accessible the report felt. One donor who relied on assistive technologies expressed gratitude for the thoughtful design, underscoring the organization's commitment to inclusion.

Case Study 2: An accessible presentation for stakeholders

The challenge
A PR agency prepared a presentation for a multinational client to discuss campaign results. With diverse attendees, including some with disabilities, the team needed to ensure everyone could engage fully with the content.

The solution
The team applied accessibility principles to their presentation:

- Logical slide titles: Each slide had a clear title to assist navigation for attendees using screen readers.
- Multimedia accessibility: Captions and transcripts were provided for video case studies featured in the presentation.
- Design considerations: Slides were formatted with high-contrast colour schemes and large, legible fonts, making them easy to follow both in person and virtually.

The impact
The client praised the presentation for its clarity and inclusivity. The accessible design also aligned with the client's values, further strengthening their partnership with the agency.

Case Study 3: A data-driven spreadsheet for decision makers

The challenge
A regional government office needed to share a budget spreadsheet with department heads to allocate resources effectively. The original spreadsheet was dense, with inconsistent formatting and unclear navigation, making it challenging for users with disabilities.

The solution
The office improved accessibility by:

- Using descriptive headers: Clear column and row headers made data navigation intuitive for screen readers.
- Avoiding merged cells: Instead, they used spacing and bold text to distinguish sections.

- Adding alt text to charts: Accompanying data visualizations included alt text summarizing trends for users unable to interpret the visuals.

The impact

The revamped spreadsheet reduced confusion and increased efficiency during budget discussions. Department heads appreciated the inclusivity and clarity, which streamlined decision-making.

Accessible documents as a foundation of communication

Accessible documents aren't just a nice-to-have, they're essential tools for fostering understanding, building trust, and respecting your audience. Whether you're drafting an annual report, creating a stakeholder presentation, or organizing a data-heavy spreadsheet, accessible design ensures your message is clear and inclusive.

Accessible documents bridge the gap between intent and understanding, ensuring no one is left behind. They reflect a commitment to inclusivity and equity, aligning with the values of respect and fairness that should guide every communicator's work.

When you prioritize accessibility, you're not just meeting compliance standards, you're expanding your audience, enhancing engagement, and creating a more inclusive world. Accessible design isn't about compromise; it's about elevating the quality and impact of your communications.

Call to action

The journey to creating accessible documents begins with small, intentional steps:

- Start small: Focus on basics like tagging, alt text and logical structure.
- Use tools: Leverage accessibility checkers in Adobe Acrobat, Microsoft Office or Google Workspace to identify and fix issues.
- Build a habit: Make accessibility a standard practice in your document creation process.

Accessibility is a mindset as much as it is a skill. By integrating accessible design into your workflow, you're not just meeting today's needs – you're shaping a more inclusive future for all. Start now and take pride in knowing your communications are truly for everyone.

KEY TAKEAWAYS

This chapter delved into the practical side of accessible communications by focusing on document accessibility. From PDFs to presentations, spreadsheets and data visualizations, we explored how professional communicators can create materials that are inclusive, effective and impactful for diverse audiences.

Summarizing the key types of accessible documents

We outlined the core types of documents that every communicator should consider:

- **Text documents**: Building content with headings, lists, alt text and meaningful links, while avoiding layout pitfalls like overusing tables or missing metadata.
- **PDFs**: The most widely used document format, requiring proper tagging, logical reading order, and alt text to ensure accessibility for all.
- **Presentations**: Structuring slide decks with clear navigation, high contrast, and captions or transcripts for multimedia content.
- **Spreadsheets**: Organizing data with headers, ensuring colour contrast in tables, and labelling interactive fields for usability with assistive technologies.
- **Graphs, charts and data visualizations**: Creating visuals that combine clarity and accessibility by using alt text, patterns and high contrast while avoiding colour dependency.

Each type of document presents unique challenges, but with the right tools and strategies, they can be transformed into powerful communication tools that reach all audiences.

Tools and resources for accessibility

We provided an overview of the tools and standards that simplify the process of creating accessible documents:

- **Software:** Adobe Acrobat, Microsoft Office Suite and Google Workspace offer robust features to support accessibility.
- **Resources:** Tools like PAC and accessibility checkers in Word and PowerPoint help identify and address barriers.

These resources empower communicators to go beyond compliance, enabling them to embed accessibility into their workflows.

Real-world applications

By examining real-world examples, we illustrated how accessible documents can make a tangible impact:

- An inclusive annual report demonstrates how to prioritize clarity and structure for diverse audiences.
- An accessible stakeholder presentation shows how thoughtful design and use of multimedia can improve engagement.
- A data-driven spreadsheet highlights how organized and accessible data visualizations support informed decision-making.

These case studies emphasize that accessible documents aren't just functional; they're foundational to effective communication.

Looking ahead

As accessibility standards evolve, communicators must adapt and continue learning. Here's how to stay ahead:

- **Stay proactive:** Monitor updates to WCAG, PDF/UA and other standards to ensure your materials remain compliant.
- **Incorporate feedback:** Regularly gather input from users who rely on accessible formats to improve your processes.
- **Invest in training:** Equip yourself and your team with the skills to create accessible documents across platforms.

This chapter reinforces that accessibility is more than a checklist – it's a commitment to inclusivity and equity. By embracing accessible design in documents, you're not just meeting legal requirements – you're opening doors for all audiences to engage with your content.

Accessible documents are the cornerstone of accessible communication. By taking small, consistent steps and leveraging the tools and strategies outlined here, you can build a future where every document serves every audience effectively and inclusively. Together, we can make accessibility the standard, not the exception, in professional communications.

References

[1] Structure with headings and lists, eCampus Ontario, https://accessibility.ecampusontario.ca/accessibility/best-practices/headings-and-lists/ (archived at https://perma.cc/FA2B-KW6H)

2   Structure with headings and lists, eCampus Ontario, https://accessibility.ecampusontario.ca/accessibility/best-practices/headings-and-lists/ (archived at https://perma.cc/EPG8-DUYJ)
3   Text spacing (Level AA), W3C, www.w3.org/WAI/WCAG21/Understanding/text-spacing.html (archived at https://perma.cc/9STV-CYDL)
4   Text spacing (Level AA), W3C, www.w3.org/WAI/WCAG21/Understanding/text-spacing.html (archived at https://perma.cc/RTG7-WGS8)
5   Guide to design and layout, Plain English Campaign, www.plainenglish.co.uk/free-guides (archived at https://perma.cc/KG74-TWQM)
6   Choosing accessible fonts: Enhancing readability and inclusivity, DigitalA11Y, www.digitala11y.com/choosing-accessible-fonts-enhancing-readability-and-inclusivity/ (archived at https://perma.cc/LR8X-QR28)
7   How to use space effectively for design accessibility, Common Ninja, www.commoninja.com/blog/how-to-use-space-effectively-for-design-accessibility (archived at https://perma.cc/4LDZ-RE99)
8   Alternative text, WebAIM, https://webaim.org/techniques/alttext/ (archived at https://perma.cc/NUU8-F2PM)
9   Master the art of accessible link text, WCAG, www.wcag.com/blog/writing-meaningful-link-text/ (archived at https://perma.cc/B5AW-FSSJ)
10 Tips to designing accessible tables, Rick Hansen Foundation, www.rickhansen.com/news-stories/blog/tips-designing-accessible-tables (archived at https://perma.cc/27ZG-7ZZ8)
11 View or change the properties for an Office file, Microsoft, https://support.microsoft.com/en-us/office/view-or-change-the-properties-for-an-office-file-21d604c2-481e-4379-8e54-1dd4622c6b75 (archived at https://perma.cc/4V6Z-M75P)
12 OpenDyslexic: A typeface for dyslexia, OpenDyslexic, https://opendyslexic.org/ (archived at https://perma.cc/2LFN-YRAN)
13 Dyslexie font, https://dyslexiefont.com/en/ (archived at https://perma.cc/A9DY-LFQA)
14 Make your PowerPoint presentations accessible to people with disabilities, Microsoft, https://support.microsoft.com/en-us/office/make-your-powerpoint-presentations-accessible-to-people-with-disabilities-6f7772b2-2f33-4bd2-8ca7-dae3b2b3ef25 (archived at https://perma.cc/X8T8-V5Y2)
15 High contrast and low vision, Perkins School for the Blind, www.perkins.org/resource/choosing-high-contrast-color-schemes-for-low-vision/ (archived at https://perma.cc/8CL9-VUPH)
16 How to choose a font for accessibility, Siteimprove, www.siteimprove.com/glossary/accessible-fonts/ (archived at https://perma.cc/KLH2-HENU)
17 Accessibility guidelines, National Disability Rights Network, www.ndrn.org/accessibility-guidelines/ (archived at https://perma.cc/76YC-9DWG)

18 The impact of motion animation on cognitive disability, TPGi, www.tpgi.com/the-impact-of-motion-animation-on-cognitive-disability/ (archived at https://perma.cc/YEV2-A3FB)
19 Make your PowerPoint presentations accessible to people with disabilities, Microsoft, https://support.microsoft.com/en-us/office/make-your-powerpoint-presentations-accessible-to-people-with-disabilities-6f7772b2-2f33-4bd2-8ca7-dae3b2b3ef25 (archived at https://perma.cc/7BSQ-4ZAW/)
20 Make your document, presentation, sheets & videos more accessible, Google Docs Editors Help, https://support.google.com/docs/answer/6199477?hl=en (archived at https://perma.cc/AX9B-W9RD)
21 Create accessible documents, spreadsheets, or presentations with Pages, Numbers, or Keynote, Apple Support, https://support.apple.com/en-ca/102031 (archived at https://perma.cc/BH2X-CSA2)
22 Accessibility best practices with Excel spreadsheets, Microsoft, https://support.microsoft.com/en-us/office/accessibility-best-practices-with-excel-spreadsheets-6cc05fc5-1314-48b5-8eb3-683e49b3e593 (archived at https://perma.cc/QB6N-R54X)
23 Creating accessible spreadsheets: Best practices, Rick Hansen Foundation, www.rickhansen.com/news-stories/blog/creating-accessible-spreadsheets-best-practices (archived at https://perma.cc/5K2K-W3JJ)
24 Set the tab order for controls, Microsoft, https://support.microsoft.com/en-us/office/set-the-tab-order-for-controls-2b37e49b-52d1-4f03-ae33-9e6d9c103c99 (archived at https://perma.cc/33DM-9NP4)
25 Creating accessible spreadsheets: Best practices, Rick Hansen Foundation, www.rickhansen.com/news-stories/blog/creating-accessible-spreadsheets-best-practices (archived at https://perma.cc/4RTT-XZ6R)
26 Improve accessibility with the Accessibility Checker, Microsoft, https://support.microsoft.com/en-us/office/improve-accessibility-with-the-accessibility-checker-a16f6de0-2f39-4a2b-8bd8-5ad801426c7f (archived at https://perma.cc/C4KA-UGRC)
27 Make your document, presentation, sheets & videos more accessible, Google Docs Editors Help, https://support.google.com/docs/answer/6199477?hl=en (archived at https://perma.cc/EX5W-T2DL)
28 An intro to designing accessible data visualizations, Sarah L Fossheim, https://fossheim.io/writing/posts/accessible-dataviz-design/ (archived at https://perma.cc/HUE5-9U7X)
29 Accessible charts: A checklist of the basics, https://analysisfunction.civilservice.gov.uk/policy-store/charts-a-checklist/ (archived at https://perma.cc/HUE5-9U7X)
30 Designing accessible dashboards for screen reader users, Tableau, www.tableau.com/blog/designing-accessible-dashboards-screen-reader-users (archived at https://perma.cc/C483-Z46A)

31 Chartbuilder, GitHub, https://github.com/Quartz/Chartbuilder (archived at https://perma.cc/NG65-34UT)
32 Datawrapper: Enrich your stories with charts, maps and tables, www.datawrapper.de/ (archived at https://perma.cc/YR6H-GS6B)
33 Venngage infographic maker, Venngage, https://venngage.com/blog/infographics-maker (archived at https://perma.cc/2SJB-TLVT)
34 Screen Reader User Survey #8 Results, WebAIM, https://webaim.org/projects/screenreadersurvey8/#pdf (archived at https://perma.cc/AB4L-T286)
35 ISO/IEC 26300-1:2015 Information technology – Open Document Format for Office Applications (OpenDocument) v1.2, www.iso.org/standard/66363.html (archived at https://perma.cc/NB7Z-NLUS)
36 Creating accessible PDFs, Adobe, https://helpx.adobe.com/ca/acrobat/using/creating-accessible-pdfs.html (archived at https://perma.cc/PD4H-6WNN)
37 What to do when OCR does not recognize text, Adobe, www.adobe.com/acrobat/hub/what-to-do-when-ocr-does-not-recognize-text.html (archived at https://perma.cc/4A3Q-WUKH)
38 PDC Accessibility Checker, PAC, https://pac.pdf-accessibility.org/en (archived at https://perma.cc/HGK5-JGY6)
39 Create and verify PDF accessibility (Acrobat Pro), Adobe, https://helpx.adobe.com/ca/acrobat/using/create-verify-pdf-accessibility.html (archived at https://perma.cc/Q2Q2-KLPQ)
40 Reading PDFs with reflow and accessibility features, Adobe, https://helpx.adobe.com/ca/acrobat/using/reading-pdfs-reflow-accessibility-features.html (archived at https://perma.cc/DM7R-MQN3)
41 GrackleDocs document and web accessibility solutions, GrackleDocs, www.grackledocs.com/en/ (archived at https://perma.cc/WU7T-KWL3)
42 PDF remediation, GrackleDocs, www.grackledocs.com/en/products-services/pdf-remediation/ (archived at https://perma.cc/V9UP-FJYB)
43 Grackle Scan, GrackleDocs, www.grackledocs.com/en/products-services/grackle-scan/ (archived at https://perma.cc/42M4-QCDE)
44 Grackle PDF, GrackleDocs, www.grackledocs.com/en/products-services/pdf-remediation/ (archived at https://perma.cc/M22A-9ZGF)
45 Digital accessibility training, GrackleDocs, www.grackledocs.com/en/products-services/digital-accessibility-training/ (archived at https://perma.cc/4WYS-3XMH)
46 Accessibil-IT, www.accessibilit.com/ (archived at https://perma.cc/EEZ3-8G5M)
47 axes4: Accessible PDF easily done!, axes4, www.axes4.com/en (archived at https://perma.cc/7KDP-TLJY)
48 axesWord, axes4, www.axes4.com/en/software-services/axesword (archived at https://perma.cc/K92W-MF5J)
49 Find and fix PDF/UA errors, axes4, www.axes4.com/en/software-services/axespdf (archived at https://perma.cc/6F7B-9ERB)

50 Check a PDF for accessibility online, axes4, www.axes4.com/en/software-services/axescheck (archived at https://perma.cc/674J-TWH6)
51 Making accessibility more accessible, axes4, www.axes4.com/en/software-services/axestraining (archived at https://perma.cc/89FR-SJ9N)
52 PDF remediation services, Allyant, https://allyant.com/pdf-accessibility-assessment-remediation/ (archived at https://perma.cc/6L8V-FHSP)
53 CommonLook PDF, Allyant, https://allyant.com/commonlook-accessibility-suite/cl-pdf/ (archived at https://perma.cc/63H7-BKH6)
54 CommonLook Office, Allyant, https://allyant.com/commonlook-accessibility-suite/cl-office/ (archived at https://perma.cc/KYY9-W9FJ)
55 CommonLook PDF Validator, Allyant, https://allyant.com/commonlook-accessibility-suite/cl-pdf-validator/ (archived at https://perma.cc/44DS-2T6J)

07

Creating accessible social media content

Love it or hate it, social media has revolutionized the way we connect, share and build communities. It's where brands tell their stories, individuals amplify their voices, and conversations happen in real time.

But are we truly speaking to everyone – or at least, everyone in the audience we're aiming for? The truth is millions of people are left out of the social media experience every day because of inaccessible content. Whether communicating on behalf of an organization or posting our individual thoughts and opinions, we have the power, and the responsibility, to change that.

Inaccessible content is harder to read for everyone. Overloading graphics with too much text, or using an attractive but low-contrast colour palette are common traps people fall into – but mean your message is ultimately less impactful for all. Creating accessible social media content isn't just about meeting guidelines or ticking boxes; it's about creating inclusion, showing respect and building trust. It's about making sure that people have the potential to fully engage with what you have to say, no matter who's scrolling.

Small actions can have a huge impact, whether adding alt text to an image, using captions on videos or simply choosing hashtags wisely.

In this chapter, we'll explore practical strategies to make your social media content more inclusive for all users. From understanding the basics of accessible design to diving into platform-specific tools and features, you'll walk away with actionable insights to apply to your next post.

Let's get started!

The importance of accessible social media content

With billions of people active on platforms like Instagram, Facebook, X (formerly Twitter), LinkedIn and TikTok, the potential for organizations to engage with diverse audiences has never been greater. Yet, within this vast digital space, accessibility is often overlooked, leaving millions of users excluded from conversations, opportunities and content. On social media, this means designing and delivering content that everyone can engage with, regardless of their ability or situation. From people with sight loss who rely on screen readers to those with hearing loss who need video captions, or someone on a train who forgot their headphones, your content should mean that no one who wants to engage with your message is left out. Social media platforms are spaces where inclusivity can either thrive or falter. The difference often lies in whether user needs are prioritized as part of a brand or organization's communication strategy.

It isn't just a matter of ethics or compliance; it's about creating better content that resonates with more people. Accessible social media content is a sign of respect for diverse audiences and how they consume our information, and a strategic advantage in today's competitive and socially conscious marketplace.

Real-world examples of exclusion and inclusion

When accessibility is overlooked

Consider a visually striking infographic posted on Instagram. While its bright colours and detailed design may catch the eye of some, someone using a screen reader won't be able to interpret its content without alternative text (alt text) or an image description. For this individual, the post might as well not exist. If someone is in an area with poor network reception, or they're out of data, they might not be able to download the image either – and that means crucial information might be lost.

Similarly, imagine a trending video shared on TikTok with engaging dialogue but no captions. A D/deaf or hard-of-hearing user scrolling through their feed will be excluded from the conversation entirely. People who are using their phone with the sound off will also miss out on the message!

A notable example of a government campaign that faced backlash due to accessibility issues is Canada's National Covid-19 Awareness Campaign in 2020. Initially, some of the materials shared on government websites and social media channels did not include alt text for images or sufficient descriptive content for videos, making them inaccessible to users with visual or auditory disabilities.[1]

The lack of accessible features led to criticism from disability advocacy groups, who highlighted that critical public health information was not reaching everyone equitably. This was especially problematic during a global health crisis when timely and clear communication was vital for public safety.

The government responded to this feedback by improving accessibility efforts, adding alt text, captions and transcripts to their materials. While it may have taken a little extra time at the beginning, including this from the outset of any campaign would avoid exclusion and ensure messages reach the intended audiences effectively – without generating negative PR!

This case serves as a reminder for communicators that accessibility is not an afterthought but a foundational aspect of effective communication, particularly in the public sector.

When accessibility is done right

Contrast that with brands that integrate accessibility into their social media strategies. A shining example is Microsoft. On X, Microsoft includes descriptive alt text for images and captions for video content and uses clear, inclusive language in its posts.[2]

During Global Accessibility Awareness Day, Microsoft even ran a campaign where employees shared their personal stories, further humanizing their commitment to inclusion.[3] Given their market share, particularly within the public sector, it clearly makes good business sense for them – it's not seen as an add-on.

Starbucks is another brand that consistently nails social media accessibility. When launching an inclusive storytelling campaign like *Starbucks Stories*, they ensured their videos are captioned and their images include descriptive alt text.[4] For National Disability Employment Awareness Month, Starbucks highlighted employees with disabilities, sharing their stories through accessible posts that used inclusive language and visual aids designed with accessibility in mind.[5] It's hard to argue against the business case when you consider the scale and success of these organizations.

These examples highlight the stark contrast between content that excludes and content that invites. When organizations approach social media with accessibility in mind, they foster a sense of belonging, build stronger connections and open the door for broader engagement.

The benefits of accessibility for engagement, reputation and audience reach

Broader audience reach

Studies show that 1 in 6 people globally identify as living with some form of disability,[6] and 1 in 4 are reported in Canada and the UK.[7][8] By making social media content accessible, you're tapping into a massive audience that many organizations often unintentionally overlook – as well as making it easier for the 1 in 12 men who are colour-blind to perceive your information.[9]

Take video captions as an example. While originally designed for people with hearing disabilities, captions also benefit people watching videos in noisy environments, non-native speakers, and anyone who prefers to consume content visually.[10] See more on this in Chapter 8. Inclusive content doesn't just benefit one specific group; it creates a better experience for everyone.

Platforms like TikTok and Instagram prioritize content that performs well with audiences.[11] The more accessible your content, the more likely it is to be engaged with and shared, increasing its visibility. Accessibility isn't just an act of goodwill; it's a way to maximize your reach and amplify your message.

Enhanced reputation and brand trust

Brands demonstrating a commitment to accessibility send a clear message: we value everyone. In an era where consumers are increasingly drawn to organizations that align with their values, what message are your communications sending? And, even if it doesn't align with your brand narrative, do you want to be accidentally excluding some of your core demographic?

Inaccessible content can lead to public backlash and damage your brand's reputation. For example, failing to caption videos or using graphics with poor contrast can spark criticism on social media. Missteps are no longer seen by many as minor oversights; they can be interpreted as indicators of a company's priorities, or lack thereof.

Conversely, accessible social media content can enhance trust and loyalty. When audiences see that your organization goes the extra mile to include them, they're more likely to engage with your content, advocate for your brand and remain loyal customers. Don't forget, the spending power of people with disabilities is over $2.6 trillion USD,[12] and that increases to over $18 trillion USD when you include their families.[13]

Legal and regulatory compliance

Many countries have accessibility legislation for digital content, including social media. For instance, the Americans with Disabilities Act (ADA) Amended Act of 2024 in the US has implications for online content. Over 4,600 ADA-related website accessibility cases were filed in 2023 alone, underscoring the legal risks of non-compliance.[14] Failure to comply with these regulations can result in legal challenges, fines and reputational damage.[15]

By prioritizing accessibility, you reduce your legal risk and position yourself as a leader in inclusive communication. It's a proactive approach that benefits your organization and ensures compliance with evolving standards like the Web Content Accessibility Guidelines.

Higher engagement metrics

Accessible content often performs better in terms of likes, shares and comments.[16] When posts are easy to read, understand and interact with, they naturally attract more engagement. Captions on videos, for instance, make content consumable for a broader range of people, boosting watch times and interaction rates.[17] Similarly, alt text allows users with sight loss to engage with image-based content, increasing overall accessibility and inclusivity.

By removing barriers, you're not just making your content accessible; you're making it engaging and memorable.

Better internal practices

Accessibility on social media doesn't just benefit external audiences; it also improves internal workflows. As mentioned in Chapter 3, by adopting accessible design and communication practices, teams become more mindful of clarity, simplicity and inclusivity in all aspects of their work. This cultural shift can lead to better decision-making, more creative solutions, and a stronger sense of purpose across the organization.

The bigger picture: Accessibility as a core value

Making your social media content accessible is all about creating meaningful connections, creating inclusivity and amplifying voices that are too often left out of the conversation. It's a reflection of your organization's values and a demonstration of your commitment to equity.

Accessibility is also a journey, not a destination.

Social media platforms evolve, new tools emerge and user expectations change. Staying ahead means continuously learning, listening to your audience and adapting your strategies to ensure everyone feels seen, heard and included.

As you read this chapter, you'll discover practical tips, tools and techniques for making your social media content genuinely accessible. After all, when everyone can engage, everyone wins.

The fundamentals of accessible social media

Creating accessible social media content ensures your message reaches everyone, regardless of their abilities. We live in a world where social media has become a dominant communication tool. Prioritizing accessibility isn't just the right thing to do; it's essential for engagement, inclusion and trust-building.

To understand how to create accessible social media content, let's consider the basics: identifying key barriers users face and exploring how accessibility guidelines, like the WCAG, apply to this ever-evolving space.

Key barriers for social media users

Social media platforms are designed for connection, conversation and creativity. Yet, for many people with disabilities, these platforms can be rife with challenges that exclude them from fully participating in the conversation. Here are some of the most common barriers.

Visual disabilities

For users who are Deafblind, blind or have low vision, images and videos on social media often lack alternative ways to convey their content. A promotional post featuring a product or event, for example, might rely entirely on visuals to communicate key information, leaving screen reader users out of the loop if alt text is missing.[18][19]

Poor colour contrast is another issue. Low-contrast visuals or text overlaying busy backgrounds can be impossible for people with sight loss to read, creating a barrier to understanding the message.

Hearing disabilities

For people who are deaf or hard of hearing, audio-based content like Instagram Stories and Reels, TikToks or live streams can pose significant challenges when captions or transcripts aren't provided. A lack of captions not only excludes these users but also misses the opportunity to engage viewers in noisy environments or those who prefer watching content on mute.[20][21]

Cognitive disabilities

Individuals with cognitive disabilities, like dyslexia, ADHD or autism, may struggle with overly complex language, cluttered layouts or rapid-paced content. Dense blocks of text in social media captions or fast, uncaptioned videos can make it difficult for them to process information effectively.[22]

Mobility and motor disabilities
Users with limited dexterity or motor disabilities may find social media apps challenging to navigate due to poorly designed interfaces, small touch targets or the lack of keyboard navigation options. These barriers can make something as simple as liking a post or tapping a button unnecessarily difficult.[23][24]

Situational or temporary disabilities
If someone is tired or stressed, their ability to process information is diminished. Don't let your message get lost amid too many details or unclear calls-to-action. If they're using their phone in a public place, or have a baby asleep on their shoulder, they may not be able to turn the volume up on their phone – so make sure those captions and descriptions are available. Perhaps they've got a cracked screen, or left their reading glasses at home, and miss that crucial tiny detail hidden in the background of that Instagram post. Make it as easy as possible for people to consume your social media!

Platform-specific limitations
While social media platforms have taken steps to improve accessibility, like introducing alt text options or automatic captions, these features are often hidden in settings or not consistently reliable. This leaves the responsibility of content creators to ensure their posts are accessible.[25]

By understanding these barriers, communicators can better anticipate the needs of their audience and create content that builds inclusion.

Accessibility guidelines overview: Applying WCAG to social media

While the Web Content Accessibility Guidelines were initially developed for websites, their principles can and should be applied to social media content. As a reminder from Chapter 2, WCAG is built on four foundational principles, often called POUR: Perceivable, Operable, Understandable and Robust.

Here's how these principles translate to social media accessibility.

Perceivable: Ensuring everyone can access content
Social media content must be presented in ways that users with different abilities can perceive. This means providing alternatives for visual or auditory elements, like:

- Alt text for images: Every image should include alt text that describes its essential information. For example, instead of 'Image of a person', you might write 'A woman holding a coffee cup and smiling at a laptop during a virtual meeting'.

- Captions and transcripts: Whether live or pre-recorded, videos should include accurate captions. For live content, consider real-time captioning tools. Provide transcripts for audio content like podcasts.
- Colour contrast: Ensure the text stands out against its background. WCAG recommends a contrast ratio of at least 4.5:1 for normal text and 3:1 for large text.

Operable: Making content easy to navigate

Operable content is designed to accommodate different ways users interact with technology. For social media, this involves:

- Keyboard-friendly content: While this is more of a platform design issue, you can help by avoiding interactive content (like complex carousels) that might be difficult to navigate with a keyboard or assistive device.
- Clear calls-to-action: Avoid vague instructions like 'Click here' or 'See this'. Be specific: 'Visit our website' or 'Register for this webinar'.
- Avoiding autoplay: Autoplaying videos can be overwhelming or disorienting for users with sensory or cognitive disabilities. Whenever possible, use static content or provide a way to turn off autoplay.

Understandable: Keeping content clear and intuitive

Understandable content ensures users can easily follow and interact with your posts. This means focusing on:

- Plain language: Write captions and posts in straightforward, jargon-free language. Break down complex concepts into digestible pieces. Refer back to Chapter 4 for best practices and tips on this.
- Consistent design: Use templates or branded visuals that are easily recognizable and navigable.
- Content clarity: Avoid cramming too much information into a single post. To organize content, use line breaks, bullet points or carousel posts.

Robust: Ensuring compatibility across platforms

Robust content works across various devices, screen sizes and assistive technologies. It is particularly important, as social media is consumed on everything from desktops to mobile phones. To ensure your content is robust:

- Test with assistive tools: Use screen readers or accessibility checkers to evaluate how different audiences perceive your content.

- Include multiple formats: If you post a complex infographic, accompany it with a plain-text summary or alt text to ensure all users can access the information. Some users may also appreciate access to the source data if you're presenting charts and graphics.

Why following these guidelines matters

Adopting accessibility practices on social media isn't just about compliance; it's about fostering genuine connections. When you take steps to remove barriers, you invite everyone to engage with your brand, message or campaign. Inclusive social media content demonstrates that you care about your audience as a whole, not just a subset of it.

Take Microsoft's social media strategy as an example: by consistently including captions, alt text and thoughtful narratives, they've built a reputation as a brand that values accessibility and inclusivity. Following these guidelines can help your organization achieve the same.[26]

Accessibility doesn't need to be overwhelming. By understanding the key barriers users face and applying WCAG principles to your social media content, you can make meaningful strides towards creating an online space where everyone feels welcome, heard and respected. Social media is one of the most powerful communication tools; why not ensure it works for everyone?

Accessible images and graphics

Images and graphics are a cornerstone of social media content, capturing attention and driving engagement faster than words alone. But what happens when these visuals exclude a portion of your audience? For many people with disabilities, inaccessible images can create significant barriers, leaving them out of the conversation. By adopting inclusive design practices, you can make your visuals more accessible, ensuring everyone can engage with and benefit from your content.

This section explores how to create accessible images and graphics, focusing on the fundamentals of alt text, the challenges of text on images, and the importance of contrast and readability.

Alt text basics: What it is, why it matters, and how to write it

Alt text (short for alternative text) is one of the most critical tools for making images accessible. It provides a written description of an image, allowing screen readers to convey the content of the visual to users who are blind or have low vision. Think of it as a way to ensure your visuals have meaning for everyone.

What is alt text?
Alt text is a description added to the HTML code of an image or through social media platforms' accessibility features. While it's invisible to sighted users viewing the image, it becomes invaluable for anyone relying on assistive technology to navigate the web or their social feeds.[27]

What is an image description?
An image description is a detailed explanation of an image designed to give people who can't see the image a clear understanding of its content. Unlike alt text, which is short and functional, image descriptions are more in-depth and often used to describe complex visuals like infographics, event photos or artistic works. They provide context, set the scene and explain visual details, helping everyone engage fully with the content. Image descriptions are often included in captions, surrounding text or accessibility notes to complement the alt text and enhance inclusivity.[28]

Breaking down the differences between alt text and an image description
The difference between alt text and an image description lies in their purpose, length and the context in which they are used.

Alt text
- Purpose: Alt text (short for 'alternative text') concisely describes an image embedded in the image's HTML or platform-specific accessibility settings. It allows screen readers to convey the image's content to users who are blind or visually impaired.
- Length: Alt text is short and to the point – generally one or two sentences. It focuses on the most critical information the image conveys.
- Where it's used: Alt text is primarily used for functional, web-based purposes. It is hidden from sighted users and is accessed by screen readers or displayed if the image fails to load.
- Example: For a promotional image of a coffee cup, the alt text might read: 'A steaming cup of coffee on a wooden table with a notepad and pen beside it.'

Image description

- Purpose: An image description is a more detailed explanation of the image's content. It provides deeper context or additional information, particularly for complex visuals like infographics, artwork or charts.
- Length: Image descriptions are longer and more descriptive, often a paragraph or more. They aim to paint a complete picture of what the image contains.
- Where it's used: Image descriptions can be included in the surrounding content, such as a social media post, blog caption or alternative content document. They are meant to complement the alt text.
- Example: For the same coffee image, an image description might read: 'The image shows a light wooden table with a spiral notebook and a black pen resting on its surface. To the left is a white ceramic mug filled with steaming coffee. The steam is softly illuminated by natural light coming through a nearby window.'

When to use each

Use alt text for essential, concise descriptions in digital content where brevity is key. Use image descriptions when the visual contains complex or additional context (e.g. infographics, event photos or promotional graphics) that needs to be conveyed in more detail.

In short, alt text is like a quick summary, while an image description is the full story. Both play a critical role in making images accessible to all users.

Why do alt text and image descriptions matter?

Imagine scrolling through your Instagram feed with visuals highlighting key statistics, but the thread lacks alt text or, in this case, an image description. A user with a screen reader won't hear those statistics; they'll hear 'Image', and that's it. The opportunity to share important insights with that user has been lost. Alt text and image descriptions bridge this gap, giving equal access to information.

HOW TO WRITE DESCRIPTIVE ALT TEXT

Writing effective alt text is an art. The goal is to provide enough detail to convey the image's purpose without overloading the description. Here are some tips:[29]

- Focus on key details: What is the image about? If it's a photo of a coffee shop, you might say, 'A barista pouring steamed milk into a latte, creating a heart-shaped pattern.'

- Avoid overexplaining: If the image is decorative or doesn't add meaningful content, it's okay to leave the alt text blank but indicate it as 'decorative' in the image settings.
- Skip phrases like 'Image of': Screen readers already identify the content as an image, so it's redundant to say, 'Image of a sunset'. Instead, describe the sunset's colours and mood: 'A vibrant orange and pink sunset over the ocean, with waves gently rolling onto the shore.'
- Consider the context: Tailor your description to the image's role in your post. For example, if the image supports a post about accessibility, you might add details about a wheelchair user navigating a cityscape.

Avoiding text on images: Best practices and alternatives

Text on images is a staple of social media content, especially for promotional posts, infographics, or inspirational quotes. However, when text is embedded in an image, it often becomes inaccessible to many users.

Why text on images can be a problem

For one, they are inaccessible to screen readers. Embedded text isn't readable by assistive technologies unless it's also included in the alt text, which can be challenging to summarize effectively. Then there's the scalability issue. Text on images may not resize well on different devices, becoming illegible on smaller screens. And finally, the language barrier. If text is baked into the image, translation tools can't process it, limiting reach for multilingual audiences.[30]

So, what are your alternatives?

Instead of embedding text in an image, include it as a caption or in the post itself. For example, if you're sharing an inspirational quote, pair the quote with an engaging visual, but keep the majority of text in the post description. You can also break complex visuals into multiple slides or carousel posts, each with its own alt text and plain-text descriptions.[31]

But, if you must include text on an image, ensure high contrast and legibility. Use large, clear fonts and avoid placing text over busy backgrounds. Adjusting your templates takes a little work to start with, but minimizing text in your images also makes for a swifter workflow in the future too! You wouldn't place your brand logo on a busy background – and neither should you do this with text.

Designing with contrast and readability

Great design isn't just about looking good; it's about being understood by everyone. Poor contrast, illegible fonts and cluttered layouts can exclude users with visual and cognitive disabilities and even those in low-light environments. By prioritizing contrast and readability, you can create visuals that are engaging and inclusive.

The importance of high contrast

Contrast refers to the difference in brightness between text and its background. It can be tempting to post using 'subtle' colour palettes, but these are harder to read for many people, who would miss your core message. Low-contrast designs, like the light grey text on a white background, are challenging to read for many users, including those with low vision or colour-blindness.[32]

CONTRAST TIPS

1. Remember the Web Content Accessibility Guidelines: Aim for a contrast ratio of at least 4.5:1 for normal text and 3:1 for large text. Tools like TPGI's Colour Contrast Analyser and WebAIM's contrast checker can help you evaluate your visuals.

2. Avoiding problematic combinations: Be mindful of colour pairings that can create challenges for colour-blind users, such as red/green or blue/purple combinations. You can use the website WhoCanUse.com to better understand what people with various colour blindness types will see.[33]

Choosing readable fonts

Typography plays a significant role in accessibility, so here's what you need to consider:[34]

- Sans-serif fonts: Use clean, simple fonts like Arial, Helvetica or Verdana, which are easier to read than ornate serif fonts.
- Size matters: Keep font sizes large enough to read comfortably, even on smaller screens.
- Spacing and alignment: Add generous line spacing and avoid justified text, which can create uneven gaps that disrupt readability.

- Avoid using special characters: Unicode text is not read clearly by screen readers, and the adjusted fonts to force formatting like bold or italic is harder to read for everyone.

Simplify visual layouts

Cluttered designs can overwhelm users, especially those with cognitive disabilities. Stick to clean, focused layouts with a clear visual hierarchy. It ensures that your message comes through without unnecessary distractions.

Accessible design is a step towards inclusion

Creating accessible images and graphics isn't just about meeting technical requirements; it's about ensuring everyone can appreciate, understand and enjoy your content. Whether it's crafting concise alt text, rethinking text placement on visuals or prioritizing contrast and readability, these practices make your content genuinely inclusive. And the best part? Accessible designs don't just help users with disabilities; they create a better experience for all. By taking these steps, you're building a more welcoming and impactful digital space for everyone.

Building inclusive social media experiences through captioning and audio accessibility

Today, video and audio content dominate social platforms. From TikToks to Instagram Reels to podcasts, this kind of media is powerful, engaging; and often inaccessible to many. This section introduces the fundamentals of captioning and audio accessibility, but we'll dive deeper into advanced strategies and tools in Chapter 8. For now, let's focus on what you need to know to get started.

The role of captions and subtitles

Captions and subtitles serve as visual representations of spoken words, sound effects, and other auditory elements within video content. They're essential for audiences who cannot rely on audio alone, but their benefits go far beyond accessibility.

Think about someone scrolling through Instagram in a quiet office, a commuter watching videos on public transit without headphones, or a student revisiting educational content to absorb information better. Captions cater to all of these scenarios, making your content universally appealing and accessible. They also boost engagement and retention. Studies show that videos with captions have higher viewership completion rates than those without.[35][36]

Captions also benefit people who are not your 'typical' audience but still want to engage. For example, captions can make content understandable for individuals learning a new language or clarify speech for those who struggle with heavy accents or background noise. Simply put, captions make your content versatile and effective.

Creating effective captions: Why 'boring' is better

Let's address a trend: the rise of 'haptic captions' or visually stylized subtitles in videos. You've probably seen captions in bright colours, funky fonts, or bouncing animations that match the tone or rhythm of the speaker. While creative, these captions can undermine accessibility.

Why? Because 'boring' captions are often the most effective. Captions are not there to dazzle; they're there to inform. Effective captions should:

- Be legible: Use a simple, sans-serif font in a size large enough to be read comfortably across devices.
- Avoid over-styling: Fancy fonts, extreme colour contrasts or animated effects can make captions hard to follow, especially for those with cognitive disabilities or visual impairments.
- Match the pacing of speech: Captions should appear on screen long enough to be read easily without lagging behind the dialogue or action.

The goal is to create captions that blend seamlessly into the viewing experience while still being accessible to everyone. If your captions distract from the message, they're not serving their purpose.[37]

Tools and tips for captioning

Fortunately, creating captions is easier than ever, thanks to a growing number of tools and platforms offering built-in or automated captioning options. However, not all tools are created equal, and automation isn't always perfect. Here's how to get it right:

- Use built-in features: Platforms like YouTube, Instagram and TikTok offer automated captioning, but these captions should always be reviewed and edited for accuracy. Automated systems often misinterpret names, accents or technical jargon, leading to errors that can confuse your audience.

- Try manual captioning tools: Software like Adobe Premiere Pro, Descript or Otter.ai allows you to edit captions for precision manually. While this requires more effort, it ensures higher accuracy and professionalism.
- Caption beyond dialogue: Don't forget to caption non-verbal sounds like [applause], [laughter] or [doorbell ringing]. These audio cues provide important context and improve the viewing experience for everyone.

Remember, captions are a critical accessibility tool, not an afterthought. Prioritizing quality and accuracy send a strong message that you value your audience's diverse needs.

Adding transcripts for audio content

While captions cater to video content, transcripts are the accessibility heroes of audio-only formats like podcasts, interviews or voice notes. A transcript is a text-based document containing the entire spoken content of an audio file, making it accessible to people who are D/deaf or hard of hearing, as well as those who prefer reading to listening.[38]

Creating transcripts is not just an act of inclusivity; it's a practical strategy. Search engines can crawl and index text-based content, making transcripts a valuable SEO tool that increases discoverability. They also make your content more versatile; someone who might not have time to listen to a whole podcast can quickly skim the transcript for key points.

EFFECTIVE TIPS FOR TRANSCRIPTS

- Be comprehensive: Include all spoken words as well as significant sound effects or cues (e.g. [soft music playing]).
- Offer multiple formats: Provide transcripts as downloadable PDFs or accessible web pages for easy access.
- Automate, then edit: Tools like Otter.ai or Rev can generate transcripts quickly but always review for accuracy. Context matters, and automation often misses subtleties like tone or intent.

Captioning and audio accessibility are fundamental to creating inclusive social media content. By making these elements a priority, you're not only expanding your audience reach but also creating a sense of belonging and trust. Whether through meticulously crafted captions or well-thought-out transcripts, your efforts to make content accessible send a powerful message: everyone is welcome here.

Start small, test your strategies, and refine your process over time. Accessibility is not about perfection; it's about progress. Each thoughtful caption and transcript you create is a step towards a more inclusive digital landscape, and that's a journey worth taking.

Writing inclusive copy for social media

When it comes to creating accessible social media content, the words you choose are just as important as the visuals or videos you include. Inclusive copywriting ensures your content connects with your entire audience, not just a select group. In this section, we'll explore the art of writing social media posts that are easy to read, sensitive to diverse experiences, and designed to foster genuine engagement. By focusing on simplicity, thoughtful language, and accessibility best practices, your posts can make everyone feel included and respected.

Plain language is powerful

We talked about plain and inclusive language in Chapter 4, but it's time to apply it to social media. When writing for social media, clarity is key. While creative, poetic, or overly complex language might feel tempting, especially for brands that want to stand out, it can alienate audiences who may struggle with cognitive disabilities, language barriers, or limited literacy skills. Plain language is not about oversimplifying; it's about ensuring everyone can understand and engage with your message.[39]

As a recap, why does plain language matter so much when it comes to social media?

For one, accessibility. Clear, concise copy is easier for everyone to understand, including people who use screen readers or translation tools. The second is engagement. Social media posts that get straight to the point tend to perform better. Audiences scroll quickly, and simple messages grab attention. And, of course, the global reach and impact. Plain language helps your message resonate across cultural and linguistic divides, making your content more inclusive on a global scale.

Plain language doesn't mean dull; it means being direct, approachable and relatable.

> **TIPS FOR WRITING IN PLAIN LANGUAGE**
>
> - Avoid jargon and slang: While trendy terms might feel fun, like 'No cap', or 'All rizz', they can confuse audiences unfamiliar with the references.
> - Keep sentences short: Aim for no more than 20 words per sentence. Break up complex ideas into smaller, digestible pieces.
> - Use action verbs: Clear, direct language like 'Learn more', 'Sign up' or 'Share your story' makes your posts easier to follow.
> - Test for clarity: Tools like Hemingway Editor can help you assess your writing's readability level. Aim for a grade 6–8 reading level for most audiences.
>
> For example, instead of saying, 'Utilize these strategies to augment your audience engagement', try 'Use these tips to grow your audience'.

Hashtag etiquette

Hashtags are essential for social media visibility but can also be accessibility pitfalls. Without proper formatting, hashtags can confuse both human readers and assistive technologies like screen readers. The solution? Use Camel Case or Pascal Case.

> **TIP**
>
> *Camel Case vs. Pascal Case: What's the difference?*
>
> Camel Case and Pascal Case are both methods of formatting text by capitalizing the first letter of each word to improve readability.[40] The key difference lies in how they handle the first word:
>
> - **Camel Case** starts with a lowercase letter, so it looks like this: #accessibleDesign.
> - **Pascal Case** starts with an uppercase letter, so it looks like this: #AccessibleDesign.
>
> When it comes to hashtags, Pascal Case is typically preferred because it's more visually distinct and easier for screen readers to interpret, ensuring accessibility for all audiences.

Why accessible hashtags are important

- **Improve readability:** For everyone, not just people with disabilities, #AccessibleCommunications is far easier to read than #accessiblecommunications.

- **Support screen readers:** Using capital letters at the beginning of each word means that screen readers correctly identify and pronounce individual words. Without it, screen readers might misinterpret the hashtag as a single, incomprehensible word.

- **Prevent unintended mishaps:** Improperly formatted hashtags can lead to embarrassing or offensive misunderstandings, as illustrated by the infamous Susan Boyle case.

REAL-WORLD EXAMPLE
Susan Boyle's hashtag mishap – #Susanalbumparty

When Susan Boyle's PR team launched a campaign to promote her new album in 2012, they created the hashtag #susanalbumparty. Unfortunately, without proper formatting, the hashtag became infamous for its unintended, risqué interpretation, sparking widespread ridicule online. What should have been a celebration of her music turned into a lesson in the importance of hashtag clarity and accessibility.[41, 42]

Had the team used Pascal Case, writing the hashtag as #SusanAlbumParty, the confusion could have been avoided. This case highlights the significance of thoughtful communication, not just for accessibility but also to protect a brand's reputation. It's a humorous reminder of how a lack of attention to detail can turn a well-intentioned campaign into a viral misstep.

Best practices for hashtags

As you plan out your next hashtag strategy, keep the following in mind:

- **Keep them short and simple:** Long hashtags are harder to read and remember.

- **Limit the number:** Overloading your post with hashtags (#like #this #example #here) can overwhelm readers and dilute your message.

- **Research first:** Check hashtags for existing usage to avoid unintended connotations or associations.

Tone and context: Words that resonate

Social media moves fast, and tone is everything. What sounds clever or edgy in one context could come across as insensitive or exclusionary in another. As communicators, it is essential to think critically about how your language resonates with diverse audiences.

Find the right tone

The tone should align with your brand's voice while remaining inclusive and respectful. Humour can be effective, but it should be handled with care. For example, jokes that rely on stereotypes or exclusivity can alienate your audience. Great comedians never 'punch down'; comedy shouldn't be at the expense of others. Instead, opt for humour that is light, relatable and inclusive.

QUESTIONS TO ASK BEFORE POSTING

- Does this post exclude anyone? While your content doesn't have to be for everyone, you shouldn't be setting out to exclude people because of their ability or protected characteristics.
- Could this be misinterpreted? Example: Cultural references or slang may not translate well across all audiences.
- Is this tone appropriate for the topic? Example: A serious topic like mental health requires sensitivity, while a product launch may allow for a more playful approach.

Inclusive language: Words matter

Again, we talked in-depth about this in Chapter 4, but it's important to bring it up here again. Be mindful of the words you choose; incorporating inclusive language into your social media copy reflects your values as a communicator.

Examples of inclusive language
- Instead of 'guys,' use 'everyone' or 'team'.
- Avoid gendered assumptions like 'she' for a nurse or 'he' for an engineer. Use gender-neutral terms when possible.

- Be mindful of ability-based language. For instance, avoid phrases like 'turn a blind eye' or 'deaf to criticism', which can unintentionally alienate people with disabilities.

Bringing our copy together

Inclusive copywriting for social media is about intention and thoughtfulness. By prioritizing plain language, formatting hashtags for accessibility, and crafting tone-sensitive, inclusive messages, you can create content that resonates with a broader, more diverse audience.

Platform-specific accessibility tips

Social media platforms are integral to communication today, each offering unique ways to connect with audiences. However, the accessibility tools and practices can vary widely between platforms. To truly engage all users, including those with disabilities, it's crucial to understand what is possible on each platform. This section provides an overview of accessibility tips tailored to the most popular platforms.

Facebook

Facebook is one of the most established and widely used platforms and has several ways to incorporate accessibility into your social media strategy.

Note the accessibility statement, 'Facebook is committed to creating a great experience for all people. Learn about the features and technologies that help people with disabilities, such as vision loss and deafness, get the most out of Facebook.'[43]

Alt text for images

Facebook allows users to add custom alt text to images. While it auto-generates alt text, it's often too generic to be meaningful. For example, 'a person outdoors' might fail to capture the context of an image meant to convey joy at a community event. Always take a moment to write a descriptive, context-rich alt text that explains why the image matters.[44]

> ### DID YOU KNOW?
>
> People who are partially sighted or have cognitive disabilities may not rely on screen readers but can still struggle to fully understand an image's content without additional context. This is why it's crucial to include alt text in the image where the platform allows, but also in the main post caption.
>
> On platforms like LinkedIn, Facebook and Instagram, adding a descriptive explanation directly into the post ensures that everyone, regardless of the tools they use, can grasp the message behind the visual. This dual approach not only makes your content more inclusive but also ensures your key message reaches and resonates with a broader audience.
>
> Note: X (formerly known as Twitter) and BlueSky have an 'ALT' badge on images that have had alt text embedded. Users can click or tap on that badge to read the description. In these cases, you do not need to add the alt text into your actual post; just make sure to embed it into the image.
>
> For those users who use a screen reader, they can skip the alt text duplication.

Video captions

Facebook offers a built-in auto-captioning tool, which is a good starting point, but it's not always accurate.[45] Review and edit captions for clarity and accuracy to ensure your message is communicated effectively. Captions are not just for people who are D/deaf or hard of hearing; they're also helpful for users scrolling through content without sound.

Avoiding autoplay videos

Autoplay videos can be jarring, especially for people with sensory disabilities or those using screen readers. Facebook allows you to disable autoplay in your settings, and as a content creator, you should avoid relying on autoplay to grab attention.[46]

> ### BONUS TIP
>
> Ensure your posts are structured with plain language and minimal jargon. Facebook's user base is diverse, so keeping it simple increases engagement across the board.

Instagram

Instagram's visual-first nature poses unique accessibility challenges, but it also provides tools to address them.

Also owned by Meta, note Instagram's remarkably similar-starting accessibility statement, 'Instagram is committed to creating a great experience for all people. Learn about the features and technologies that help people with disabilities, such as vision loss and deafness, get the most out of Instagram.'[47]

Alt text for images

Instagram has a feature to add custom alt text when uploading photos. This feature is often overlooked, but it's critical for making your content accessible.[48] For instance, instead of saying 'a dog', you might write, 'A golden retriever puppy playing with a red ball in a grassy park'.

> **NOTE**
>
> Screen reader users hear the image first before they hear your caption. It's imperative that you include alt text in your image to avoid any context being lost to the built-in auto-generating alt text application trying to decipher what the image is all about.

Captions and descriptive posts

Not all users will engage with your images visually; many rely on captions to understand the story. Use your captions to provide context and details that might not be apparent from the image alone. Additionally, keep captions concise but descriptive, as overly lengthy text can overwhelm some users.

Avoiding text-only posts

While text overlay on an image might look aesthetically pleasing, it's often inaccessible to screen readers. If you must use text on images, ensure it has high contrast and include the same information in your caption.

X (formerly Twitter)

X is known for its brevity, but that doesn't mean accessibility should take a back seat.

Note X's accessibility statement, 'Here at X, our mission is to give everyone the power to create and share ideas and information instantly without barriers, including people with disabilities/disabled people. We have a dedicated group of cross-functional inclusive designers and engineers, with and without lived experience of disability, focused on providing the best experience regardless of device, platform, or disability by incorporating established guidelines and best practices.'[49]

Alt text for images

Whenever you include an image in a tweet, take a moment to add alt text. X provides up to 1,000 characters for alt text, allowing for detailed descriptions. For example, instead of writing 'a pie chart', you could say, 'A pie chart showing 60 per cent of respondents prefer vanilla ice cream, 30 per cent prefer chocolate, and 10 per cent prefer strawberry.'

Hashtag etiquette

Use Pascal Case or Camel Case for hashtags (e.g. #AccessibleCommunications instead of #accessiblecommunications). This improves readability for everyone, including screen readers and people with cognitive disabilities. It also avoids the kind of confusion made famous by the #susanalbumparty hashtag fiasco, as we already talked about earlier in this chapter.

Concise and clear writing

Since X limits your character count, focus on plain language. Be direct and avoid abbreviations or slang that might not be universally understood.

> **DID YOU KNOW?**
>
> When creating content on social platforms, you should avoid using external fonts, fancy headings or bolding generated by third-party tools. These styles may look interesting visually, but they can be hard to read for lots of people, and assistive technologies like screen readers can't interpret them properly, leaving some of your audience excluded.
>
> Instead, use the platform's native tools for formatting. By sticking to what's provided in the root platform, you ensure that your content is accessible and readable to all users, regardless of their abilities. Accessible design starts with simplicity!

LinkedIn

As a platform for professionals, LinkedIn requires clear, concise and inclusive communication to engage its audience effectively.

Note LinkedIn's accessibility statement, 'LinkedIn is a place where every member of the global workforce can find opportunity. Whatever your goals, ideas and abilities are, we're here to help you succeed. No two LinkedIn members are the same – and it's that diversity which makes our community so great. We're on a journey to make accessibility and inclusive design part of our core principles, building accessibility from the ground up and testing our products with assistive technology to make sure that everyone can use LinkedIn to advance their professional goals.'[50]

Image descriptions and alt text

LinkedIn supports custom alt text for images, but many users still neglect this feature. Adding alt text ensures your posts are accessible to everyone, especially when sharing infographics or charts.

LinkedIn carousels

It's possible to add alt text to images on LinkedIn carousels, although they present a number of usability challenges for some users and should really be avoided – simple image formats and captioned videos present a better experience.[51] It was announced that the functionality would be phased out, but as of early 2025 the format remains active.

Clear calls-to-action

Whether you're sharing a job posting or an industry insight, ensure your call-to-action (CTA) is simple and easy to understand. For example, use 'Click here to apply' rather than vague phrases like 'Check this out'. There's also a phenomenon about 'link in comments' to boost engagement on posts; while there are multiple blogs and debates about whether this works or not, sometimes that comment can be hidden under a 'relevant vs. recent' filter that appears to deliberately obscure the link to keep people on the platform.

> **BONUS TIP**
>
> When uploading videos, always include captions, open or closed captions. Many LinkedIn users consume content during work hours, often with their device muted.

TikTok and YouTube

Video-first platforms like TikTok and YouTube present unique opportunities for accessibility, but they also require careful planning.

TikTok's accessibility statement says, 'At TikTok, we're committed to maintaining an inclusive environment and supporting our diverse community. Inclusivity is important to us because when people feel included, they're more comfortable expressing themselves authentically, creating content, and engaging with others. Being truly inclusive means building products and tools for everyone. Our cross-functional teams work with our creator community, as well as disability organizations and advocates to help ensure TikTok is accessible to everyone.'[52]

Captioning tools

Both TikTok and YouTube offer auto-captioning features to users. While helpful, these tools often make errors, especially with technical jargon or accents. Take the time to edit auto-generated captions or upload your own for better accuracy.

Audio descriptions

For visually complex content, consider adding audio descriptions. While not every video will require this, they are invaluable for conveying visual details to viewers who are Deafblind, blind or have low vision.

Clear and concise content

Keep your videos focused and ensure your key messages are easy to grasp. For TikTok, where brevity is key, consider overlaying text summaries of your main points in addition to captions.

> **BONUS TIP**
>
> When designing thumbnail images for YouTube, use high-contrast colours and legible fonts to ensure they're easy to see and understand.

Tailoring accessibility to each platform

Each social media platform has its quirks and features, but the goal of accessibility remains the same: to ensure everyone, regardless of ability, can engage with your content. By understanding and using the tools available on each platform, you not only expand your audience but also build a reputation for inclusivity and care.

Remember, accessible social media content doesn't just benefit people with disabilities; it creates a better experience for everyone.

Common pitfalls and how to avoid them in accessible social media content

It can be easy to think that creating accessible social media content is just about following a checklist. However, it's more than that; it's about making deliberate, thoughtful choices that ensure everyone can engage with your content. However, even with the best intentions, there are common pitfalls that can unintentionally exclude parts of your audience. Here are some of the most common accessibility missteps and how to steer clear of them.

Overuse of emojis: Why moderation and placement matter

Emojis have become an integral part of online communication. And really, who doesn't love a well-timed emoji from time to time? They add personality, enhance tone and make posts feel fun and conversational. But when it comes to accessibility, too much of a good thing can quickly become a problem.

The problem

For users relying on screen readers, each emoji is read out loud by its official name. For example, the 🎉 emoji is read as 'party popper' and the 🤔 emoji is read as 'thinking face'. When emojis are overused or placed mid-sentence, they disrupt the natural flow of text, making it harder for the user to focus on the actual message. Additionally, some emojis may not be accurately interpreted by all screen readers, especially if they are newly introduced or culturally specific.[53]

> **THE PROBLEM IN ACTION**
>
> Imagine a post that reads:
>
> 'We're so excited 🎉🎉🎉 to announce our new product launch 🎊🎊🎊 happening next week!'

A screen reader would interpret this as:

'We're so excited party popper, party popper, party popper to announce our new product launch rocket, rocket, rocket happening next week!'

This creates a frustrating experience for the listener, detracting from the intended message.

Emojis and cognitive load

For individuals with cognitive disabilities, interpreting the meaning of emojis, especially when used in sequences or without accompanying text, can add unnecessary complexity. Emojis often rely on context, and their intended tone can be misinterpreted without clear cues. A string of ambiguous emojis can leave some users unsure of the message being conveyed.[54]

For example, a series like 🌀💧🍎 could mean something playful to some but be entirely unclear to others. Even something as simple as combining emojis like 🏆+💪 can leave room for interpretation, adding unnecessary cognitive strain.

Cultural and contextual misunderstandings

Emojis don't always translate universally. The meaning of an emoji can vary depending on cultural context, age group or even platform. For example, the 🙏 emoji can be interpreted as praying hands, a high-five, or simply gratitude, depending on the user and cultural background. Misunderstandings around emojis can lead to confusion, or worse, miscommunication that alienates your audience.

Case study: The thumbs-up emoji – A misunderstood symbol across generations

The thumbs-up emoji 👍, a symbol many associate with agreement, approval or encouragement, recently sparked debate. While older generations use it as a quick, positive response, younger users, particularly Gen Z, view it as dismissive or passive-aggressive in certain contexts. This generational divide highlights how even small communication tools, like emojis, can be interpreted differently depending on the audience and cultural context.[55]

The issue In October 2022, discussions erupted on social media and forums like Reddit, where younger users claimed that the thumbs-up emoji felt cold or sarcastic in professional and personal interactions. They argued that it lacked the emotional nuance of a more thought-out reply or other emojis, such as a heart or smile. For instance, responding to a message with just 👍 could be seen as curt, or even rude, rather than affirming.

Psychologists argue that this misunderstanding stems from a lack of shared norms between generations. For older generations, the thumbs-up emoji might signal simple agreement, or a job well done, but for Gen Z, it can appear as though the sender is uninterested or unwilling to engage in deeper communication. This disconnect creates friction, especially in workplace communications.[56]

Implications for professional communicators The controversy over the thumbs-up emoji underscores the importance of understanding audience perception when choosing visual or written language in professional settings. While emojis can enhance tone and relatability, misinterpreting their meaning can lead to unintentional tension, particularly in multigenerational workplaces.

Takeaways
- Context is key: The thumbs-up emoji can feel positive or dismissive depending on the situation and audience. When in doubt, clarify your intent with additional context or a more personalized response.
- Know your audience: In professional communications, consider the generational and cultural norms of your team. What feels efficient to one group may seem impersonal to another.
- Embrace nuance: Emojis should support, not replace, thoughtful communication. When communicating approval or agreement, consider pairing emojis with text for clarity and warmth.

This case highlights a broader lesson in accessible and inclusive communications: language, even in its smallest forms, should be approached thoughtfully to ensure it resonates with diverse audiences.

BEST PRACTICES FOR USING EMOJIS[57]

- Use emojis sparingly: Limit the number of emojis in a single post. Stick to one or two to emphasize key points without overwhelming the message.
- Know your alt text sources: Understand that the alt text for emojis can vary depending on the platform, browser and device being used. This inconsistency means your intended meaning might not come across universally. Refer to resources like emojipedia.org to check how specific emojis are described to ensure your choice aligns with your message.

- Place emojis at the end of sentences: When you do use emojis, place them at the end of a sentence or phrase. This minimizes disruption for screen readers, as users will first hear the important text before the emoji name is read aloud.
- Avoid emoji-only posts: Never rely solely on emojis to convey a message. For example, a post that says '🎉🎉🎉' without accompanying text leaves screen reader users and many others guessing the context. Always pair emojis with descriptive text.
- Test for screen reader accessibility: Before posting, use a screen reader to hear how your emojis are interpreted. This can help you understand how your post sounds to users relying on assistive technology.
- Be mindful of tone and context: Ensure that the emojis you use align with the tone and meaning of your post. Avoid sequences that could confuse or alienate your audience.
- Consider alternatives: Sometimes, words or punctuation marks can achieve the same effect without the complications of emojis. For instance, instead of 'Great job 💯👋,' you could write, 'Great job! Outstanding work'.
- Avoid using emojis as bullet points. It's disappointing when platforms like LinkedIn don't offer rich text formatting, but using a hyphen is better than an emoji for screen readers.
- Don't list a string of emojis in your handle or username on platforms – every time a screen reader notes your name, the user will receive a repetitive list.

Striking the right balance

Emojis can make your social media content more engaging and relatable, but accessibility should always come first. By being intentional with your emoji use, you can ensure your content remains inclusive and clear for all audiences. Think of emojis as a garnish, not the main dish. Used sparingly, they can add flavour to your posts without overshadowing the essential message.

Remember, accessible communication isn't about avoiding fun or creative elements; it's about making sure everyone, regardless of ability, can enjoy and engage with your content.

When in doubt, ask yourself: Does this emoji enhance understanding or create a barrier? If in doubt, it's better to leave it out.

Ignoring colour contrast in visual content

Colour is a powerful tool in social media design. It grabs attention, conveys mood and reinforces branding. But poor colour contrast can exclude individuals with low vision, colour blindness or other visual disabilities.[58]

The problem

Text that blends into the background or colour combinations that are difficult to distinguish can make your visuals unreadable. For example, light grey text on a white background or red text on a green background can create significant barriers for users with visual or cognitive disabilities.

How to avoid this pitfall

1. Follow contrast standards: WCAG recommends a contrast ratio of at least 4.5:1 for normal text and 3:1 for large text.[59] Use free tools like the TPGI's Colour Contrast Analyser or WebAIM's Contrast Checker to evaluate your visuals.
2. Use high-contrast combinations: Stick to text and background pairings that are easy to read, like black text on a white or off-white background, or yellow text on a dark blue background.
3. Test your content: View your posts on different devices and in various lighting conditions to ensure readability across platforms.

By prioritizing contrast, you not only improve accessibility but also enhance the overall visual impact of your content.

Relying solely on automated accessibility tools

Automated accessibility tools are incredibly useful for identifying issues in your social media content, like missing alt text or poor contrast. However, they're not foolproof. Relying solely on these tools can lead to missed nuances and a false sense of security.[60]

The problem

Automation can't fully capture the context or intent of your content. For example:

- An automated tool may flag a low-contrast graphic as compliant, but it can't judge whether the text is readable in real-world conditions.

- Auto-generated alt text might describe an image as 'a person standing' without conveying the critical context, such as 'A teacher standing in front of a whiteboard, explaining a math problem'.

Automated tools also struggle with complex content like infographics, GIFs or videos, which require manual adjustments to ensure accessibility.

How to avoid this pitfall
- Pair automation with human oversight: Use tools like Facebook's auto-alt text feature or TikTok's auto-captioning as a starting point, but always review and edit for accuracy and completeness.
- Test your content manually: Use screen readers (like NVDA or VoiceOver) to experience your content as your audience would. This helps you catch nuances that automated tools might miss.
- Stay educated: Accessibility standards like WCAG are constantly evolving. Regularly update your knowledge to ensure your content aligns with best practices.

Automation is a helpful ally, but it's the human touch that ensures your content is truly inclusive.

Building a habit of accessibility

Avoiding these common pitfalls doesn't have to feel overwhelming. Here are some actionable steps to make accessibility a natural part of your social media workflow:

- Create checklists: Use a pre-posting checklist that includes tasks like adding alt text, testing contrast and reviewing captions.
- Leverage platform tools: Familiarize yourself with accessibility features on platforms like LinkedIn, Instagram and TikTok. For example, use Instagram's alt text field or TikTok's auto-captioning feature.
- Seek feedback: Engage with users who rely on assistive technologies and ask for their input. Their insights can help you refine your approach and identify areas for improvement.

By addressing these issues, you're ensuring your content is more engaging, effective and open. Accessible social media doesn't just benefit individuals with disabilities; it creates a better experience for all users, which, in turn, builds trust, loyalty and a broader reach.

Each thoughtful decision, whether it's limiting emojis, improving contrast or pairing automation with human oversight, brings you closer to creating a more inclusive digital space. Let accessibility be the foundation of your social media strategy, not an afterthought. Everyone deserves a seat at the table, and by avoiding these missteps, you're making sure there's room for all.

> **KEY TAKEAWAYS**
>
> Social media is one of the most powerful tools for connection and communication in our modern world. But as we've explored in this chapter, it's also a space that often leaves people behind when accessibility isn't prioritized. From the basics of alt text and captioning to avoiding common pitfalls like low contrast or overuse of emojis, we've covered actionable strategies to ensure your content is engaging and inclusive.
>
> Accessible social media content isn't just about compliance; it's about respect, inclusivity and creating meaningful connections with all members of your audience. By making thoughtful decisions, like writing descriptive alt text or leveraging platform-specific accessibility tools, you're showing that your brand values every individual's voice and perspective.
>
> The key takeaway? Accessible social media is better social media. It's more engaging, more relatable, and a true reflection of your commitment to inclusivity.

References

1. Disabled Canadians feel excluded from COVID-19 messaging, CityNews Ottawa, https://ottawa.citynews.ca/2020/03/18/disabled-canadians-feel-excluded-from-covid-19-messaging-2176110/ (archived at https://perma.cc/VP3D-M5AD)
2. Microsoft profile, X (formerly known as Twitter), https://x.com/Microsoft (archived at https://perma.cc/CAY7-852Q)
3. Continuing to talk, think and learn about inclusion, Microsoft, https://news.microsoft.com/en-ca/2021/05/19/sharing-our-learnings-to-create-a-more-accessible-world/ (archived at https://perma.cc/2BGJ-JFP5)
4. Starbucks profile, Instagram, www.instagram.com/starbucks/ (archived at https://perma.cc/U27D-6VE2)
5. Starbucks post, LinkedIn, www.linkedin.com/posts/starbucks_this-month-starbucks-and-our-disability-activity-7217177644151320576-htzt/ (archived at https://perma.cc/LNZ6-8MPY)

6 Disability, World Health Organization, www.who.int/news-room/fact-sheets/detail/disability-and-health (archived at https://perma.cc/BQ98-RCRJ)

7 Disabled people in the world: Facts and figures, Okeenea, www.inclusivecitymaker.com/disabled-people-in-the-world-in-2021-facts-and-figures/ (archived at https://perma.cc/U4RK-8V3S)

8 Family Resources Survey: Financial year 2022 to 2023, GOV.UK, www.gov.uk/government/statistics/family-resources-survey-financial-year-2022-to-2023/family-resources-survey-financial-year-2022-to-2023#disability-1 (archived at https://perma.cc/NSL5-E285)

9 Colour Blind Awareness, www.colourblindawareness.org/ (archived at https://perma.cc/SH4F-FLJ3)

10 M A Gernsbacher. Video captions benefit everyone, *Policy Insights from the Behavioral and Brain Sciences*, 2 (1), 195–202 https://pmc.ncbi.nlm.nih.gov/articles/PMC5214590/ (archived at https://perma.cc/WZ83-6UGR)

11 Everything you need to know about social media algorithms, Sprout Social, https://sproutsocial.com/insights/social-media-algorithms/ (archived at https://perma.cc/5GV8-MSFU)

12 Unlocking the value of the disability market with new 2024 report, The Return on Disability Group, www.newswire.ca/news-releases/unlocking-the-value-of-the-disability-market-with-new-2024-report-886192337.html (archived at https://perma.cc/7L2J-4JBE)

13 Unlocking the value of the disability market with new 2024 report, The Return on Disability Group, www.newswire.ca/news-releases/unlocking-the-value-of-the-disability-market-with-new-2024-report-886192337.html (archived at https://perma.cc/XRQ6-PUZJ)

14 2023 ADA web accessibility lawsuit statistics: Full report, ADA Site Compliance, https://adasitecompliance.com/2023-ada-web-accessibility-lawsuit-statistics-full-report/ (archived at https://perma.cc/BC9M-U69S)

15 Title II regulation supplement current as of October 8, 2024, US Department of Justice, www.ada.gov/assets/pdfs/title_ii_reg_update.pdf (archived at https://perma.cc/CM6C-3DUH)

16 Top tips for enhancing social media accessibility for all users, Brandwatch, www.brandwatch.com/blog/social-media-accessibility/ (archived at https://perma.cc/F89X-N3KT)

17 Subtitled success: How social media algorithms favor video content with captions, Amberscript, www.amberscript.com/en/blog/social-media-algorithms-video-content/ (archived at https://perma.cc/QFE4-XVH6)

18 Accessibility for people who are deafblind: Strategies for inclusion, Level Access, www.levelaccess.com/blog/understanding-assistive-technology-how-do-deaf-blind-people-use-technology/ (archived at https://perma.cc/7B3U-LGUX)

19 The frustrations of social media, Blind People Don't Mingle, www.blindpeopledontmingle.com/post/the-frustrations-of-social-media (archived at https://perma.cc/9VA9-223E)

20 This deaf woman perfectly illustrated what it's like for deaf people to watch videos without captions, and it's a wakeup call, Buzzfeed, www.buzzfeed.com/alexalisitza/deaf-video-caption-simulation (archived at https://perma.cc/S76E-7UB7)
21 Captions for deaf and hard-of-hearing viewers, National Institute on Deafness and Other Communication Disorders, www.nidcd.nih.gov/health/captions-deaf-and-hard-hearing-viewers (archived at https://perma.cc/6CQB-6QU7)
22 Designing digital content for users with cognitive disabilities, General Services Administration – Section 508, www.section508.gov/design/digital-content-users-with-cognitive-disabilities/ (archived at https://perma.cc/3C7A-4CJT)
23 Why touch target size matters for accessible UX design, Medium, https://medium.com/design-bootcamp/why-touch-target-size-matters-for-accessible-ux-design-333508313b21 (archived at https://perma.cc/ZK78-KKNU)
24 Mobile accessibility barriers for assistive technology users, Smashing Magazine, www.smashingmagazine.com/2024/02/mobile-accessibility-barriers-assistive-technology-users/ (archived at https://perma.cc/N894-ERU9)
25 M A Raymond, H Smith, L Carlson and A Gupta. An examination of digital accessibility within social media platforms: Problems for vulnerable consumers and policy implications, *Journal of Advertising Research*, 64 (4), 430–50. https://doi.org/10.2501/JAR-2024-026 (archived at https://perma.cc/C6EF-28BM)
26 Our accessibility approach, Microsoft, www.microsoft.com/en-us/accessibility/approach (archived at https://perma.cc/WT4M-BYBA)
27 Image alt text: What it is, how to write it, and why it matters to SEO, HubSpot, https://blog.hubspot.com/marketing/image-alt-text (archived at https://perma.cc/F3GT-QUK9)
28 What is this 'image description' thing all about? Birdability, www.birdability.org/blog/what-is-this-image-description-thing-all-about (archived at https://perma.cc/QGE8-EABV)
29 Writing image descriptions, Accessible Social, www.accessible-social.com/images-and-visuals/writing-image-descriptions (archived at https://perma.cc/NW4G-A3F2)
30 Designing accessible text over images: Best practices, techniques, and resources (Part 1), Smashing Magazine, www.smashingmagazine.com/2023/08/designing-accessible-text-over-images-part1/ (archived at https://perma.cc/4UEY-KQJC)
31 Best Practice 1.2 – Avoid images of text (Advanced level), Digital Policy Office for the Government of the Hong Kong Special Administrative Region of the People's Republic of China, www.digitalpolicy.gov.hk/en/our_work/digital_government/digital_inclusion/accessibility/promulgating_resources/maahandbook/best_practices/maa_best_practices_1-2.html (archived at https://perma.cc/9JA8-UGXF)
32 Choose colours and contrast carefully, eCampus Ontario, https://accessibility.ecampusontario.ca/accessibility/best-practices/colours/ (archived at https://perma.cc/X2K2-8EXB)

33 Who can use this color combination, WhoCanUse, www.whocanuse.com/ (archived at https://perma.cc/F6PJ-GKFV)
34 The role of typography in designing for accessibility, Hypha HubSpot Development, www.hyphadev.io/blog/the-role-of-typography-in-designing-for-accessibility (archived at https://perma.cc/D9GY-LD7W)
35 Why video captions are key to greater engagement and showing up in more searches, Crisp, https://crisp.co/video-captions-and-transcripts/ (archived at https://perma.cc/L6GP-SDDE)
36 Studies find captions can improve focus on video content, 3PlayMedia, www.3playmedia.com/blog/studies-find-captions-improve-engagement/ (archived at https://perma.cc/KU96-ZSN2)
37 These side-by-side videos will make you rethink your captioned videos, Meryl Evans, https://meryl.net/why-captioned-videos-are-important/ (archived at https://perma.cc/UKT3-24FU)
38 Transcripts, W3C, www.w3.org/WAI/media/av/transcripts/ (archived at https://perma.cc/J4NL-QGBR)
39 What are the benefits and challenges of using plain language in social media posts and campaigns? Dan Wilson – LinkedIn, www.linkedin.com/advice/1/what-benefits-challenges-using-plain-language-1e (archived at https://perma.cc/B2KB-K7V2)
40 Pascal Case vs. Camel Case explained, Built In, https://builtin.com/articles/pascal-case-vs-camel-case (archived at https://perma.cc/KB7X-C5U4)
41 Twitter fail: Susan Boyle's accidental adult party invite, SBS News, www.sbs.com.au/news/article/twitter-fail-susan-boyles-accidental-adult-party-invite/tp98r4dtm (archived at https://perma.cc/JF3V-AGV5)
42 Hashtags at 10 – remembering the most disastrous one of all, NME, www.nme.com/blogs/hashtags-twitter-10-birthday-susan-boyle-2127822 (archived at https://perma.cc/7E2R-V5PL)
43 Accessibility, Facebook, www.facebook.com/help/273947702950567/ (archived at https://perma.cc/PH4J-ZE7A)
44 How do I edit the alternative text for a photo on Facebook? Facebook, www.facebook.com/help/android-app/214124458607871 (archived at https://perma.cc/9TUT-ZP8U)
45 About auto-generated captions on Facebook, Facebook, www.facebook.com/business/help/385195769594602 (archived at https://perma.cc/PE2A-RKBU)
46 Stop videos from playing automatically in your Feed on Facebook, Facebook, www.facebook.com/help/1406493312950827/ (archived at https://perma.cc/J76C-AHN2)
47 Accessibility, Instagram, https://help.instagram.com/308605337351503 (archived at https://perma.cc/QWH5-P9AM)
48 Edit the alternative text for a post on Instagram, Instagram, https://help.instagram.com/503708446705527 (archived at https://perma.cc/XG9N-D4FV)

49 Accessibility at X, X, https://help.x.com/en/resources/accessibility
50 Accessibility, LinkedIn, www.linkedin.com/accessibility (archived at https://perma.cc/ZP58-G5C7)
51 Navigating the accessibility challenges of LinkedIn carousels, Intopia, https://intopia.digital/articles/navigating-the-accessibility-challenges-of-linkedin-carousels/ (archived at https://perma.cc/EG6D-ZXZ5)
52 Accessibility, TikTok, www.tiktok.com/accessibility/en
53 Emoji, Accessible Social, www.accessible-social.com/copy-and-formatting/emoji (archived at https://perma.cc/9LPV-BXTW)
54 Making content usable for people with cognitive and learning disabilities, W3C, www.w3.org/TR/coga-usable/ (archived at https://perma.cc/HR9U-G32E)
55 Gen Z have cancelled the thumbs up emoji and here's why you should worry, Forbes, www.forbes.com/sites/johnbbrandon/2022/10/16/gen-z-have-canceled-the-thumbs-up-emoji-and-heres-why-we-should-worry/ (archived at https://perma.cc/FL9K-FHVK)
56 What's so wrong about using the thumbs-up emoji? *Psychology Today*, www.psychologytoday.com/ca/blog/language-in-the-mind/202211/whats-so-wrong-about-using-the-thumbs-up-emoji (archived at https://perma.cc/7XXK-4RN4)
57 Emoji, Accessible Social, www.accessible-social.com/copy-and-formatting/emoji (archived at https://perma.cc/TJA5-G7YK)
58 Check text and background for sufficient color contrast, Deque University, https://dequeuniversity.com/tips/color-contrast (archived at https://perma.cc/J63R-UWX9)
59 Contrast (minimum): Understanding SC 1.4.3, W3C, www.w3.org/TR/UNDERSTANDING-WCAG20/visual-audio-contrast-contrast.html (archived at https://perma.cc/Q2AX-H5KW)
60 Automated accessibility testing gets you on the way, but doesn't find all the problems, Medium, https://chrisheilmann.medium.com/you-cant-automate-accessibility-testing-9f278ab6b7a (archived at https://perma.cc/T5TU-Q6PK)

08

Making videos and podcasts for everyone

In the previous chapter, we explored the importance of accessible social media and how simple adjustments can open conversations, connect communities and make digital spaces more inclusive. Now, let's dive into those widely used mediums, videos and podcasts. These content types can add rich, dynamic layers to our messages but often come with unique accessibility challenges.

Imagine tuning into a podcast, but the sound quality is off, and there's no transcript, or watching a muted video with no captions.[1] For many with accessibility needs, these gaps make engaging with content difficult, if not impossible. It's not just those with additional needs who use these either. Use of captions and subtitles is actually growing in popularity, particularly among younger audiences.[2]

Sound quality matters. Poor audio undermines the integrity of your messaging and can even make people find you less trustworthy. It's reported that the quality of audio influences whether you believe what you hear[3] – and a study suggests that in court, poor audio quality leads to people viewing evidence and witnesses less favourably.[4]

But just like with other media formats, small steps can make all the difference.

In this chapter, we'll cover practical ways to make video and audio content more accessible to everyone. From captions and transcripts to thoughtful visual descriptions, each strategy enhances inclusivity without losing creativity or impact – and in many cases will increase the impact of your message. By making these adjustments, you're not just meeting a standard; you're reaching a broader audience in a more meaningful way.

Ready to take your videos and podcasts to the next level?

Planning for accessibility in videos and podcasts

Creating accessible video and podcast content starts with understanding the diverse needs of your audience. We often think we know our users, but the truth is, we may not fully grasp the range of accessibility needs they bring with them. Some viewers may have permanent disabilities, while others might be experiencing situational or temporary challenges, like watching a video in a noisy place or while caring for a child.

By planning with accessibility in mind, we don't just reach a wider audience, we make our content welcoming, engaging and easier for everyone to experience.

Whether you're creating a how-to video, an interview podcast, or a brand story, designing for accessibility from the start makes your work more inclusive and effective.

Here's how to build accessibility into each step of your video and podcast planning.

Understanding accessibility needs for video and podcast content

Knowing your audience's needs is essential to creating content that resonates with everyone. However, you may not always know the specific accessibility requirements of each viewer or listener, so it's crucial to apply these best practices universally. By considering a range of potential needs from the outset, you prevent unintentional barriers and create a better experience for all.

You may have viewers who are D/deaf or hard of hearing, people who are blind or have low vision, or those with cognitive disabilities. Each of these groups benefits from specific accessibility features, like captions, audio descriptions and clear structure.

KEY POINTS

Audio descriptions

Audio descriptions provide a narrative which describes important visual elements in a video.

Transcript

A transcript provides a word-for-word written account of what is said in a video or audio track.

Captions

Captions display the words and important sounds (like laughing, or significant background noises) which are featured on the audio track.

Open captions

Open captions are built permanently into video content and cannot be turned off.

Closed captions

Closed captions are captions that viewers can turn on or off depending on their preferences or needs.

Even if you believe you understand your typical audience, your content might reach new viewers and listeners with varying needs. Applying universal accessibility principles ensures that your content is open to everyone.

Let's consider cooking videos. Without captions, viewers who are hard of hearing may miss key instructions. Without audio descriptions, viewers with low vision may not understand visual steps, like what a dish should look like at each stage. By anticipating these needs and building in accessibility, you make your content more usable by everyone.

Scripting and storyboarding with accessibility in mind

Planning for accessibility includes creating scripts and storyboards that incorporate essential accessibility elements. By scripting for inclusivity, you build a foundation that makes your content accessible from the start.

What should you be considering in the scripting and storyboarding phase of your video or podcast production?

Include descriptions of key visuals: When planning a video, write into the script descriptions of important visual elements that need explanation for those who are blind or with low vision. For example, instead of just saying, 'Look at this chart', describe it briefly: 'The chart shows a steady increase in views over the past year.'[5] [6]

Plan for clear dialogue and avoid overlapping voices: Make sure the voices don't overlap in podcasts, as it can make them hard to follow. Clear, uninterrupted dialogue is essential for creating accurate transcripts and easy-to-understand audio.[7]

Structure content for consistency: Plan your episodes or video segments to follow a predictable, easy-to-follow format. For instance, podcasts might start with an introduction, cover main points, and end with a recap. This helps people with cognitive disabilities process and retain information.[8]

Setting up for high-quality audio and visuals

Accessible content relies on clear audio and visuals. Poor sound quality or hard-to-see visuals can be a barrier for all users, especially those with sensory disabilities.[9]

When you're planning your content, you want to ensure:

- You use high-quality microphones and record in quiet settings. Laptop microphones are rarely good enough for recording clear audio – although the mic on your mobile device may be good enough. Clear, background-noise-free audio is essential, particularly for people who rely on transcripts or may have auditory processing challenges.

- For videos, ensure good lighting and avoid cluttered backgrounds. This will make the visuals clearer for all viewers, including those with low vision.

- Make sure your audio or voiceover doesn't contradict any text that's displayed on the screen. Keeping your content to one idea at a time will make it easier to follow for everyone, particularly neurodiverse audiences.

- If using text on screen, ensure high contrast between text and background. Choose simple fonts and use large, readable text for accessibility.

> Think about a tech tutorial video. These types of videos benefit from high-quality visuals that show each step clearly, and have readable on-screen text. High-contrast visuals and legible fonts make it easier for people with low vision or colour blindness to follow along.

Plan for captions and transcripts

Captions and transcripts are essential for making audio and video content accessible. Including them in your planning process ensures they're ready when your content is published.

Plan to include captions for spoken dialogue and important sounds (like [laughter] or [music plays]) to provide full context. Captions help viewers who are D/deaf or hard of hearing and others watching in environments where they can't use sound.[10]

For podcasts and videos, provide word-for-word transcripts that capture spoken content and significant audio cues. Transcripts allow people who prefer reading or have hearing impairments to engage with the content.[11]

> Let's use a travel podcast for this example. Including audio descriptions of places and sounds can reach more people by providing a complete transcript. Listeners can refer to the transcript for clarity and revisit any part of the episode later.

Plan for audio descriptions in visual content

Audio descriptions narrate important visual elements in a video, ensuring people who are blind or have low vision can follow along. Planning audio descriptions into your video structure makes these elements more natural and seamless.

Identify scenes or actions central to the message during the planning phase. For example, in a video where visuals demonstrate a product's features, plan for brief verbal descriptions of what's happening on screen.[12]

Integrate audio descriptions in the script where natural pauses occur. It keeps the flow smooth and inconspicuous for all viewers.

> For example, a video showcasing a new gadget might include audio descriptions like, 'The phone's screen displays a vibrant blue background with icons arranged in a grid', giving viewers who are blind or with low vision essential context.[13]

Design graphics and visual elements for accessibility

Visuals are powerful in videos and podcasts (for promotional graphics or episode notes). So, how can you plan your graphics to be accessible to all?

First, provide alternative text for images on social media and websites to ensure screen reader users can understand what the visuals convey, which we've already talked about in our previous chapters.

Use simple, readable fonts in high-contrast colours to make sure all viewers, including those with sight loss, can easily read on-screen text or graphics.

Make sure your visual elements don't rely on colour alone to convey meaning.

And finally, consistent branding helps viewers recognize your content and aids cognitive accessibility. It's not just for the likes of Apple, Google and Coca Cola;[14] planning your visual elements to follow a predictable format helps viewers navigate and recognize your content.

> Think about a YouTube thumbnail. When it has a high-contrast title text against a simple background, it is easier to read and attracts more viewers, especially those with low vision.

Make accessibility part of your publishing process

Planning for accessibility doesn't end with simply creating your video or podcast. It's equally important to ensure your publishing process supports accessibility features.

If hosting videos on your own website, use players that support closed captions, keyboard navigation and screen reader compatibility.

When you're posting content, include information on the available accessibility features. Mention that captions, transcripts or audio descriptions are available to encourage engagement.

> In the description of a video uploaded to YouTube, include a note like, 'This video includes captions and an audio description. A transcript is available on our website.' This tells viewers that the content is accessible and guides them to additional resources.

Why accessibility planning matters for all audiences

It's true that captions, transcripts and audio descriptions directly serve people with disabilities, but they also enhance usability for everyone.

Captions help viewers in noisy environments, transcripts make podcasts accessible at work or on the go, and clear visuals support understanding for all.

Accessibility isn't just an add-on; it's a way to ensure everyone can engage fully regardless of their abilities or environment. When you make accessibility an integral part of planning, you create a more connected, inclusive and effective experience for your audience.

Video accessibility

Creating accessible video content means thinking beyond just what you want to say. It's about designing video experiences that work for everyone, including people who may have disabilities or unique viewing needs. We will explore the specifics of accessible video design, including captions, audio descriptions, visual accessibility and the importance of choosing an accessible video player. As we covered earlier in this chapter, thoughtful planning in these areas ensures that your video content reaches and resonates with as many people as possible.

Script with clear dialogue and descriptive language

Writing your script with descriptive language and clear dialogue helps ensure that everyone, including viewers with sight loss, understands what's happening on screen. This approach means thinking beyond visual cues and embracing more detailed narration.

First, you want to consider descriptive language. Imagine someone is listening without seeing. If you're showing something visually significant, like a graph or a demonstration, describe it clearly in your narration.

> For instance, instead of just saying, 'Look at this,' say something like, 'This graph shows a steady increase in engagement over time.'
> Specific descriptions like this help audiences who are blind or with low vision, or maybe just not in front of the screen at that time, to understand the key takeaways, especially when they can't see what's happening.[15]

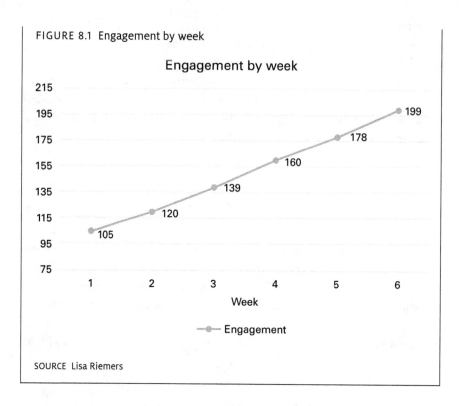

FIGURE 8.1 Engagement by week

SOURCE Lisa Riemers

We also need to consider natural integration of descriptions. Describing visuals should feel like a natural part of your script, not an afterthought. In video production, we call this 'integrated description'.[16] We'll go into more detail on this later in this chapter.

> We're going to use the cooking video example again. Instead of just listing ingredients, you might say, 'Now I'm pouring a cup of milk into the mixing bowl.'

This approach integrates visuals into the narrative, providing context for everyone, including those who rely on audio cues alone.

Planning for clear, descriptive dialogue at the script stage ensures that everyone, regardless of ability, has an equal experience and can follow along without missing key information.

Structured layouts and on-screen text

Structure is crucial in creating accessible video content. Without a logical flow, viewers can quickly become lost, especially if they have cognitive disabilities or are trying to absorb a lot of new information.

Let's start with creating a logical sequence. Plan a sequence that guides viewers smoothly through the content. Break down complex information into smaller sections, each with a clear focus.

For example, if you're covering three main points, introduce each point with a title card or a verbal cue. This structure provides 'mental anchors' that help viewers stay on track.

On-screen text is a powerful tool to reinforce spoken content. Display key points, statistics or important terminology alongside narration to strengthen the message. However, keep the on-screen text simple and avoid overloading the screen with too much information, which can be visually overwhelming and hard to follow.[17]

> Imagine a video on financial planning that breaks down a complex concept like budgeting basics. By displaying each step in the budgeting process as a separate on-screen point, viewers can visually and mentally process each part more easily.

But keep in mind, while eye-catching visuals can be engaging, too many graphics, rapid movements or detailed animations can distract from the main message and overwhelm some viewers. Focus on a clean, simple design that allows viewers to follow the core message without too much visual clutter.

Structured layouts and on-screen text support all viewers by making the video easy to follow and reinforcing important information. This approach allows the content to feel organized, focused and accessible.

Thoughtful use of music and sound effects

Music and sound effects can add emotional depth and atmosphere to a video, enhancing the viewing experience. However, when overused or misused, these elements can unintentionally create barriers for viewers who rely on clear audio.

When choosing background music, consider its volume and tone. Background music should be subtle and should never overpower the spoken content. For people with hearing impairments or those who rely on captions, loud music or sound effects can obscure the dialogue, making it hard to follow the message. Test different audio levels to find a balance where the music adds depth without drowning out the main content.[18]

Sound effects can add context or highlight actions but should be used purposefully. For example, a subtle 'ding' when making a key point can add emphasis without distraction. Avoid sounds that may confuse or distract viewers from the main narrative.

Also consider the emotional tone you want to set. Upbeat music can energize a video, while a slower tempo might convey calm. Choose music and effects that align with your message, but remember that not everyone experiences sound the same way.

For instance, research published in the *Neuroscience & Biobehavioral Reviews* found that 50 per cent to 70 per cent of people with autism or sensory sensitivities may find loud or sudden sounds distressing.[19] When planning music and sound effects, consider what might make the viewing experience comfortable and inclusive for all.

> Let's use the example of an instructional video about meditation technique. It has a quiet, calming background track that can enhance the peaceful tone without overshadowing the instructor's voice. Soft sounds or subtle transitions between sections can guide viewers smoothly, setting a relaxed pace for the content.

Open versus closed captions and when to use them

Captions have become a core element of accessible video content, and they're essential for ensuring that everyone can engage with your message. Captions make video accessible not only to people who are D/deaf or hard of hearing but also to viewers watching in noisy places (or quiet places with their device on silent), non-native speakers, or anyone who benefits from visual reinforcement.

While it's tempting to think of captions as simply text on a screen, understanding the nuances between open and closed captions – and when to use each type – can significantly enhance the viewer experience.[20]

Let's explore these two types of captions, when to use them, and how to craft captions that make your videos genuinely accessible.

Closed captions (CC): Flexibility and user control

Closed captions are captions that viewers can turn on or off depending on their preferences or needs. On most platforms, closed captions can be toggled by selecting the 'CC' icon, allowing users to choose when to use them. This flexibility is one of the major advantages of closed captions, making them a good choice for a wide range of content and audiences.

Closed captions work well in scenarios where people are in control of their viewing environment. They're ideal for platforms like YouTube, Vimeo and streaming services, where users can adjust the video's audio or visual settings. Since they're optional, they don't disrupt the visual experience for those who may not need them, but they're readily available for those who do.[21]

They also offer greater accessibility and control to viewers who may not necessarily need captions, but prefer to use them. According to 2023 surveys from YouGov, most under 30s in the US and UK prefer to watch TV with subtitles on, even in their native language. For instance, someone watching a video while commuting might turn on captions rather than listen with headphones. Similarly, non-native speakers may use closed captions to better follow along, especially when faced with fast dialogue or unfamiliar accents. However, not all users like to use subtitles, as they find them distracting.[22]

TIPS FOR USING CLOSED CAPTIONS

1 Most major platforms support closed captions, but the way they handle captions can vary. YouTube offers auto-generated captions that can be edited for accuracy, while other platforms, like Vimeo, require you to upload a caption file manually. **Note**: Auto-generated captions will not help with your SEO or Google search ranking.

2 If you're using auto-generated captions, double-check them. Automated captions often miss the mark, especially with industry jargon, accents, brand or product names or quick dialogue.[23]

3 Some platforms, like YouTube, allow you to add closed captions in multiple languages. If you're catering to an international audience, providing multilingual captions is a great way to enhance accessibility and inclusivity.

Open captions: Guaranteed visibility in every setting

Open captions are a type of caption that's 'burned into' the video, meaning they're permanently embedded and can't be turned off. It makes open captions always visible to viewers, which can be beneficial in specific situations where sound might not be accessible or where you want to ensure captions are always on.

Open captions work well in contexts where sound is often muted or where viewers might not know how to turn on closed captions. Social media is a prime example: platforms like Instagram, TikTok and Facebook autoplay videos without sound by default. Open captions ensure that viewers immediately understand what's happening, regardless of whether they activate sound.

These types of captions are also valuable for videos displayed in public or noisy environments, such as digital signage, waiting rooms or event spaces. For instance, if you're displaying a promotional video at a conference booth, open captions can help ensure that your message is accessible even in a bustling, noisy environment.

However, open captions usually are not, by their very nature, readable by screen reading software, as they're a built-in part of the picture. Make sure you also have an accessible transcript available.

TIPS FOR USING OPEN CAPTIONS

1. Since open captions are always visible, choose a font style and size that's clear, even on small screens. Sans-serif fonts like Arial or Verdana are typically easier to read. Ensure high contrast between the caption text and background.

2. Open captions work best when they're brief and to the point. Break up long sentences into shorter phrases to avoid overwhelming the screen with too much text at once.

3. Since open captions can't be turned off, be mindful not to obstruct key visuals or action on the screen. Position the captions in a way that's readable without detracting from the video's visuals.

4. If your video is to be played at a conference, you may want to position your captions at the top of the screen, so it's not obscured by speakers on stage.

Best practice: When to choose closed versus open captions

A general rule of thumb is to use closed captions for most video content because they offer the greatest flexibility and viewer control. Closed captions work well on streaming platforms, educational videos, tutorials and most general-purpose content. However, open captions are ideal for short videos on social media, advertisements, or any situation where sound may be off by default.

Use **closed captions** for:

- Vimeo or YouTube videos
- streaming content
- e-learning platforms
- any content where viewers may want to choose their own caption experience

Use **open captions** for:

- social media feeds
- public displays
- any context where sound might be muted, and you want to guarantee accessibility

What makes captions effective?

Captions aren't just about transcribing spoken words; they're about creating a comprehensive experience everyone can understand and enjoy.

Let's break down the elements of good captions:[24]

1 **Synchronization with audio:** Captions should align precisely with spoken words and sounds in real time. Delays between spoken dialogue and captions can make it challenging for viewers to follow along.

   How-to tip: Use video editing software like Adobe Premiere or platforms like YouTube's captioning tool that allows you to adjust timing for accuracy manually.

2 **Speaker identification:** Identify who's speaking in videos with multiple speakers, especially when the speaker isn't visible. Simple identifiers like [Sarah] or [Narrator] help viewers keep track of the conversation and context.

How-to tip: Place speaker names in brackets before the dialogue to make it clear who's speaking. Avoid overloading captions with unnecessary details but include enough information for clarity.

3 **Describing non-verbal sounds:** Non-verbal sounds like laughter, music or ambient noise provide context and emotion to the scene. Including descriptions of these sounds helps viewers who can't hear them understand the full experience.

How-to tip: Use brackets for sound descriptions, such as [laughter] or [background music playing]. Keep descriptions brief but specific enough to capture the scene's atmosphere.

4 **Pacing and line breaks:** Captions which are too fast or lengthy can be hard to read, especially for those with cognitive or visual processing difficulties. Use line breaks and pacing to make captions easier to follow.

How-to tip: Captions should be kept to about 42 characters per line and with a maximum of 2 lines per subtitle cell. Break up long sentences naturally to match speech patterns, ensuring each line is digestible and comfortable to read.

TIPS FOR CRAFTING EFFECTIVE, ENGAGING CAPTIONS

1 **Prioritize clarity over creativity**: When writing captions, clarity is key. While it might be tempting to get creative with language, remember that captions are a functional tool. Aim for straightforward, clear wording that captures the essence of what's being said.

2 **Be mindful of cultural nuances and language**: If your content will reach a global audience, keep cultural and linguistic differences in mind. For instance, idioms or slang may not translate well. Work with a professional to ensure cultural accuracy if your video is captioned in multiple languages – and bear in mind that some languages will read from left to right, while others read from right to left.

3 **Test your captions on multiple devices**: Different devices can display captions in various ways. Test your captions on desktops, tablets and phones to ensure readability. Captions that look fine on a large screen might need adjustments on a smaller one.

4. **Make use of captioning tools and software**: Many captioning tools, like Descript, Rev and YouTube's Caption Editor, make the process easier and more efficient. Some tools can generate auto-captions, which you can then refine for accuracy. Professional captioning services can also ensure top-notch quality if you're handling content with complex dialogue or industry-specific terminology.

When you plan captions early in your video production process, you can make intentional choices that keep them in mind throughout. For instance, you can plan for areas of the screen to remain free from important visuals, so captions don't obscure key information. Integrating captions into your production workflow from the beginning can streamline the entire process and result in a smoother, more polished final product.

Audio descriptions: Post-production versus integrated

Creating inclusive video content means designing experiences that everyone can fully enjoy and understand, including people who are blind or have low vision. Audio descriptions are an essential tool in this effort. These descriptions narrate important visual elements, allowing viewers to follow along with key visuals like facial expressions, scene changes and other non-verbal cues that help convey the story or message.

When it comes to audio descriptions, there are two main types to consider: post-production described audio and integrated described audio. Each has its strengths, depending on the content type, audience and platform.

KEY POINTS

Audio descriptions narrate important visual elements.

Post-production described audio is recorded and added after the video has been filmed.

Integrated described audio weaves descriptions directly into the main audio track of the video.

This section dives into the unique benefits of each method, when to use them, and practical tips for making audio descriptions a seamless part of your video content.[25]

What are audio descriptions and why are they important?

Audio descriptions provide verbal narration of essential visual details that enhance understanding, particularly for people who are blind or have low vision. They serve as an additional layer of context, filling in the visual information that isn't captured through dialogue alone.

Audio descriptions aren't new. Consider the difference in coverage between live televised sporting fixtures, versus the additional audio descriptions that radio pundits might offer. Radio broadcasters offer additional context to help listeners visualize who is in play and what they're doing, whereas TV commentators let the visuals do a lot of the talking. Think of your audio descriptions a little like you're a sports journalist offering a radio broadcast of your content.

For instance, in a suspenseful video scene, the audio description might say, 'The main character tiptoes down a dark hallway, glancing nervously over his shoulder,' which gives viewers who are blind or low vision insights into the tension and mood they would otherwise miss.[26]

Why audio descriptions matter

1 By adding audio descriptions, you're creating a more inclusive experience that respects and accommodates the needs of all viewers.
2 Audio descriptions make your content accessible to a wider audience, boosting engagement and reach.
3 In some regions, audio descriptions are required for accessibility compliance, especially for public-facing organizations or institutions.

Now, let's explore the two types of audio descriptions and how to choose the right one for your content.

Post-production described audio

Post-production described audio is recorded and added after the video has been filmed. In this approach, a separate narrator or voiceover artist describes key visual elements during pauses in dialogue or natural breaks in the audio.[27]

This type of audio description is commonly used for:

- **narrative films and TV shows** where the visual storytelling is complex, and audio descriptions would disrupt the pacing if integrated directly
- **promotional and marketing videos** where certain scenes or visuals need extra context but shouldn't interrupt the primary message or brand voice

Advantages of post-production described audio

Post-production audio descriptions can be added as a separate audio track that users can turn on or off, depending on their needs. This feature is especially valuable on platforms like YouTube and Vimeo, which allow multiple audio tracks, providing viewers with the flexibility to customize their experience.

Additionally, by recording audio descriptions separately, you can avoid disrupting the natural flow and pacing of the main narrative. This is particularly important in content where mood and timing are critical, like a suspenseful film or an ad with a specific tone.

Finally, because post-production audio descriptions are recorded independently, they can be crafted to fit exactly where there are pauses, allowing for a more precise level of detail. This means you can fit in more descriptive language without compromising the primary audio.

TIPS FOR CREATING EFFECTIVE POST-PRODUCTION AUDIO DESCRIPTIONS[28]

1. Plan for audio descriptions in pre-production: Even if you're adding audio descriptions afterwards, planning for them early is helpful. Identify scenes that may need description and consider building in a few extra pauses in the script for these descriptions. This makes it easier to fit them into natural breaks later.

2. Keep descriptions concise and relevant: Since post-production descriptions are typically inserted during pauses, brevity is key. Avoid overloading the viewer with unnecessary detail. Focus on what's essential for understanding the scene or story, like facial expressions, body language or significant visual cues that affect comprehension.

3. **Use a professional voiceover artist**: A clear, steady voice enhances the effectiveness of audio descriptions. Hire a professional voiceover artist who can provide consistent pacing and articulation, making the descriptions easy to follow. The narrator's tone should complement the content – serious for dramas, lively for upbeat content, and so on.

4. **Test on multiple platforms**: Once added, test the audio descriptions on platforms that support optional audio tracks. Make sure the descriptions sync well with the primary audio and that the option to toggle them on or off works smoothly. Platforms like YouTube and some streaming services support this feature, but not all do, so confirm compatibility.

Integrated described audio

Integrated described audio, on the other hand, weaves descriptions directly into the main audio track of the video. These descriptions are part of the original narrative and are designed to fit seamlessly within the dialogue.[29]

Integrated described audio is ideal for:

- **instructional and tutorial videos** where step-by-step descriptions are needed to explain visual actions, such as a cooking or DIY video
- **educational content** where visual elements are directly related to the information being conveyed, like explaining how to perform an exercise or navigate a software interface

Advantages of integrated described audio

Integrated descriptions fit naturally into the content, enhancing clarity without requiring a separate audio track. In tutorials or instructional videos, descriptions become part of the explanation, allowing viewers to follow along easily.

Since the descriptions are built into the primary audio, there's no need for additional audio tracks. Integrated audio is ideal for platforms that don't support multiple audio options, such as Instagram or TikTok.

Integrated descriptions ensure that viewers always have access to the information, regardless of platform or settings. All users get the same cohesive experience in educational content without needing extra clicks or adjustments.[30]

Tips for creating effective integrated descriptions[31]

Script with descriptions in mind When planning instructional or educational content, build descriptions directly into the script. For example, in a yoga tutorial, you might say, 'Now step your right foot forward between your hands and look up towards the sky', rather than just showing the movement.

Use clear and simple language Keep descriptions straightforward and avoid jargon, especially for instructional content aimed at a general audience. Use familiar language that everyone can understand, enhancing comprehension for all viewers.

Practice timing with the primary content Integrated descriptions must fit naturally within the flow of the main content. Practice recording to ensure the pacing feels organic and that there's no awkward overlap between descriptions and dialogue. For example, in a recipe video, ensure the description of adding ingredients lines up with each action.

Consider audience needs for descriptions In educational content, assume some viewers may have limited familiarity with the material. Descriptions should focus on important visual details but also provide a sense of the broader context. For example, in a software tutorial, don't just describe the screen – mention which button to press and what will happen next.

When to use post-production versus integrated descriptions

Knowing when to use each type of audio description depends largely on the nature of your content and your audience's needs.[32]

By planning the type of audio description that best suits your content, you can create a seamless, inclusive experience for all viewers.[33]

Tips for making audio descriptions a part of the planning process[34]

Identify key visual elements early
Determine what visuals are crucial for understanding the content. Think about details that convey emotion, action or information – such as a character's expression, a change in scenery or a key action step. Make a list of these elements in the script to guide your descriptions.

TABLE 8.1 A quick guide to the differences between post-production and integrated described

Post-production descriptions	Integrated description
Best for narrative content where descriptions might disrupt pacing.	Best for instructional and educational videos where descriptions fit naturally into the dialogue.
Ideal for videos on platforms that support separate audio tracks.	Works well on platforms that don't support multiple audio tracks.
Great for content where detailed, vivid descriptions enhance viewer comprehension.	Ideal for content where descriptions enhance clarity without breaking the flow.

Collaborate with a team

If possible, involve individuals who are blind or have low vision in your planning process. Their insights can help you prioritize what to describe, as they'll know firsthand which elements enhance understanding.

Create a test audience

Before finalizing, show your video to a test audience that includes people with diverse needs. Ask for feedback on the clarity, pacing and helpfulness of the audio descriptions to fine-tune the final product.

Update and adapt descriptions as needed

Over time, audiences may offer feedback on the clarity and effectiveness of your descriptions. Be prepared to make updates based on user feedback to continuously improve the accessibility and quality of your video content.

The bigger picture: Why audio descriptions matter

Audio descriptions are more than just an accessibility feature – they're a bridge that connects viewers to the full experience of your content. By offering well-crafted audio descriptions, you're helping viewers engage on a deeper level, making your video more enjoyable, informative and inclusive.

With thoughtful planning and the right approach, audio descriptions become a natural part of the viewing experience. They make a statement: that your content is meant for everyone, no matter their ability to see visual details. In an increasingly diverse and connected world, audio descriptions are one of the most impactful ways to ensure that no one is left out of the story you're telling.

Visual accessibility

Visual accessibility ensures that everyone, regardless of visual disabilities, can fully engage with and understand your content. For many people, vision-related barriers make viewing or interpreting certain visual elements on screen challenging. However, by paying close attention to colour contrast, text size and flashing content, you can make sure that your videos, images and graphics are accessible to the broadest possible audience. These seemingly small adjustments can have a significant impact, transforming content from difficult to enjoyable and accessible.

Let's explore best practices for creating visually accessible content and provide practical tips and tricks for designing with inclusivity in mind.

Colour contrast: Ensuring text and visual elements stand out

Colour contrast is one of the most critical aspects of visual accessibility. It's about ensuring that text and essential visuals are distinguishable from their background, which is especially important for people with low vision, colour blindness or other visual impairments. Poor colour contrast can make text unreadable and images hard to interpret, turning what should be engaging content into a frustrating experience.[35]

Why colour contrast matters

People with low vision or certain types of colour blindness may find it difficult to distinguish between similar colours. For example, a light grey font on a white background can be unreadable to someone with low vision. Similarly, people with red-green colour blindness may struggle to differentiate between red and green elements. Effective colour contrast allows content to be easily viewed and read by everyone, creating a more inclusive experience.

Best practices for colour contrast

Follow WCAG colour contrast ratios The Web Content Accessibility Guidelines (WCAG) recommend specific colour contrast ratios to ensure readability. The guidelines suggest a minimum contrast ratio of 4.5:1 for regular text and 3:1 for large text (typically considered 18-point or larger). For visually impaired users, higher contrast ratios can make a significant difference.[36]

Use contrast checkers Contrast-checking tools like the TPGi's Colour Contrast Analyser or WebAIM Contrast Checker allow you to test text's contrast against backgrounds to ensure it meets accessibility standards. These tools provide instant feedback on whether your colour choices are accessible and suggest ways to improve them.

Choose high-contrast colour combinations When designing content, aim for high contrasts. Black text on an off-white background or white text on a dark blue background are classic, high-contrast combinations that are easy on the eyes and accessible to a broad audience. Avoid low-contrast pairs, like light grey on white or pastel on pastel.[37]

Consider colour blindness Use tools like the Color Oracle or Sim Daltonism to simulate how people with different types of colour blindness view your content. This can help you identify potential problem areas and adjust colours to make them distinguishable for everyone.

Avoid colour as the sole indicator For graphics, charts or other visuals, avoid relying solely on colour to convey information. For instance, if you're using red and green to show positive and negative changes in a data chart, consider adding symbols, patterns or labels to differentiate them. This way, even viewers with colour blindness can interpret the information correctly.[38]

TIPS FOR ENSURING GOOD COLOUR CONTRAST

- **Plan ahead**: Choose a consistent colour palette for your brand or video series that meets accessibility standards from the outset. This prevents the need for adjustments later.

- **Test on different screens**: Colours can appear differently on various devices. Test your content on a phone, tablet and computer screen to make sure it's accessible across platforms.
- **Highlight key points with high contrast**: Use high contrast for headers, titles and other critical information so viewers can easily identify and retain key takeaways.

Text size: Making content readable and scannable

Text size is another essential element of visual accessibility. For many people with low vision, small or cramped text can make content difficult, if not impossible, to read. Ensuring that text is large enough and spaced well can make all the difference in readability and engagement.[39]

Why text size matters

Small text can be a significant barrier for people with low vision, those using smaller screens, or individuals who may struggle with reading due to cognitive disabilities. By designing with larger, clear text, you ensure that everyone can read and understand the information without needing to zoom in or strain their eyes.

Best practices for text size

Follow WCAG guidelines for text To ensure readability, the WCAG recommends a minimum font size of 18 points for large text and 14 points for regular body text. The text should be legible without zooming in on smaller devices, like smartphones or tablets.[40]

Use readable fonts Choose sans-serif fonts like Arial, Helvetica or Verdana, often easier to read on screens than serif fonts. Avoid overly decorative fonts, which can be challenging to decipher, especially in smaller sizes. Italicized fonts also tend to be harder to read than regular fonts so use them sparingly.

Provide adjustable text size If possible, allow viewers to adjust the text size on your website or platform. Many content management systems and website builders offer options to increase or decrease font size, which can be a valuable accessibility feature.

Spacing and line height Ensure that your text has adequate spacing between lines (1.5x line height is a good rule of thumb) and between paragraphs. Proper spacing prevents text from looking cramped, making it easier to read and scan.

TIPS FOR ACCESSIBLE TEXT SIZES

- **Avoid all caps for long text**: Text in all capital letters is harder to read and can slow down comprehension. Use all caps sparingly if you must use them at all, but avoid it for full paragraphs.[41]
- **Break up long blocks of text**: Large blocks of text can be overwhelming. Break them up with bullet points, lists or headers to make content easier to digest.
- **Test on different screen sizes**: As with colour, check that your text size is accessible across devices. What looks great on a computer screen may be too small on a phone, so make sure your text is readable on both.

By following these text size guidelines, you're helping ensure that viewers of all abilities can comfortably read and engage with your content.

Flashing content: Avoiding triggers and discomfort

Flashing content, while often used for dramatic effect, can pose significant risks to viewers with photosensitive epilepsy or other sensory sensitivities. Rapid flashing or strobe-like effects can trigger seizures or cause discomfort, making avoiding or minimizing flashing content in videos and animations essential.[42]

Why avoiding flashing content matters

According to the Epilepsy Foundation, around 3 per cent of people with epilepsy have photosensitive epilepsy, meaning their seizures are triggered by flashing or flickering lights.[43] Additionally, flashing content can be uncomfortable or overwhelming for people with sensory processing disorders, ADHD or autism. By being mindful of flashing effects, you ensure your content is safe and comfortable for all viewers.

Best practices for flashing content[44]

Follow WCAG flash thresholds To reduce the risk of seizures, the WCAG recommends that any flashing content not exceed three flashes per second.

Avoid content that flashes or flickers rapidly, as this is a common trigger for photosensitivity.

Include a warning If flashing content is unavoidable, provide a clear warning at the beginning of the video, informing viewers of the flashing content and allowing them to skip it. This lets people with photosensitivity decide whether to proceed or avoid the content.

Reduce flashing or use alternatives Replace flashing effects with other visual elements, such as fades or dissolves. Animated transitions and effects can still be visually engaging without the risks associated with flashing.

Consider viewer comfort Flashing lights or rapid movements can be distressing for viewers with sensory sensitivities. By minimizing these effects, you're creating content that's accessible and respectful of your audience's comfort.

> TIPS FOR AVOIDING FLASHING CONTENT
>
> - **Use slow transitions**: Instead of quick flashes, use gradual transitions, like fades or zooms, which can add visual interest without posing a risk.
> - **Test with viewers who have sensory sensitivities**: If possible, ask for feedback from viewers with sensory sensitivities to confirm that your content is comfortable and accessible.
> - **Opt for static or minimal animations**: Static images or animations with gentle movements are often safer for visually engaging content without the risks of flashing.

Putting it all together: Designing for visual accessibility

Creating visually accessible content means considering each aspect – colour contrast, text size and flashing content – from the perspective of diverse viewers. Here's a quick summary of how to implement each of these elements:

- **Colour contrast:** Use tools to check compliance with WCAG standards to ensure high contrast between text and background. Choose bold colours that make important elements stand out, and avoid relying on colour alone to convey information.

- **Text size:** Use a readable font size, allowing for adjustable text size if possible. Break up text into smaller sections, use headers, and avoid all caps for readability.
- **Flashing content:** Avoid or minimize flashing effects, especially those that exceed three flashes per second. If flashing is essential, provide clear warnings and consider alternatives to keep your content safe for all viewers.

By incorporating these practices into your content creation process, you create videos, graphics and images that respect and accommodate everyone. Making these adjustments isn't just about meeting guidelines; it's about making your content accessible and enjoyable for everyone, regardless of their visual abilities. With a little extra thought and planning, you can design with inclusivity in mind and make your content a welcoming experience for all.

Accessible video players: YouTube, Vimeo and beyond

Video has become one of the most popular and engaging online communication methods. But to ensure that video content is accessible to everyone, it's not just about what's in the video itself – it's also about where and how it's viewed. Choosing an accessible video player, like YouTube, Vimeo or others, is essential to creating an inclusive experience that allows all users to engage with your content.

Accessible video players provide features that help people with disabilities navigate, understand and interact with video content. Let's examine some of the most widely used video players, exploring their accessibility features and offering tips for making the most of each platform.

Why accessible video players matter

Before diving into individual platforms, it's important to understand why accessible video players matter. Video players serve as the interface between your content and your audience. If that interface isn't accessible, even the best captions, audio descriptions or high-contrast visuals won't reach everyone who could benefit from them. Accessibility in video players can help people with various needs, such as:

- **deaf and hard-of-hearing viewers** who need captions

- **blind or low-vision users** who rely on screen readers and keyboard navigation
- **people with mobility issues** who may need keyboard shortcuts for control
- **viewers with cognitive disabilities** who benefit from intuitive layouts and clear controls

An accessible video player ensures that everyone can interact with your content in ways that work for them, regardless of their device.

YouTube

YouTube is one of the most popular video platforms worldwide, and it offers a variety of accessibility features that make it a strong choice for inclusive video sharing. However, while it's a solid option for accessibility, there are some nuances to keep in mind.

Accessibility features on YouTube[45]

Closed captions and subtitles: YouTube provides robust closed captioning options, including automatically generated captions. Creators can edit these captions to ensure accuracy or upload their own caption files. You can also add subtitles in multiple languages, making content more accessible for non-native speakers.

Transcripts: YouTube automatically generates transcripts from the captions. Viewers can view these transcripts alongside the video, allowing for a searchable text version of the spoken content.

Keyboard accessibility: YouTube's player can be controlled via keyboard shortcuts, enabling users to play, pause, adjust volume and navigate without a mouse. This is helpful for people with motor impairments who rely on keyboard navigation.

Adjustable playback speed: Users can control playback speed, which can be particularly useful for people with cognitive disabilities who may need to slow down the video to understand it better.

Multiple audio tracks: YouTube allows creators to upload multiple audio tracks, which can help add audio descriptions as an optional feature for viewers who need them.

> ### TIPS FOR USING YOUTUBE ACCESSIBLY
>
> - **Edit auto-generated captions**: YouTube's automatic captions can be a helpful starting point but are often inaccurate. Take the time to edit auto-generated captions to ensure accuracy, especially with complex terms, names or accents.
> - **Provide detailed descriptions in video titles and descriptions**: Since YouTube is widely used on screen readers, include a detailed summary in the video description to give additional context to visually impaired users who may not be able to access all visual content.
> - **Encourage interaction with transcripts**: Let viewers know they can access the transcript feature. A brief mention in the video description or at the start of the video can help viewers navigate the content more easily.

Vimeo

Vimeo is a popular platform known for its high-quality video streaming and customizable player. While it doesn't have the same level of automatic accessibility features as YouTube, it does offer some valuable tools for creators looking to ensure their videos are accessible to a broad audience.

Accessibility features on Vimeo[46]

Closed captions and subtitles: Vimeo supports closed captions and allows creators to upload their own caption files. Unlike YouTube, however, Vimeo doesn't generate automatic captions unless you pay for its extra features, so creators using its free services are responsible for creating and uploading captions.[47]

Multiple language options: Vimeo enables creators to upload captions in multiple languages, making it a good choice for audiences in diverse linguistic regions.

Keyboard controls: Vimeo also supports keyboard shortcuts for playing, pausing and adjusting volume, helping viewers with motor disabilities navigate the video content.

Video embedding options: Vimeo's robust embedding options allow creators to control how videos are displayed on other websites. This includes the ability to customize the player controls, which can improve accessibility on platforms where Vimeo videos are embedded.

> **TIPS FOR USING VIMEO ACCESSIBLY**
>
> - **Create and upload accurate captions**: Since Vimeo lacks automatic captioning, generating high-quality captions manually or through third-party software is crucial. Tools like Rev or Descript can help produce accurate caption files.
>
> - **Customize the player for better accessibility**: Vimeo allows for a range of customizations, including removing unnecessary controls or clutter. Use this to create a cleaner, more accessible player that's easier to navigate.
>
> - **Link to transcripts if possible**: Since Vimeo doesn't provide automatic transcripts, consider linking to a transcript file in the video description. This can help viewers who prefer to read or need text-based content.

Wistia

Wistia is another video platform for professional and business use. Known for its high-quality playback and customization options, Wistia also provides some accessibility features, though it lacks certain built-in options like automatic captions.

Accessibility features on Wistia[48]

Closed captions: Like Vimeo, Wistia allows users to upload their own caption files. The captions are customizable so that you can adjust the appearance for better readability.

Keyboard controls: Wistia supports keyboard navigation, making it accessible for viewers who can't use a mouse.

Transcript linking: While Wistia doesn't generate transcripts, you can include links to transcripts in the video description, giving viewers an alternative way to engage with the content.

Adjustable speed control: Wistia offers adjustable playback speeds, which can benefit viewers who need content delivered slower or faster.

> **TIPS FOR USING WISTIA ACCESSIBLY**
>
> - **Ensure captions are clear and legible**: Wistia allows for caption customization. Choose a high-contrast colour for text and background to ensure captions are easy to read.

- **Provide external transcripts**: Since Wistia doesn't support in-player transcripts, consider creating a downloadable transcript or linking it directly in the video description.
- **Optimize player settings for accessibility**: Wistia provides various player customization options. Make use of them to create an uncluttered, easy-to-navigate interface that improves accessibility for all viewers.

Facebook and Instagram

Facebook and Instagram are social media platforms that differ slightly from YouTube and Vimeo in terms of functionality and features. Since they're heavily visual and often consumed on mobile devices, accessibility considerations are even more important.

Accessibility features on the Meta platforms[49]

Autoplay with muted sound: Both platforms autoplay videos with the sound muted. This is an excellent reason to use open captions, as many viewers will rely on them without sound.

Closed captions: Facebook and Instagram allow closed captions, though they need to be uploaded by the creator. Instagram supports captions on IGTV, Stories and Reels, and Facebook supports captions on uploaded videos.

Alt text for images: Although this is a still-image feature, Facebook and Instagram allow users to add alt text. This can be useful for thumbnail images or for context in posts accompanying videos.

TIPS FOR ACCESSIBLE VIDEO ON SOCIAL MEDIA

- **Use open captions for wider accessibility**: Since many viewers won't turn on sound, open captions (always visible) ensure everyone can follow along, even if they don't unmute the video.
- **Provide descriptions in the post text**: Use the accompanying post text to describe key points or visuals in the video, giving low-vision users an additional way to understand the content.
- **Add alt text to thumbnails**: Include alt text for any thumbnails or cover images. This helps visually impaired users understand what the video might be about before playing it.

Selecting the right platform for your audience

Choosing the right accessible video player depends on a variety of factors, including your target audience, the type of content you're creating, and your technical capabilities.

So, when do you use each platform?

- **YouTube:** Ideal for broad audiences, especially if you want built-in captioning and automatic transcripts. Best for content that benefits from community engagement and ease of access.
- **Vimeo:** Great for businesses and brands who want a clean, customizable player. Ideal for high-quality videos where you can provide your own captions and need professional-grade presentation.
- **Wistia:** Best for brands that require advanced marketing integrations and professional playback quality. Useful for high-impact, business-focused content.

Creating accessible podcasts

Podcasts are powerful storytelling tools that allow us to share ideas, connect with audiences, and bring voices from around the world into our daily lives. But just like any other form of media, podcasts need to be accessible to ensure everyone can enjoy, engage and participate fully. Making podcasts accessible goes beyond just recording good audio; it means designing each aspect of the listening experience with inclusivity in mind.

Creating accessible podcasts isn't just about meeting guidelines; it's about widening your reach, respecting diverse needs, and ensuring that your stories and insights are accessible to everyone. By embracing these principles, you're creating better content and building a more inclusive and connected community around your podcast.

Let's dive in!

Podcast content design: Clarity and structure for accessibility[50]

Creating accessible podcast content begins with the basics: clarity and structure. Even if your podcast covers complex topics or takes a conversational approach, how you design and deliver the content can make a significant difference in how well all listeners – including those with disabilities – can engage with it.

Good content design ensures that your message is clear and enhances the overall listening experience, making your podcast more enjoyable and inclusive.

Accessible podcasting requires some additional planning and intentional choices, especially around clear speech and structured, well-scripted content.

So, how do we do it?

The importance of clear speech in podcasts

The foundation of any accessible podcast is clear, understandable speech. It's the primary way you communicate with your listeners, and how you deliver your message can make a huge difference to accessibility.

Why clear speech matters

Clarity in speech is essential for listeners with hearing disabilities, auditory processing disorders, or those listening in noisy environments. Mumbling, rapid-fire speech or inconsistent volume can make it hard to follow what's being said. Additionally, clear speech helps your audience retain information and stay engaged, making the content more memorable and impactful.

Best practices for clear speech[51]

Maintain a consistent volume level Keep your microphone at a consistent distance and maintain a steady volume throughout the recording. This helps avoid volume spikes or dips that can confuse or frustrate listeners. If your podcast involves multiple speakers, ensure each voice is balanced in volume so that no one voice overshadows another.

> **Tip:** Check that your guests are using their intended microphone, and not the built-in mic that is picking up the whirring of their laptop fan. Use a pop filter (a shield that protects your microphone) and monitor your volume during recording to maintain a consistent audio level. Most editing software also includes tools to adjust volume, so check your final mix to make sure it's even.

Pace yourself and avoid rushing Speak at a measured pace that's neither too slow nor too fast. Rushing through ideas, especially when excitement builds, is a common issue in podcasts. While a natural flow is important, don't speak too quickly, as this can make it difficult for listeners to keep up.

> **Tip**: Imagine speaking directly to one listener. This approach naturally slows down your pace and creates a more conversational tone, which can help make the content feel accessible and relatable.

Enunciate clearly without overdoing it   Pronounce words clearly, especially complex terms or jargon that may be unfamiliar to listeners. However, avoid over-enunciating or exaggerating your speech, which can sound unnatural and distracting.

> **Tip**: Practice reading parts of your script aloud to ensure clear pronunciation – or repeat yourself if it's an unscripted conversation. If you do stumble over a word, try rephrasing it with a simpler synonym or breaking it down into easier-to-pronounce parts.

Consider your audience's language proficiency   Remember that some of your listeners may not be native speakers or may be new to the subject matter. Using straightforward language and avoiding slang or idioms can improve comprehension for everyone.

> **Tip**: When using industry-specific terms, briefly explain them. This ensures everyone can follow along, regardless of their familiarity with the topic.

Tools for clear speech

Investing in good recording equipment can make a huge difference in capturing clear, high-quality audio. Here are a few tools to consider:

- **Microphones**: A quality microphone ensures your voice is captured clearly. Dynamic microphones minimize background noise, while condenser microphones capture a fuller range of vocal tones.
- **Editing software**: Audacity or Adobe Audition allows you to remove background noise, balance audio levels and adjust pacing.
- **Speech practice apps**: Apps like Voice Pitch Analyzer or Speech Tools can help you monitor your speaking speed and clarity.

Scripted content: Why structure matters

While some podcasts are entirely conversational, accessible podcasts benefit from at least a loosely structured script. Structured, well-thought-out content provides consistency, ensuring listeners with cognitive disabilities or those who prefer a more organized format can easily follow along.

Why scripts and structure are important[52]

For some listeners, especially those with cognitive disabilities, a clear structure makes processing and retaining information easier. Scripts also help speakers stay on track, reducing filler words, tangents and awkward pauses that can disrupt the flow of information. Having a plan in place lets you create content that's focused, coherent and easier for all listeners to follow.

Types of scripted content

There's no single way to script a podcast. Some formats work best with a fully written script, while others benefit from a bullet-point outline that allows for a more conversational tone. Here's a look at different approaches and how each can make your content more accessible.

Full scripts for informative podcasts Using a full script is beneficial if your podcast covers detailed or complex information – such as legal updates, scientific research, or step-by-step guides. It ensures accuracy, clarity and consistency in delivering facts and keeps listeners from getting lost.

> **Tip**: Practice reading from your script before recording to make it sound natural. Insert conversational language and occasional asides to avoid a robotic tone, which adds warmth and personality.

Bullet-point scripts for conversational podcasts If your podcast includes multiple hosts or guests, bullet-point scripts can keep the conversation on track without feeling overly rehearsed. Bullet points allow flexibility, giving speakers room to add spontaneous comments while ensuring they hit all the key points.

> **Tip**: In a bullet-point script, include transition cues like 'let's dive into...' or 'next, we'll explore...' to help structure the conversation and give listeners a sense of progression.

Topic-based structure for panel discussions Dividing the content into specific topics for podcasts with multiple guests or panel discussions can help keep the conversation focused. Introduce each topic clearly and allow each participant a turn to speak, preventing listeners from feeling overwhelmed or confused.

> **Tip**: Summarize each section before moving to the next. A simple 'to recap' statement reinforces the main points and prepares listeners for the next segment.

Organizing podcast episodes for consistency

Listeners are more likely to return to your podcast if they know what to expect each time. Establishing a consistent episode structure is a small but impactful way to make your podcast more accessible, especially for listeners with cognitive disabilities who benefit from predictable formats.[53]

Intro and outro consistency Start each episode with a brief, consistent introduction. Mention the episode's topic and introduce any guests or hosts. A familiar structure makes new episodes feel recognizable and easy to navigate.

> **Tip**: Keep intros short but informative. In a few sentences, set the tone and provide context for what listeners will learn or experience.

Segmented episodes Break episodes into clear segments, especially for longer podcasts. For example, a news podcast might have 'Top Stories', 'Deep Dive' and 'Listener Q&A' sections. This segmented approach allows listeners to anticipate what's coming next, making it easier to process the content.

> **Tip**: Use musical cues or brief pauses between segments to signify transitions. These audio cues create a natural rhythm and help listeners identify when a new topic is beginning.

Recaps and summaries Summarize the main points at the end of each segment or episode. This reinforces the key takeaways and helps listeners with memory challenges or cognitive processing difficulties retain information.

> **Tip**: Use phrases like 'let's quickly recap' or 'the main points today were...' to cue listeners into summary mode.

Crafting accessible language and tone

The language you use matters as much as the structure. Accessible language makes your podcast easier to understand, especially for listeners with cognitive disabilities or non-native speakers.[54]

Keep language simple and direct Avoid complex jargon or overly technical language unless it's essential. If you need to use technical terms, explain them briefly. Accessible language doesn't mean dumbing down content; it means making complex ideas understandable for a broad audience.

> **Tip**: Pretend you're explaining the topic to a friend who's unfamiliar with it. This approach keeps your tone approachable and the language clear.

Use a friendly and engaging tone Speak in a conversational, friendly tone that makes listeners feel welcome. A warm tone improves accessibility by reducing any sense of intimidation or distance. Even if your podcast is about serious topics, using an empathetic tone can help make content more accessible.

> **Tip**: Smile while you speak – it may sound silly, but it actually comes across in your voice and creates a more welcoming atmosphere.

Avoid overloading with information   It's easy to pack too much information into a podcast episode, but overloading listeners can be counterproductive. Stick to a few main points and elaborate as needed. If your topic is complex, consider breaking it into multiple episodes.

> **Tip**: Explain complex ideas using examples or metaphors. They're relatable and help listeners form a clearer understanding of abstract concepts.

Designing accessible podcast content isn't just about clear speech and structured scripting; it's about putting yourself in the listener's shoes and considering how they might experience your content. With attention to clarity, pacing, language and structure, you can create an engaging, understandable and enjoyable podcast.

As you work to make your podcast more accessible, remember that these adjustments don't just benefit people with disabilities – they enhance the experience for everyone. Accessible content is simply better, designed thoughtfully and with inclusivity. By prioritizing accessibility in your podcast design, you create a welcoming space for all listeners to enjoy and connect with your message.

Transcripts: The cornerstone of accessible podcasting

Transcripts are a powerful tool in accessible podcasting, serving as the written counterpart to your audio content. They provide a textual version of everything spoken and heard in an episode, allowing a broader audience to engage with your podcast, including people who are deaf or hard of hearing, non-native speakers, and those who simply prefer reading to listening. Additionally, transcripts enhance searchability, improve SEO and create a resource that's easy to reference and share.

Creating high-quality transcripts isn't just a matter of typing out dialogue; it's about designing a text version of your podcast that's accessible, readable and effective.

It's time to explore the different types of transcripts, tips for creating detailed and accurate transcripts, and various formatting options to make sure they're accessible to all audiences.[55]

The importance of detailed transcripts

A detailed transcript provides more than just the words spoken. It also includes descriptions of non-verbal elements, speaker identification, sound cues and even emotional undertones when relevant. For someone reading instead of listening, these additional details help recreate the podcast experience, bridging the gap between audio and text.

Why detail matters in transcripts

Think of detailed transcripts as a roadmap of your episode. They help readers understand what's being said and how it's being said. For example, in an interview podcast, moments of laughter, sighs, or pauses can convey as much as spoken words. Including these non-verbal elements can give readers a fuller experience, allowing them to pick up on tones and nuances they might miss otherwise:

- **Audience inclusivity**: Transcripts that capture the complete context benefit people who are deaf, hard of hearing, or have auditory processing disorders. Detailed transcripts provide context beyond words, improving understanding for non-native speakers.

- **Content depth**: By including detailed descriptions, you're not only making the content accessible, but you're also deepening the reader's experience. It's a way to capture the mood and intent behind what's being said.

Best practices for creating detailed transcripts[56, 57]

Include non-verbal sounds Non-verbal sounds like *[laughter]*, *[sigh]*, or *[applause]* add depth to a transcript, allowing readers to understand the atmosphere. If a sound affects the context or mood of the conversation, it's worth including.

> **Tip**: Keep non-verbal sounds in brackets to make them easily distinguishable. For example: *[laughter]* or *[background music fades out]*. This keeps them separate from spoken text and easy to scan.

Identify each speaker clearly Speaker identification is crucial for maintaining clarity, especially in multi-speaker formats. Start each section with the speaker's name (or role, like 'Host' or 'Guest'), followed by a colon. This way, readers can follow the flow of conversation without confusion.

> **Tip**: Use consistent speaker labels, such as 'Host' and 'Guest', or simply the names of the speakers. Avoid abbreviations like 'H' or 'G', which can confuse readers.

Capture tone and emotion when relevant   Emotions and tones can significantly impact meaning. For instance, if someone says, 'I'm fine', with a sigh, that sigh may add context that changes the meaning. If relevant, consider capturing these emotional tones in brackets, like *[sighs]* or *[sarcastically]*.

> **Tip**: Don't overdo it – use tone markers sparingly and only when they add value. For example, in a humorous podcast, you might include *[jokingly]* or *[laughing]* where appropriate.

Transcribe sound effects and music cues   Background music and sound effects often set the scene for narrative or storytelling podcasts. Including cues like *[upbeat music playing]* or *[rain falling]* can give readers a sense of atmosphere and immersion.

> **Tip**: Place sound effects and music cues in italics to make them visually distinct. For example, *[sombre piano music begins]* or *[door slams]*.

Accessible formats for transcripts

A transcript isn't fully accessible unless presented in a format that's easy to read, navigate and access across devices. An accessible format considers screen reader compatibility, clear font choices, and options for different viewing preferences.

Key accessible formats for transcripts
Plain Text (TXT) files   Plain text files are simple and lightweight, making them accessible on virtually any device. While they lack formatting options, plain text files are highly compatible with screen readers.

> **Tip**: Plain text files are useful for quick access without fancy formatting. They're also handy for mobile users needing a lightweight format for faster loading.

Web-based transcripts Many podcasters provide web-based transcripts that are accessible on their website. This format allows for easy reading and navigation, especially if the page is well-designed with headings and accessible text.

> **Tip**: Ensure your website is accessible and that transcripts are easy to find. Consider adding a dedicated 'Transcripts' section so users don't have to search extensively to locate them.

Interactive transcripts Interactive transcripts are synced with the audio, allowing users to click on a section of text and jump to that exact point in the audio. This is particularly beneficial for educational podcasts, where listeners may want to reference specific sections.

> **Tip**: Some podcasting platforms, like Descript, provide tools to create interactive transcripts. These tools can enhance the user experience, making switching between text and audio easier.

PDFs and Word documents PDFs and Word documents are familiar formats to many although they're not always immediately accessible, depending on how they're made. Word documents tend to be more accessible than PDFs from the outset and provide familiar formatting options to make sure they're easy to read. Make sure your documents have a logical structure with headings, lists and clear navigation. Screen reader users rely on this structure to understand the flow of the text.

> **Tip**: If you use a PDF, ensure it's tagged. Tagging organizes the content in a way that's readable by screen readers, providing a clear hierarchy of headings and lists.

Formatting options for readability and accessibility[58]

Consider how the transcript is presented once you've decided on a format. Thoughtful formatting can enhance readability, especially for users with visual or cognitive disabilities.

Essential formatting elements

Clear, readable fonts Choose a simple, sans-serif font like Arial, Verdana or Helvetica for web-based and PDF transcripts. These fonts are generally easier to read on screens than decorative or serif fonts.

Tip: Use a font size of at least 12–14 points. For readers with low vision, larger fonts are more accessible and reduce eye strain.

Headings and subheadings Use headings and subheadings to structure longer transcripts, especially if your episode covers multiple topics. Headings help users navigate the text quickly, particularly for screen reader users.

> **Tip**: If the transcript is on a website, use H1, H2 and H3 tags for headings. This hierarchy helps screen readers identify sections and makes the content easier to scan.

Line breaks between speakers Including a line break between speakers or different sections improves readability and makes it easier to follow the conversation. This is especially important in multi-speaker transcripts where dialogue can be dense.

> **Tip**: Use a blank line or double-spacing between speakers. CSS styling can help create a clean, readable layout for web-based transcripts.

Numbering or timestamps for long transcripts For lengthy episodes, add timestamps periodically (every 5–10 minutes) or for each speaker change. Timestamps make it easier for readers to follow along and find specific parts of the transcript.

> **Tip**: If you're using timestamps, consistently format them. Place them in brackets at the beginning of each section, like *[10:15]*, to indicate the time in the podcast.

Bolds and italics for emphasis Use bold text for speaker names and italics for non-verbal sounds or background music cues. These visual cues help separate dialogue from sound effects, making the transcript more engaging and easier to follow.

> **Tip**: Don't overuse bold or italics, as excessive formatting can be distracting. Use them strategically to enhance readability without overwhelming the reader.

Using technology and tools for efficient transcription

Creating detailed transcripts can be time-consuming, but a variety of tools can make the process faster and more accurate. Here are some options to streamline your workflow:[59]

Automated transcription software Tools like Descript, Otter.ai and Rev use AI to generate transcripts quickly. While automated transcription saves time, these tools aren't perfect, so manual editing is necessary for accuracy.

> **Tip**: Start with automated transcription to save time, then review and edit for accuracy. Pay special attention to complex words, names or industry-specific terms that AI might misinterpret.

Human transcription services If accuracy is critical, consider hiring a human transcription service, which can provide highly accurate, detailed transcripts. Many services offer captioning and transcription packages tailored for accessibility.

> **Tip**: When choosing a service, check its accessibility standards and ask if it includes features like speaker identification and sound cues in its transcripts.

Interactive transcription tools   Interactive transcription tools, like Sonix or Trint, allow you to edit transcripts while listening to the audio. This feature can save time and improve accuracy, especially if you need to add timestamps or correct speaker labels.

> **Tip**: Use interactive tools if you plan to create synchronized transcripts for a website or app. They make it easier to link text with audio.

Transcripts are more than just an accessibility add-on – they're a resource that can enhance your podcast's reach, SEO and value. By focusing on detailed, accessible formats and thoughtful formatting, you create a transcript that's genuinely beneficial to your audience.

An accessible podcast is a podcast for everyone. Embracing transcripts as an integral part of your workflow makes your content inclusive and invites a broader audience to connect, engage and share in the experience. When it comes to accessible communication, that's what it's all about – reaching more people, building connections and ensuring everyone has a seat at the table.

Accessible podcast players: Making sure everyone can listen

For most podcast listeners, finding and playing an episode is as easy as opening their favourite app and pressing play. But for listeners with disabilities, this process can be far more complex. Accessible podcast players bridge the gap, ensuring that everyone – regardless of ability – can enjoy podcasts in a way that's convenient, easy and engaging. In this section, we'll explore some of the major podcast players – like Apple Podcasts, Spotify, Google Podcasts and others – and dive into the accessibility features each platform offers.

As podcast creators and listeners, it's essential to understand the strengths and limitations of these platforms to help ensure a seamless experience for all users. You may syndicate your podcast across multiple platforms – but how do these podcast players measure up in terms of accessibility?

Why accessible podcast players matter

An accessible podcast player isn't just a nice-to-have feature; it's crucial for allowing people with disabilities to navigate, play and control their listening experience.

Podcast players need to be designed with accessibility in mind for listeners who rely on screen readers, keyboard navigation or other assistive technologies.

The primary aspects of accessibility in podcast players include:

- **Screen reader compatibility:** Ensuring that menus, buttons and playback controls are easily interpreted by screen readers, allowing users with vision impairments to navigate the app.
- **Keyboard navigation:** Making it possible for users to control the player using only a keyboard, which is important for individuals with motor impairments.
- **Clear, intuitive layouts:** Minimizing complexity in the user interface helps listeners with cognitive disabilities more easily interact with the app.
- **Playback speed control:** Allowing users to adjust playback speed benefits people with auditory processing disorders or non-native speakers who may need to slow down content for comprehension.

> **Tip**: Regardless of platform, podcast creators should ensure that episode titles and descriptions are concise and clear. Avoid filler words in titles, as screen readers will read each word out loud.

Considering these aspects, let's examine how some of the most popular podcast players support accessibility.

Platform: Apple Podcasts

Apple Podcasts is one of the most widely used podcast players. It's known for its generally strong accessibility features. Apple has a long-standing commitment to accessibility across its products, and this focus is evident in its podcast app.

Accessibility features[60]
VoiceOver compatibility Apple Podcasts is fully compatible with VoiceOver, Apple's built-in screen reader. VoiceOver allows users to navigate the app, read episode descriptions, and easily control playback. Users can swipe or tap to hear elements read aloud, making it possible to interact with the app without sight.

> **Tip**: As a podcast creator, consider writing clear and descriptive episode titles and descriptions. This helps VoiceOver users understand what the episode is about with minimal effort.

Siri integration For listeners who use Siri, Apple Podcasts integrates with Apple's voice assistant, making it possible to control the app with voice commands. Users can ask Siri to play specific episodes, subscribe to shows or skip forward or backward without needing to touch their device.

> **Tip**: Listeners can enhance their experience by using Siri shortcuts. For example, creating a shortcut for 'Play my latest episode' can simplify navigation even further.

Adjustable playback speed and skip controls Apple Podcasts offers adjustable playback speeds and skip intervals. Listeners can choose from various playback speeds, making it easy for those with auditory processing needs to slow down or speed up the audio. Additionally, users can customize skip forward and skip back intervals to suit their preferences.

> **Tip**: Encourage listeners to try different playback speeds. Mentioning this feature briefly in your show could benefit listeners who may not know it's available.

Keyboard shortcuts On iPads with an external keyboard or Mac computers, Apple Podcasts offers keyboard shortcuts to control playback, volume and navigation. This feature is particularly helpful for users with limited mobility who may find touch navigation challenging.

> **Tip**: Make your audience aware of these shortcuts, as they can significantly enhance accessibility for listeners using non-touch devices.

APPLE PODCASTS ACCESSIBILITY LIMITATIONS

While Apple Podcasts performs well in terms of accessibility, some areas could be improved, particularly in playlist organization and customizable display settings for users with cognitive or visual processing challenges. Also, some users may not use any Apple accounts, so relying on the Apple universe might rule out a proportion of your audience.

Platform: Spotify

Spotify has emerged as one of the top podcast platforms, boasting a vast library and a sleek user interface. While it does have accessibility features, Spotify's primary focus has historically been on music, which means its podcast accessibility options are somewhat limited compared to Apple Podcasts.

Accessibility features[61]

Screen reader compatibility   Spotify is compatible with both VoiceOver on iOS and TalkBack on Android, meaning users with visual impairments can navigate and control the app. The screen reader will read out buttons, track information and menus.

Playback speed options   Spotify offers playback speed adjustments, allowing users to listen from 0.5x to 3x. This feature is beneficial for people who process information at different speeds and for users who may want to consume content quickly or slowly.

> **Tip**: Encourage your audience to experiment with playback speed. It can help listeners who need to slow down the audio to absorb the content better.

Hands-free voice commands (limited)   While Spotify has some voice command capabilities (e.g. Hey Spotify on mobile devices), they're relatively limited. These commands can play music or podcasts but may not offer the same level of control as Siri or Google Assistant.

> **Tip**: If your listeners are on Android, encourage them to try using Google Assistant to navigate Spotify hands-free.

Spotify accessibility limitations

Spotify's accessibility options are still evolving, and some features, such as comprehensive voice control, are limited. Additionally, the interface can feel visually cluttered, which may pose challenges for users with cognitive disabilities. It's a powerful app, but it's not as intuitive or streamlined for accessibility as other platforms.

Other accessible podcast players worth exploring

In addition to Apple and Spotify, several other podcast players prioritize accessibility:

Overcast: Overcast offers a clean, user-friendly interface with features like Smart Speed (which shortens silences) and Voice Boost (which makes voices clearer). These tools enhance audio accessibility, and the app is compatible with VoiceOver for easy navigation.[62]

Castbox: Castbox has a range of accessibility features, including playback speed adjustment, a sleep timer and customizable notifications. It's compatible with screen readers and has a visually clear interface, making it a solid choice for accessible podcasting.[63]

Pocket Casts: Pocket Casts supports screen readers, adjustable playback speeds and intuitive navigation. It also offers options to trim silence and boost volume, improving audio clarity for listeners with hearing loss.[64]

Audible: Known for audiobooks, Audible also offers podcasts with accessibility features like VoiceView screen reader support on Amazon devices and playback customization options. Its visually clean interface and adjustable text size suit listeners with low vision.[65]

Key takeaways

Creating accessible content isn't just a matter of compliance; it's about making sure your message reaches and resonates with as many people as possible.

In Chapter 8, we dived into video and audio content and examined the steps needed to make these mediums accessible and inclusive. With video and podcasting growing as essential tools in digital communication, ensuring accessibility is crucial to avoid leaving anyone out of the conversation.

> **KEY TAKEAWAYS**
>
> - **Plan accessibility from the start**: Begin with accessibility in mind, identifying your audience's diverse needs and ensuring scripts, captions and transcripts are ready for inclusive content.
> - **Clear scripting and quality production**: To enhance accessibility and engagement, use clear dialogue, descriptive language and high-quality visuals and audio.
> - **Captions and transcripts**: Captions and transcripts are essential tools. Use open captions on platforms where sound is off by default and closed captions for flexibility. Include transcripts for podcasts to expand accessibility.
> - **Audio descriptions**: Add audio descriptions to narrate important visual details for those who are blind or have low vision, choosing post-production or integrated descriptions based on content type.
> - **Optimizing visual accessibility**: To support users with visual disabilities, focus on high-contrast visuals and readable text sizes, and avoid flashing content.
> - **Choose accessible players**: Use platforms like YouTube or Apple Podcasts that offer accessibility features like screen reader compatibility, adjustable playback speeds, and closed captions.

References

1. Survey: Why America is obsessed with subtitles, Preply, https://preply.com/en/blog/americas-subtitles-use/ (archived at https://perma.cc/SN95-NCXV)
2. Young viewers prefer TV subtitles, research suggests, BBC News, www.bbc.co.uk/news/entertainment-arts-59259964 (archived at https://perma.cc/SLJ9-7CPW)
3. The quality of audio influences whether you believe what you hear, USC Today, https://today.usc.edu/why-we-believe-something-audio-sound-quality/ (archived at https://perma.cc/7A2L-XY4X)
4. E Bild, A Redman, E J Newman, B R Muir, D Tait and N Schwarz. Sound and credibility in the virtual court: Low audio quality leads to less favorable evaluations of witnesses and lower weighting of evidence, *Law and Human Behavior*, 45 (5), 481–95, https://doi.org/10.1037/lhb0000466 (archived at https://perma.cc/FB88-BEBA)

5 Creating accessible videos: Best practices for video accessibility, Soona, https://soona.co/blog/best-practices-for-video-accessibility (archived at https://perma.cc/N6EM-MHD5)
6 Accessibility for storyboards, LCA Spotlight, www.youtube.com/watch?v=Cg7oh6IbIn0 (archived at https://perma.cc/6J8L-EB82)
7 More than transcripts: Accessibility in podcasting, Simplecast, https://blog.simplecast.com/more-than-transcripts-accessibility-in-podcasting (archived at https://perma.cc/424X-SRSR)
8 How to structure your podcast in 5 steps, Buzzsprout, www.buzzsprout.com/blog/podcast-structure (archived at https://perma.cc/WE58-SFGT)
9 Audio content and video content, W3C, www.w3.org/WAI/media/av/av-content/ (archived at https://perma.cc/FF8Z-N936)
10 Captions/subtitles, W3C, www.w3.org/WAI/media/av/captions/ (archived at https://perma.cc/8ZBK-ME9Y)
11 Transcripts, W3C, www.w3.org/WAI/media/av/transcripts/ (archived at https://perma.cc/465H-AKK4)
12 Description of visual elements, W3C, www.w3.org/WAI/media/av/description/ (archived at https://perma.cc/2A9U-8AF7)
13 Audio descriptions: What they are and how they work, Continual Engine, www.continualengine.com/blog/audio-descriptions/ (archived at https://perma.cc/78N9-E8V5)
14 Interbrand's best global brands 2024, https://interbrand.com/best-brands/ (archived at https://perma.cc/BW6R-58TC)
15 How to write the perfect audio description script (AD), Inclusive Communication Services, https://inclusiveasl.com/inclusive-communication-services-guides/how-to-write-the-perfect-audio-description-script-ad/ (archived at https://perma.cc/8XNW-VTDE)
16 Description of visual information, W3C, www.w3.org/WAI/media/av/description/ (archived at https://perma.cc/U2S9-9GZW)
17 Video accessibility guide for content creators and viewers, Adobe, https://blog.adobe.com/en/publish/2021/12/10/video-accessibility-guide-for-content-creators-and-viewers (archived at https://perma.cc/TD9M-Z4X7)
18 The accessibility of background music for people with disabilities, LinkedIn – Tom Babinszki, www.linkedin.com/pulse/accessibility-background-music-people-without-tom-babinszki/ (archived at https://perma.cc/H52F-QPAC)
19 A review of decreased sound tolerance in autism: Definitions, phenomenology and potential mechanisms, Elsevier, www.sciencedirect.com/science/article/abs/pii/S0149763420306722 (archived at https://perma.cc/XE6M-UBH8)
20 The difference between closed and open captions, HappyScribe, www.happyscribe.com/blog/en/the-difference-between-closed-captions-and-open-captions (archived at https://perma.cc/S39A-62DX)
21 The ultimate guide to closed captioning, 3PlayMedia, www.3playmedia.com/learn/popular-topics/closed-captioning/ (archived at https://perma.cc/2VUL-MFXZ)

22. Most American adults under 30 prefer watching TV with subtitles — even when they know the language, YouGov, https://today.yougov.com/entertainment/articles/45987-american-adults-under-30-watching-tv-subtitles (archived at https://perma.cc/9QNN-D7SB)
23. Use automatic captioning, YouTube Help, https://support.google.com/youtube/answer/6373554?hl=en (archived at https://perma.cc/E9A4-ZK4K)
24. DCMP Captioning key: Standards and guidelines, 3PlayMedia, www.3playmedia.com/blog/dcmp-closed-captioning-standards/ (archived at https://perma.cc/DWC6-FXSB)
25. What's the difference between integrated described video and traditional described video, Described Video Canada, https://describedvideocanada.com/whats-the-difference-between-integrated-described-video-and-traditional-described-video/ (archived at https://perma.cc/452X-XH4N)
26. Post production described video (DV), Accessible Media Inc., www.ami.ca/described-video-dv (archived at https://perma.cc/FGC2-ANDD)
27. Post production described video best practices, Accessible Media Inc., www.ami.ca/sites/default/files/2020-07/PP_Described_Video_Best_Practices_0.pdf (archived at https://perma.cc/677Y-RUK4)
28. Post production described video best practices, Accessible Media Inc., www.ami.ca/sites/default/files/2020-07/PP_Described_Video_Best_Practices_0.pdf (archived at https://perma.cc/C2CA-KLE4)
29. Integrated described video best practices, Accessible Media Inc., www.ami.ca/sites/default/files/2020-07/Integrated-Described-Video-Best-Practices.pdf (archived at https://perma.cc/TY9D-YLTL)
30. Integrated described video, Accessible Media Inc., www.ami.ca/sites/default/files/2020-07/IDV%20White%20Paper_0.pdf (archived at https://perma.cc/9N36-75UY)
31. Integrated described video best practices, Accessible Media Inc., www.ami.ca/sites/default/files/2020-07/Integrated-Described-Video-Best-Practices.pdf (archived at https://perma.cc/B4XZ-5973)
32. Described video vs audio description: What's the difference? 3PlayMedia, www.3playmedia.com/blog/described-video-vs-audio-description-whats-the-difference/ (archived at https://perma.cc/8VGZ-9LJA)
33. Integrated described video best practices, Accessible Media Inc., www.ami.ca/sites/default/files/2020-07/Integrated-Described-Video-Best-Practices.pdf (archived at https://perma.cc/JPR2-SG93)
34. The ultimate guide to audio description, 3PlayMedia, www.3playmedia.com/learn/popular-topics/audio-description/
35. The ultimate video accessibility checklist, Recite Me, https://reciteme.com/news/video-accessibility-checklist/ (archived at https://perma.cc/429G-WRZ6)
36. Understanding SC 1.4.3: Contrast (minimum) (Level AA), W3C, www.w3.org/WAI/WCAG21/Understanding/contrast-minimum.html (archived at https://perma.cc/9C5X-D4ZG)

37 High contrast and low vision, Perkins School for the Blind, www.perkins.org/resource/choosing-high-contrast-color-schemes-for-low-vision/ (archived at https://perma.cc/4GJB-4LNQ)
38 3 common color accessibility issues one can easily avoid, Deque, www.deque.com/blog/3-common-color-accessibility-issues-one-can-easily-avoid/ (archived at https://perma.cc/Q7W2-Q8US)
39 Accessibility requirements for people with low vision, W3C, www.w3.org/TR/low-vision-needs/ (archived at https://perma.cc/G66X-TUP3)
40 Contrast (minimum) understanding SC 1.4.3, W3C, www.w3.org/TR/UNDERSTANDING-WCAG20/visual-audio-contrast-contrast.html (archived at https://perma.cc/6EG8-8JAX)
41 Why text in all caps is hard for users to read, UX Movement, https://uxmovement.com/content/all-caps-hard-for-users-to-read/ (archived at https://perma.cc/Y5YU-GKBJ)
42 Why Netflix warns flashing, fast edits can trigger seizures, *Psychology Today*, www.psychologytoday.com/ca/blog/the-fallible-mind/202112/why-netflix-warns-flashing-fast-edits-can-trigger-seizures (archived at https://perma.cc/ST5N-QKEC)
43 Photosensitivity and seizures, Epilepsy Foundation, www.epilepsy.com/what-is-epilepsy/seizure-triggers/photosensitivity (archived at https://perma.cc/35FK-NEVM)
44 Three flashes or below threshold – understanding SC 2.3.1, W3C, www.w3.org/TR/UNDERSTANDING-WCAG20/seizure-does-not-violate.html (archived at https://perma.cc/K2NH-JM5C)
45 YouTube accessibility: How to make your videos more accessible, Purple Goat Agency, www.purplegoatagency.com/insights/youtube-accessibility-how-to-make-your-videos-more-accessible/ (archived at https://perma.cc/YR4Y-YJ5E)
46 Video accessibility at Vimeo: What you need to know, Vimeo, https://vimeo.com/blog/post/accessibility-updates-to-the-vimeo-player (archived at https://perma.cc/ZF7W-MGV6)
47 Add subtitles & closed captions to video automatically, Vimeo, https://vimeo.com/features/auto-caption (archived at https://perma.cc/HF4T-QRX4)
48 Make your videos more accessible for everyone, Wistia, https://wistia.com/product/accessibility (archived at https://perma.cc/6D7X-G44J)
49 Accessibility, Facebook, www.facebook.com/help/273947702950567 (archived at https://perma.cc/C54D-NNHS)
50 Make your podcasts more accessible, Pacific Content, https://pacific-content.com/make-your-podcast-more-accessible/ (archived at https://perma.cc/6GV4-PJM9)
51 Tips to speak clearly and be understood, UHN, www.uhn.ca/PatientsFamilies/Health_Information/Health_Topics/Documents/Tips_to_Speak_Clearly_and_Be_Understood.pdf (archived at https://perma.cc/7LBY-RVWY)

52. Making podcasts accessible: Tips for engaging a diverse listener base, ADA Site Compliance, https://adasitecompliance.com/making-podcasts-accessible-tips-engaging-diverse-listener-base/ (archived at https://perma.cc/D55H-JDAN)
53. How to plan your podcast episodes, Medium, https://medium.com/diy-podcasts/how-to-plan-your-podcast-episodes-e5ac9a249c5b (archived at https://perma.cc/4DGN-8ZPN)
54. How can you write podcast scripts that are accessible to all listeners? LinkedIn, www.linkedin.com/advice/1/how-can-you-write-podcast-scripts-accessible-all-listeners-dhvlc (archived at https://perma.cc/W5VC-568Z)
55. The power of podcast transcripts for SEO and accessibility, Wavve, https://wavve.co/the-power-of-podcast-transcripts-for-seo-and-accessibility/ (archived at https://perma.cc/F27T-PHJ2)
56. 11 tips to create perfect transcripts, SmartScribe, www.smartscribe.co/blog/11-tips-to-create-perfect-transcripts/ (archived at https://perma.cc/7EAV-KZ5N)
57. Transcripts, W3C, www.w3.org/WAI/media/av/transcripts/ (archived at https://perma.cc/KMP4-5Q6X)
58. Boost podcast accessibility & engagement with transcripts – How to guide, Top 5 Accessibility, https://top5accessibility.com/blog/boost-podcast-accessibility-engagement-with-transcripts-how-to-guide/ (archived at https://perma.cc/WRF7-X92Y)
59. 8 best automatic transcription tools for 2024, Otter.ai, https://otter.ai/blog/best-automatic-transcription-tools?7bd4a6f3_page=1&84d5663d_page=2 (archived at https://perma.cc/5QW6-EKYV)
60. Get started with accessibility features on iPhone, Apple, https://support.apple.com/en-ca/guide/iphone/iph3e2e4367/ios (archived at https://perma.cc/VN9K-HQPQ)
61. Accessibility center, Spotify, www.spotify.com/us/accessibility (archived at https://perma.cc/Q7DP-JW5C)
62. Overcast: This accessible iOS app brings sunny weather to podcast listeners, American Federation for the Blind, https://afb.org/aw/15/9/15536 (archived at https://perma.cc/DU5M-UE9Z)
63. Explore your Castbox – User guide, Castbox, https://helpcenter.castbox.fm/portal/en/kb/articles/castbox-user-guide (archived at https://perma.cc/W5SZ-AWSX)
64. Accessibility, Pocket Casts, https://support.pocketcasts.com/knowledge-base/accessibility/ (archived at https://perma.cc/VCE8-JHYL)
65. This UX designer helps to make audible more accessible for all, Audible, www.audible.com/about/newsroom/this-ux-designer-helps-to-make-audible-more-accessible-for-all (archived at https://perma.cc/W7UB-NW2B)

PART THREE

Looking towards the future

As we move towards a world that increasingly relies on digital connections, the landscape of accessible communications is evolving at lightning speed. Part 3 of this book, 'Looking towards the future', invites us to step back and examine where accessibility is headed – not just as a compliance requirement but as an essential framework for innovation, inclusion and equity. While many organizations recognize this importance, communicators often face challenges in making accessibility a consistent priority among stakeholders.

We'd love to see a future where accessibility is no longer confined to technical standards or a niche concern; it's a transformative lens through which we can rethink communication entirely. In this section, we'll explore how emerging technologies, global trends and evolving cultural expectations reshape how we engage audiences. We'll also reflect on how communicators can lead the charge, using accessibility as a catalyst for creative solutions that resonate with diverse audiences.

While this vision has its challenges, this section invites you to imagine a future where accessible communications are seamless, intuitive and an integral part of every interaction. We know that the journey isn't always going to be linear or straightforward. While assistive technology continues to advance, we'll need to navigate both promising innovations and solutions that fall short of accessibility needs.

We'll examine the role of artificial intelligence in simplifying accessibility tasks, the global push for more inclusive policies, and the creative possibilities that arise when accessibility is a driving force rather than an afterthought.

But this isn't just about technology or policy – it's about people. The future of accessible communications depends on creating meaningful connections that transcend barriers. It's about designing experiences that not only accommodate but empower individuals to engage fully and authentically.

As you read this section, consider the potential of accessibility to meet today's challenges and pave the way for a more inclusive tomorrow. Together, let's envision a future where accessible communications are not only the standard but also a source of inspiration, collaboration and progress. The journey continues towards a future where everyone's voice is heard, and every story can be shared.

The future of accessible communication isn't just something to react to – it's something we can shape. Chapter 9 challenges you to see what's ahead not as a set of hurdles but as a chance to lead and inspire. Because the work you do today doesn't just make a difference now – it helps build a more inclusive tomorrow. A tomorrow that's better for business, too.

09

Future challenges and opportunities: How to stay ahead of the curve

The world of communication is constantly changing. New technologies emerge, regulations evolve and audience expectations shift. What worked yesterday might not work tomorrow, and if we want to create accessible content, we need to stay ahead of the curve.

But accessibility isn't just about keeping up. It's about leading the way, making sure no one gets left behind as the digital world grows. The good news? Every shift presents new opportunities to build a more inclusive future. From AI-driven content tools to expanded legislation, there's never been a more important time to advocate for accessibility in everything we create.

This chapter is all about looking towards the future and exploring what's next. We'll examine the biggest challenges on the horizon, the most exciting opportunities and, most importantly, how communicators can stay proactive instead of playing catch-up.

By the end of this chapter, you'll walk away with insights, strategies and practical steps to keep accessibility at the heart of your work, no matter where the future takes us.

The next frontier: Emerging technologies and accessibility

The future of communication is unfolding before our eyes. AI, augmented reality, voice assistants and whatever's coming next are revolutionizing the way we engage with content. But here's the thing: if these technologies aren't built with accessibility in mind, they risk leaving people behind.

For communicators, this is both exciting and challenging. We have more tools than ever to create meaningful, inclusive experiences, but only if we use them the right way. Automated captions, AI-generated content and immersive digital experiences all hold incredible potential, but they also come with risks: bias, exclusion and barriers that weren't there before.

So, what does this mean for us? We need to stay informed and proactive, and push for accessibility at every stage, whether we're choosing tech tools, developing content strategies or advocating for better industry standards.

This section explores what's next, what to watch out for, and how we can ensure that technology works for everyone, not just a select few.

AI and automation: A powerful tool, but not a perfect solution

Artificial intelligence and automation are reshaping how we approach accessibility in communications. We're seeing tools like auto-generated captions and AI-powered alt text being used to make content more accessible, but they're far from flawless. AI may be an incredible assistive tool, but it still needs human oversight to ensure content is accurate, inclusive and respectful. And not all tools are created equal.

The opportunities: AI as an accessibility game-changer

AI has opened new doors for making content more accessible:

- *Automated captioning and transcription:* AI-powered captioning tools like YouTube's auto-captions and Otter.ai make it easier than ever to transcribe speech into text, helping D/deaf and hard-of-hearing users engage with video and audio content.[1]
- *Alt text generators:* Platforms like Facebook and Instagram use AI to automatically generate image descriptions, giving screen reader users some level of context.[2]
- *AI-driven content optimization:* AI-powered accessibility checkers can flag readability issues, poor contrast and missing accessibility elements, helping communicators improve their materials.[3]

These tools can provide incredible efficiency, as they can process vast amounts of content in seconds, potentially reducing manual workloads and increasing accessibility at scale.

The challenges: AI still misses the mark

For all its benefits, AI is not a perfect solution:

- *Inaccurate captioning:* Auto-captions can misinterpret words, slang and accents, changing the meaning of dialogue and creating confusion for viewers.[4]

- *Lack of context and nuance:* AI struggles with context, often generating alt text that's vague, misleading or just plain wrong (e.g. 'image may contain a tree' when it's a picture of a group of people at an event).[5]
- *Cultural and linguistic bias:* AI models are trained on existing data, which means they can reinforce biases or exclude non-mainstream dialects, languages and perspectives.[6]

All of this is to say, while AI is a valuable tool, it should never replace human judgement, especially in areas as critical as accessibility.

How to stay ahead: AI and human collaboration
As communicators, we need to understand AI's strengths and limitations to use it effectively. Here's how:

- Use AI as a starting point, not the final product. Always review and edit AI-generated content for accuracy and inclusivity.
- Advocate for better AI training. Encourage platforms and developers to refine their AI models, making them more responsive to diverse needs.
- Test with real users. Work with people who rely on accessibility features to ensure AI-powered tools meet their needs.

AI isn't the future of accessibility; it's part of it. The real power lies in combining automation with human insight to create digital experiences that are truly inclusive.

Expanding accessibility through virtual and augmented reality

Virtual reality (VR) and augmented reality (AR) are transforming how we experience information, learn new skills, and engage with digital content. These technologies offer exciting opportunities to make education and communication more engaging and interactive, from training simulations to immersive storytelling. But as VR and AR continue to grow, one question remains: Who gets to participate?

The opportunities: A new way to learn and engage
VR and AR have the potential to break down traditional barriers to access by creating more inclusive and engaging learning environments:

Education and training: Virtual classrooms and AR-enhanced textbooks offer interactive, multisensory learning experiences, helping students of all abilities engage with complex topics.[7]

Professional development: VR job training provides hands-on experience in controlled environments, helping people practice tasks before applying them in real-world settings.[8]

Accessible storytelling: Immersive experiences allow users to step into another person's perspective, fostering greater empathy and understanding across different lived experiences.

Navigating the physical environment: Using a combination of AR and AI, users can be presented with audio descriptions of the world around them. From recognizing people to objects and hazards, the potential is huge.

These technologies could redefine accessibility if they're designed with inclusion in mind.

The challenges: Who's being left behind?

Despite their potential, many VR/AR experiences remain inaccessible to people with disabilities. Some of the biggest challenges include:

Visual and hearing barriers: Many VR/AR experiences lack captioning, audio descriptions or screen reader compatibility, making them difficult to navigate for users who are blind, low-vision, D/deaf or hard of hearing.[9] Headsets aren't always designed for glasses wearers in mind, either, which can exclude a high proportion of potential users.

Physical and motor challenges: VR often requires precise hand movements or standing mobility, making it unusable for those with mobility impairments.[10]

Cognitive overload: Fast-moving, complex VR environments can overwhelm users with neurodivergent needs, leading to disorientation or sensory overload.[11]

Cost and availability: While these technologies will likely drop in price as they become more widely used, there's a huge barrier to entry for many people who cannot afford to buy these new products.

When accessibility is an afterthought, entire communities are excluded from the future of digital engagement.

The future of voice and gesture-based interfaces

Voice search and hands-free technology, including smart assistants like Alexa and Google Assistant and gesture-controlled devices, are transforming how we interact with digital content. For many, these tools provide a seamless, efficient way to navigate the digital world, whether asking for directions, setting reminders, or searching for information online. For people with mobility disabilities or vision loss, voice-controlled devices can be a game-changer, allowing them to access technology without relying on traditional screens or keyboards.[12,13]

However, these technologies are far from perfect. Many voice interfaces still struggle to accurately recognize diverse speech patterns, including regional accents, speech disabilities or non-standard verbal communication. Users with conditions like Amyotrophic Lateral Sclerosis (ALS), cerebral palsy or stuttering often experience frustration when voice assistants fail to understand their commands.[14,15] Voice interfaces also rely on users learning to use, and being able to remember, the right commands, which can be a challenge for those with cognitive disabilities. Additionally, non-verbal users remain excluded entirely from this form of interaction, highlighting the need for more adaptive AI solutions that recognize diverse modes of communication.

To stay ahead of these challenges, communicators, developers and accessibility advocates must test voice interfaces for inclusivity. It means ensuring speech recognition models are trained on diverse voices and pushing for multimodal input options that go beyond voice, such as text-based or gesture-driven commands. As hands-free technology becomes increasingly integrated into our daily lives, prioritizing inclusivity will determine whether it enhances accessibility or reinforces existing barriers.

A global shift towards stricter accessibility regulations?

Around the world, many governments and jurisdictions are tightening regulations to ensure digital content, communications and public services are accessible to all. From the European Accessibility Act (EAA) to updates in WCAG guidelines, organizations that fail to meet standards face fines, legal challenges and reputational risks.

This shift isn't just about compliance; it's about creating a more inclusive digital world. As regulations evolve, communicators must stay ahead of the curve, understanding what's required, how to implement best practices, and how to future-proof their content and platforms.

Changing laws and policies: What communicators need to know

As legislation and the political landscape continues to evolve in this arena, it's vital that communications professionals continue to champion accessible communications which are easier to read for everyone. Organizations that fail to comply with accessibility regulations risk more than just fines; they risk alienating audiences, damaging reputations and missing out on growth opportunities.

REAL-WORLD EXAMPLE

Ireland is setting a strong example for enforcement. Under its implementation of the EAA, designated compliance authorities will be responsible for ensuring businesses adhere to accessibility laws. These authorities have the power to:[16]

- direct businesses to comply with accessibility requirements
- investigate complaints and take enforcement action against non-compliant organizations
- facilitate legal processes for individuals who have experienced digital barriers

Failing to comply with accessibility regulations in Ireland is not just a reputational risk, as it carries serious financial and legal penalties:

- A fine of up to €5,000 and/or imprisonment for up to 6 months in case of a summary conviction.
- A fine of up to €60,000 and/or imprisonment of up to 18 months in case of an indicted conviction.

Ireland's approach signals that accessibility enforcement is not just a recommendation but a legal obligation, and we hope that other EU member states follow suit with strict penalties.

Keeping up with evolving accessibility policies requires proactive strategies. Here's how communicators can ensure their content remains compliant and inclusive:

- Stay informed. Laws are changing rapidly, and ignorance isn't an excuse for non-compliance. Follow accessibility advocacy groups, government updates and industry news to stay ahead.
- Conduct regular accessibility audits. Evaluate websites, social media content, emails and digital documents against WCAG and other relevant standards. Regular audits help identify issues before they become legal liabilities.

- Make accessibility a core part of content strategy. It means incorporating user-centred design from the start, like using clear templates, alt text, captions, accessible PDFs and readable text.
- Train your team. Ensure that designers, writers and digital content creators are educated on best practices. Investing in training helps prevent costly compliance issues down the line.
- Work with experts. Accessibility consultants, legal advisers and digital accessibility specialists can help organizations navigate changing laws and implement sustainable solutions.

Compliance isn't just about avoiding penalties; it's about doing the right thing. Organizations that prioritize accessibility now will be better positioned to lead, innovate and build lasting trust with their audiences – wider audiences who are positioned to spend their money with those organizations too.

The rise of complex infographics and data storytelling

Infographics and data visualizations have become essential tools for breaking down complex topics and making information more digestible. Whether it's a heat map showing climate change patterns, a financial trends dashboard, or an interactive election results graphic, data storytelling shapes how we understand the world.

However, as these visualizations become more intricate and sophisticated, they also become less accessible to many people, particularly those who use screen readers, have cognitive disabilities or experience colour blindness. Inaccessible data storytelling risks excluding audiences, distorting information and failing to comply with accessibility regulations.

So, how do we make complex infographics and data storytelling accessible?

Challenges in data accessibility

Screen reader limitations: Most screen readers can only interpret text-based content, meaning detailed visual representations like graphs, pie charts and data dashboards become invisible to users with sight loss. Without accessible alternatives, critical insights are lost.[17]

Cognitive load and readability: Complicated infographics with dense text, excessive numbers or unclear visuals can be overwhelming, especially for individuals with cognitive disabilities like dyslexia, ADHD or brain injuries. Information overload can make data difficult to process and retain.[18]

Colour dependence: Many data visualizations rely solely on colour coding (e.g. green means increase, red means decrease), which can be problematic for users with colour blindness or those viewing content on low-contrast screens.[19]

How to stay ahead: Best practices for accessible data storytelling
Provide alternative text descriptions: Every infographic, chart or graph should have clear alternative text or long descriptions explaining the key takeaways.

EXAMPLE

Instead of: Sales growth by region: [pie chart image].

Use: Pie chart showing North America leading with 45 per cent sales growth, followed by Europe at 30 per cent and Asia at 25 per cent.

For highly complex data, consider providing a linked text-based summary that walks users through the findings without relying on visuals.

Offer data in multiple formats: Not everyone engages with data the same way. To maximize accessibility, provide data in raw text format (tables or bullet points summarizing key data); downloadable spreadsheets with properly labelled headers; and audio descriptions for video-based data presentations.

Use high-contrast colours and patterns: To make charts readable for all users, you should:

- ensure a minimum contrast ratio of 4.5:1 (WCAG standard)
- avoid using red and green together (a common issue for colour blindness)
- use patterns, textures, or symbols instead of relying on colour alone (e.g. striped bars for one category, solid bars for another)

Prioritize simplicity in design: The best data visualizations are clear, direct and easy to interpret:

- Use concise labelling rather than excessive annotations.
- Choose simple fonts and avoid decorative or all upper-case text.
- Present one key message per infographic; don't overload users with too much data at once.

The role of inclusive design in the future of communications

Too often, accessibility is treated as a box to check at the end of a project, a final step in content creation, website development, or marketing campaigns. But true accessibility isn't about meeting minimum legal requirements; it's about creating experiences that work for everyone from the start.

Content becomes more inclusive, usable and effective. This approach isn't just about compliance; it's about building better, more equitable experiences for all users.

Why accessibility needs to be part of design thinking

1 It's easier to do it right from the start: Fixing accessibility after a product is built or collateral has been produced can be expensive and time-consuming. Retrofitting a website, adding captions to videos after production, or rewriting content to be more inclusive takes more effort than designing with user needs in mind from the beginning.
2 It results in better UX for everyone: Accessible design benefits everyone, not just people with disabilities:
    - Clear, structured content helps all users navigate a page more easily.
    - High-contrast and readable fonts improve visibility for anyone in low-light conditions.
    - Keyboard-friendly navigation isn't just useful for screen readers – it helps power users and mobile device interactions too.
3 It drives innovation: Many features we take for granted today, like voice assistants, captions and screen magnification, were designed to support people with disabilities but became mainstream tools. By embedding accessibility into early-stage thinking, communicators and designers can spark new ideas that improve usability for all.

How to embed accessibility in design conversations

Make accessibility a core principle
When planning a project, ask: How will this work for someone using a screen reader? For someone with low vision? For someone who relies on captions?

By making these questions non-negotiable, accessibility becomes part of the foundation, not an afterthought.

Involve people with disabilities in user testing

The best way to ensure accessibility? Ask the people who need it most.

Engage people with disabilities in research, testing and design reviews to get direct feedback on what works and what doesn't.

Push for accessible UX/UI design

Communicators play a role in shaping digital experiences – so it's important to be part of conversations about website design, branding and platform choices:

- Advocate for clear, easy-to-read typography and colour contrast.
- Push for mobile-friendly layouts that support adaptive technologies.
- Ensure navigation is intuitive for keyboard users and assistive tech.

Train teams to think accessibly

Designers, developers and communicators shouldn't be working in silos; accessibility training should be integrated across all teams. When everyone understands the basics, inclusive design becomes a collaborative effort, not just a specialist's job.

Chapter wrap up

The way we communicate is constantly evolving, but one thing remains the same: accessibility is not optional. It's the foundation of inclusive, effective and impactful communication.

As PR and communications professionals, we have the power to shape narratives, build connections and influence change. But that power also means responsibility, ensuring every message, campaign and strategy reaches and resonates with all audiences without barriers.

Accessibility isn't just about compliance or checking a box. It's about respect, equity and the ability for everyone to engage with the content we create fully. It's about understanding that the digital and communications landscape will continue to shift, but our commitment to inclusion must remain constant.

The path forward: What's next?

So, how do we stay ahead?

Stay informed: Legislation, technology and best practices will continue to change. Commit to lifelong learning.

Stay engaged: Accessibility is an ongoing conversation. Connect with experts, advocates and communities leading the way.

Stay proactive: Don't wait for accessibility to be an afterthought – integrate it into everything from day one.

Stay an advocate: Use your influence to push for accessibility beyond compliance and into a core organizational value.

Stay safe: Being an advocate can be exhausting. Make time to look after yourself, connect with others, and know that you're trying to make things better than before.

Wrapping up the book: The bigger picture

Throughout this book, we've explored the why and how of accessible communications, from digital content to social media, branding, to strategy. But now, it's up to you.

Because accessibility doesn't stop here; it's a journey.

Whether you're refining your content strategy, training your team or writing a report, every step you take towards inclusion makes a difference.

By leading the way, you're improving accessibility and shaping a future where communications are truly for everyone.

References

1. Voices from industry access for deaf and hard of hearing individuals in informational and educational remote sessions, Assistive Technology Industry Association, www.atia.org/wp-content/uploads/2022/08/ATOB-V16.2-Ballenger.pdf (archived at https://perma.cc/9SYW-SSNF)
2. How to write alt text and image descriptions for the visually impaired, Perkins School for the Blind, www.perkins.org/resource/how-write-alt-text-and-image-descriptions-visually-impaired/ (archived at https://perma.cc/FU6C-M3W2)

3. Accessibility and AI tools, The University of British Columbia, https://learningdesignviews.educ.ubc.ca/accessibility-and-ai-tools/ (archived at https://perma.cc/SU3X-HEEB)
4. Maximizing impact with auto-captions: The crucial role of human review, Amara Accessibility Media, https://blog.amara.org/2024/03/06/maximizing-impact-with-auto-captions-the-crucial-role-of-human-review/ (archived at https://perma.cc/XT4N-SXZN)
5. Be careful when using A.I. for alternative text, Bureau of Internet Accessibility, www.boia.org/blog/be-careful-when-using-ai-for-alternative-text (archived at https://perma.cc/JD4C-BVBN)
6. AI generates covertly racist decisions about people based on their dialect, Nature, www.nature.com/articles/s41586-024-07856-5 (archived at https://perma.cc/CL6J-3URL)
7. Interactive textbooks: The future of learning with AR, Let's Nurture, www.letsnurture.ca/blog/technology/interactive-textbooks-the-future-of-learning-with-ar/ (archived at https://perma.cc/D786-THZ9)
8. Opportunities for accessible virtual reality design for immersive musical performances for blind and low-vision people, ACM Digital Library, https://dl.acm.org/doi/fullHtml/10.1145/3607822.3614540 (archived at https://perma.cc/VT92-CW2B)
9. Inclusive AR/VR: Accessibility barriers for immersive technologies, DMT Lab, Birmingham City University, https://arxiv.org/pdf/2304.13465 (archived at https://perma.cc/UU63-CVJD)
10. Inclusive AR/VR: Accessibility barriers for immersive technologies, DMT Lab, Birmingham City University, https://arxiv.org/pdf/2304.13465 (archived at https://perma.cc/8QDH-4WQX)
11. Inclusive AR/VR: Accessibility barriers for immersive technologies, DMT Lab, Birmingham City University, https://arxiv.org/pdf/2304.13465 (archived at https://perma.cc/3APB-WSV8)
12. The best smart assistive devices for people with disabilities, Wirecutter, www.nytimes.com/wirecutter/reviews/best-assistive-smart-home-technology-for-disabled/ (archived at https://perma.cc/Z6ZX-N2XP)
13. The role of assistive technology in digital inclusion, Level Access, www.levelaccess.com/blog/assistive-technology/ (archived at https://perma.cc/L5H7-VZC6)
14. Voice assistants don't understand us. They should, *The New York Times*, www.nytimes.com/2021/09/22/opinion/voice-assistants-accessibility-disability.html (archived at https://perma.cc/T9UN-3MG6)
15. Tech firms train voice assistants to understand atypical speech, *The Wall Street Journal*, www.wsj.com/articles/tech-firms-train-voice-assistants-to-understand-atypical-speech-11614186019 (archived at https://perma.cc/8747-6HSL)

16 Ireland digital accessibility laws: EAA and beyond, TPGi, www.tpgi.com/ireland-digital-accessibility-laws-eaa-and-beyond/ (archived at https://perma.cc/EP4Y-KUEU)
17 The accessibility of data visualizations on the web for screen reader users: Practices and experiences during COVID-19, ACM Digital Library, https://dl.acm.org/doi/10.1145/3557899 (archived at https://perma.cc/466T-W8WN)
18 Centering accessibility in data visualization, Urban Institute, www.urban.org/sites/default/files/2022-12/Do%20No%20Harm%20Guide%20Centering%20Accessibility%20in%20Data%20Visualization.pdf (archived at https://perma.cc/FN36-8BRH)
19 5 tips on designing colorblind-friendly visualizations, Tableau, www.tableau.com/blog/examining-data-viz-rules-dont-use-red-green-together (archived at https://perma.cc/UNQ9-CUS5)

CHECKLISTS

A checklist for plain language

Audience

- ☐ Am I clear on the audience for this content?
- ☐ What is the user need?

Content

- ☐ Is active voice used where appropriate?
- ☐ Have I avoided complex words unless they're needed?
- ☐ Have technical terms and acronyms been spelt out?
- ☐ Are there any clichés or jargon words that could be removed?
- ☐ Is content broken into paragraphs with clear headings?
- ☐ Have sentences been kept short – and definitely less than 25 words?
- ☐ Have links got useful actionable text – no 'click here' here?

Format

- ☐ Is the font a readable size?
- ☐ Do I know how this content will look in-situ?
- ☐ Do I have appropriate descriptions for any images or graphics?

Accessible social media content checklist for communicators

Ensuring social media content is accessible helps create an inclusive online space where everyone, regardless of ability, can engage with your content. Use this checklist to make your posts, visuals and videos more accessible across platforms.

Text and copy

- ☐ **Plain language** – Have I kept sentences clear, concise and jargon-free?
- ☐ **Links** – Have I used meaningful link text, e.g. 'Learn more about accessibility' instead of 'Click here'?
- ☐ **Hashtags** – Have I used capital letters for each word in my hashtags? (e.g. #AccessibleContent instead of #accessiblecontent)?
- ☐ **Special characters** – Have I avoided using special characters or excessive emojis in place of words that may not be read properly by assistive technology?
- ☐ **Content warnings** – Have I provided trigger warnings or content warnings (e.g. CW: Flashing Lights) when necessary?

Images and graphics

- ☐ **Alternative text** – Have I added descriptive alt text to images that conveys the key visual details (avoiding vague descriptions like 'image of a person')?
- ☐ **Contrast** – Have I ensured high contrast between text and background for readability?
- ☐ **Text overlays** – Have I avoided using images with text overlays unless the text is also provided in the caption?
- ☐ **Templates** – Do my templates prioritize readability and minimize distractions?
- ☐ **Infographics** – Are infographics clear, structured and have accompanying alt text or a text-based description?

Videos and multimedia

- ☐ **Captions** – Have I provided accurate captions for all video content (not just auto-generated ones, which can be inaccurate)?
- ☐ **Transcript** – Have I included a transcript for video and audio content so users can read along?
- ☐ **Audio descriptions** – Have I used audio descriptions to describe important visual elements for people who are blind or have low vision?
- ☐ **Avoid flashing lights** – Have I made sure videos don't include flashing lights or rapid movements that may trigger seizures, and provided warnings if necessary?

Engagement and interaction

- ☐ **Response tone** – Are my responses to comments and messages inclusive, with respectful language and tone?
- ☐ **Capitalization** – Have I avoided excessive use of CAPS LOCK, as it can be harder to read and may be interpreted as shouting?
- ☐ **GIFs** – Have I checked that any GIFs I've used do not have flashing content that could trigger seizures?
- ☐ **Emoji placement** – Have I used emojis sparingly and placed them at the end of sentences rather than in the middle of text?
- ☐ **Screen reader testing** – Have I tested posts with a screen reader to ensure readability and accessibility?

Platform-specific considerations

- ☐ **Instagram and Facebook** – Have I written descriptive captions and added alt text for images?
- ☐ **X** – Have I used alt text for images and avoided ASCII art or complex emoji combinations?
- ☐ **LinkedIn** – Have I made sure document uploads have accessible formatting, including structured headings and alt text? Have I provided an alternative format (e.g. description in the post) for any words saved in carousel images?
- ☐ **TikTok and Instagram Reels** – Have I included closed captions and avoided heavy reliance on on-screen text?
- ☐ **YouTube** – Have I provided detailed video descriptions and manually reviewed auto-generated captions for accuracy?

Accessible video content checklist

Creating accessible video content ensures that all audiences, including those with disabilities, can fully engage with and understand your message. Use this checklist to make sure your videos meet accessibility standards and provide an inclusive viewing experience.

Pre-production

- ☐ **Script** – Have I included descriptions of key visual elements?
- ☐ **Clarity of speech** – Do speakers use clear, concise language and avoid excessive jargon?
- ☐ **Avoid flashing content** – Have I reduced or eliminated flashing lights and rapid movements that could trigger seizures?
- ☐ **Text readability** – Have I planned for any on-screen text to be large, high-contrast and displayed long enough to be read comfortably?

Audio and captioning

- ☐ **Open or closed captions** – Have I provided accurate, synchronized captions for all dialogue, sound effects and relevant audio cues?
- ☐ **Auto-captions review** – Have I checked any auto-generated captions for accuracy?
- ☐ **Transcript** – Have I provided a downloadable transcript with all spoken content, descriptions of key visuals, and important sounds?
- ☐ **Audio description** – Have I provided an additional track describing important visual elements for blind or low-vision users, if it's not included within the script?

Visual considerations

- ☐ **Contrast and readability** – Have I checked the colour contrast between text and background for on-screen elements?
- ☐ **Legible font choice** – Have I used sans-serif fonts (e.g. Arial, Verdana) at a readable size?
- ☐ **Consistent speaker identification** – Have I indicated who is speaking if multiple speakers are present?
- ☐ **Avoid excessive animations** – Have I made sure transitions and animations are smooth and not distracting for neurodivergent viewers?

Playback and distribution

- ☐ **Accessible media player** – Does the video player support captions, keyboard navigation and screen readers?

- ☐ **Multiple formats** – Have I offered alternative viewing options, such as a text transcript or an audio-only version?
- ☐ **User controls** – Can users can pause, stop or adjust playback speed easily?
- ☐ **Test with assistive technology** – Have I checked video accessibility using screen readers, captioning tools and other assistive tech?
- ☐ **Provide alternative contact** – Have I offered an email or contact method for users to request additional accessibility accommodations?

INDEX

ABIDE 16
   see also belonging
ableist language 93, 112–13, 151, 206
academic writing 94, 108
accessiBe 49–50
Accessibil-IT 175
accessibility 1, 3, 16, 18, 23, 41, 48
Accessibility Act (2017) 40
accessibility checkers 49, 78, 79, 107, 142, 193, 278
   Adobe Acrobat 169–70, 173
   Microsoft Excel 161, 164
   Microsoft Office Suite 173
   Microsoft PowerPoint 157
   Microsoft Word 152
   PDF (PAC) 31, 169
Accessibility Commissioner 37
Accessibility for Manitobans Act (2013) 39
Accessibility for Ontarians with Disabilities Act (AODA) (2005) 27, 37, 38–39, 48
Accessibility Insights 61
accessibility myths 78–79
accessibility statements 44
Accessible British Columbia Act (2021) 40
Accessible Canada Act (ACA) (2019) 35–38, 45
accountability 47, 65, 68, 72, 73, 83
achievable goals 68
acronyms 97
Act to Secure Handicapped Persons in the Exercise of Their Rights (1978) 40
action plans 67–71, 84
action verbs 203
active voice 96, 127
ADA (1990) 25, 27, 33–35, 48
ADA (Amended) (2024) 189
ADHD 191, 246
adjustable text size 245
Adobe 174
Adobe Acrobat 167, 173, 174, 176
   Accessibility Checker 169–70, 173
Adobe Audition 255
Adobe InDesign 166, 167
Adobe Premiere 32, 235
Adobe Premiere Pro 201
Adobe Reader 170

advocacy 41, 61, 69, 75, 77, 187–88, 189, 278, 279, 287
ageist language 112, 113
AI (artificial intelligence) 15, 47, 61, 264, 278–79
   see also generative AI; Grammarly
Alexa 281
Allyant 176
alternative (alt) text 31, 135–36, 152, 157–58, 163–65, 168, 179, 228, 252, 278
   and AI (automation) 15, 49, 217
   e-commerce 70
   Microsoft 188, 194
   social media 192, 194–97, 206–07, 208, 209, 210, 214
American Psychological Association (APA) 115, 116, 117
Americans with Disabilities Act (ADA) (1990) 25, 27, 33–35, 48
Americans with Disabilities Act (ADA) (Amended) (2024) 189
ampersands ('and' sign) 105
Android 13, 268
animations 28, 32, 156, 200, 231, 246, 247
annual reports 31, 81, 166, 177
anonymous feedback 117
Apple 13
Apple Keynote 157–58
Apple Podcasts 265, 266–68
ARIA 76
Arial font 139
assistive technology 5, 12–15, 24, 133, 193
   see also accessibility checkers; screen readers
Associated Press 114
ATMs 42
Audacity 255
Audible 269
audience reach 5, 24, 62, 64, 188–89
audio announcements 17
audio content 17, 32, 73–74, 156, 157, 191, 223–70, 293
   see also transcripts
audio description recording practice 241
audio descriptions 32, 50–51, 211, 224, 227, 237–43, 280

audits 44, 49, 68–69, 75, 80–81, 116, 282
augmented reality 279–80
Australia 45
Australian Human Rights Commission 45
author information 153
autism 232, 246
auto-captions 157, 200, 208, 217, 233, 250, 278
auto-play features 157, 193, 207, 234, 252
automation 49–50, 69, 170–71, 216–17, 264, 278–79
 see also auto-captions
axesCheck 176
axes4 175–76
axesPDF 175
axesTraining 176
axesWord 175

Barnes & Noble 26
Basic Act for Persons with Disabilities 45–46
belonging 16, 17, 117
bereavement 110–11
Beyoncé 26
bio conditions 8
 see also physical accessibility
biophysical model of disability 8
blindness 5, 25–26, 191, 249
 see also colour blindness
BlueSky 207
bold type 125, 133, 153, 178, 264
bookmarks 171
Boyle, Susan 204
braille displays 14, 33
brand reputation (reputational risk) 25, 26, 30, 47, 60–61, 64, 70, 189
branding 228
British Columbia 40
bullet points 100, 126, 128–29, 137, 150, 193, 215, 246, 256–57
burnout 110
business cases 24–26, 64
business communications 94
buy-in 63–65, 83

Calibri font 153
calls to action 73, 126, 179, 193, 210
Camel case 73, 203, 204, 209
Canada 5, 6, 24, 187–88
 legislation 27, 35–41, 45, 48
Canada.ca 104
Canadian Radio-television and Telecommunications Commission 37
Canadian Transportation Agency 37
capitalization (caps) 114, 128, 204, 246

caption length 236
captions 24, 50–51, 136–38, 226–27, 232–37, 251
 auto-captions 157, 200, 208, 217, 250, 278
 closed 225, 249, 250, 252
 open captions 225, 252
 real-time 32
 social media 188–89, 191–93, 199–201, 207, 208, 210, 211, 217
cascading style sheets 133
Castbox 269
cells 159
 merged 160, 178
 protection of 161
Center for Inclusive Design and Innovation 115
champions 75
channel selection 10, 101
charity model of disability 8, 9
Chartbuilder 165
charts 162–65, 177, 180, 194
ChatGPT 107
checklists 217
Chrome 170
Claude 107, 164
clear speech 254–55
clear versus complex words 97
clichés 98, 111
clickable content 126
closed captions 225, 233, 235, 249, 250, 251, 252
cognitive bias 94
cognitive disabilities 191, 249, 281
 see also ADHD; autism; dyslexia
cognitive load (overload) 110, 213, 239, 259, 280, 283
Coles Supermarket 26
collaboration (team-work) 71–73, 242
Color Oracle 244
colour 10, 153, 163–64, 284
colour blindness 5, 142, 244
colour contrast 32, 156, 162
 presentations 73
 social media 191, 193, 198, 216
 video content 243–45, 247
 web design 132–33, 141–42
colour contrast analysers 78, 159, 164, 198, 216, 244
Colour Contrast Checker (WebAIM) 133, 164, 198, 216, 244
columns 151, 159, 168–69
CommonLook Office 176
CommonLook PDF 176

CommonLook PDF Validator 176
complex communications 92, 97
compliance 23, 27, 39, 47–53, 62, 64, 70, 80, 189–90, 283
    see also non-compliance
condenser microphones 255
Conscious Style Guide, The 117
consistency 226, 257–58
consultancies 69
consultation (engagement) 37, 41, 80, 190
consumer electronics 42
content creator (designer) training 76
Content Design London Readability Guidelines 100
content management systems 153
content structure 226, 231
    content length 100–01
    see also clickable content
continuous improvement 50, 83
Convention on the Rights of Persons with Disabilities (2006) 9
conversational podcasts 256–57
Covid-19 awareness campaigns 187–88
creativity 50–51, 70
credibility 112, 118
Crystal Mark accreditation 100
cultural sensitivity 93, 114, 205, 213, 236, 279
culture xvii, 2, 59–86
culture-first mindset 62–63
'curse of knowledge' 94
customer feedback 82
customer loyalty 70
customer satisfaction metrics 80
customer service 38, 43, 82
customer touchpoint audits 69
cybersecurity 110

D&I 15
    see also diversity; inclusion
daily workflows 71–75, 81, 84, 190
dashboards 164
data 103, 159, 178–79
data validation rules 160
data visualization 162–65, 180, 283–84
    see also graphics; images
Datawrapper 165
deadlines 68, 71
deafblindness 191
deafness 5, 248
decorative fonts 140, 153, 245
decorative images 136
DEI 16, 116
    see also diversity; inclusion
Deque Systems 25

Descript 201, 237, 251, 262, 264
descriptive language 229–30
design thinking 51, 285–86
developer training 76
dialogue clarity 225, 229–30
digital accessibility 11–15, 17, 26–27, 42, 43
    ACA 37
    ADA 34–35
    AODA 39
    see also technology (IT)
digital platform audits 69
Digital.gov 104
disability 3–9, 10, 109, 192
Disability Act (2005) 46
Disability Discrimination Act (1992) 45
Disability Discrimination Act (DDA) (1995) 44, 45
disability-led workshops 65
disability statistics 5, 24, 62, 64, 188–89
diversity 15, 16, 116–17
diversity and inclusion 15
diversity, equity & inclusion (DEI) 16, 116
document properties (metadata) 153, *154*
documents 73, 81, 148–81
    templates for 71, 74
    see also reporting
Domino's Pizza 25–26
Dragon NaturallySpeaking 13
dynamic microphones 255
dyscalculia 91
dyslexia 5, 90, 142, 153, 155
Dyslexie 153, 155

e-commerce 41, 43, 70
e-learning 76, 235
Easy Read 108, 109
economic impact 5–6, 24
Edge 170
editing software 255
    see also Hemingway Editor
education 65, 75, 84, 115–16, 181, 217, 240, 241, 282
    see also training
education sector 70, 279
emails 73, 74
    email addresses 132
embedded alt text 207
embedded fonts 167
emoji-only posts 215
emoji placement 215
emojipedia.org 214
emojis 212–15
empathy 63
employee morale 61, 82

employee onboarding 75
employee retention 70
engagement (consultation) 37, 41, 80, 190
environmental context 10
epilepsy 246
Equality Act (2010) 44
Equality and Human Rights Commission 45
Equality Commission for Northern Island 45
equity 16, 118
error reduction metrics 77
ethics 26–27
ethnically inclusive language 114
European Accessibility Act (EAA) (2019) 27, 41–44, 45
European Union (EU) 41
    Web Accessibility Directive (2016) 43
event accessibility 67, 69, 70, 72
exclamation marks 106
exclusion, economic impact of 5–6
experts 69, 98, 102–03, 283
extended image descriptions 137–38
'eye candy' images 136
eye-tracking systems 14

F-patterns 125–26
Facebook 206–07, 217, 234, 252, 278, 292
false claims 49–50
false positives (negatives) 49
familiar language 92, 241
Federal Trade Commission 49–50
feedback (feedback loops) 37, 74, 77, 80–82, 96, 116–17, 158, 217, 242, 247
Fenty Beauty 26
figurative expressions 105
financial risk 64
    see also lawsuits
findable content 103
flashing content 28, 32, 246–47, 248
Flesch-Kincaid scores 106
flexibility 51, 117
focus groups 82, 116
fonts 139–40, 153, 155–56, 162, 177, 198, 200, 228, 245, 263
    embedded 167
    font size 10, 32, 73, 168–69, 172
    sans-serif 32, 234
form accessibility (completion) 28, 31, 172
Format Object 157, 158
Format Picture 157, 158
format selection 10, 33
    number (numeral) 104–05, 126, 149
forward slash symbols 106
Fox News Network 25
front-loaded content 103

full podcast scripts 256
functionality descriptors 135–36

GDP 5
Gen Z 213–14, 233
gender-identity 114–15
gender-neutral language 92, 114–15, 151, 205
gendered language 112, 113
generative AI 107, 164–65
gesture-based technology 281
Global Accessibility Awareness Day 64, 188
glossaries 98
goal (objective) setting 68, 69–70, 71
Google Assistant 268, 281
Google Docs 73, 152, 167, 173
Google Gemini 107
Google Lighthouse 69, 80
Google Mobile-Friendly Test 141
Google Sheets 161, 164, 173
Google Slides 157, 173
Google Trends 95
Google Workspace 173
Government Digital Service 45
Grackle PDF 175
Grackle Scan 175
Grackle Service 174
Grackle Sheets 161
Grackle Training 175
GrackleDocs 152, 174–75
Grammarly 107
'grandfathered in' 114
graphics 194–99
    see also charts; graphs
graphs 137, 138, 160, 162–65, 177, 180, 194
grief 110–11
growth mindset 77–78, 117
guest speakers 77
Gunning Fog Index 106

hands-free voice commands 268, 281
haptic captions 200
Hasbro 26
hashtags 73, 203–04, 209
header rows 159, 168–69
headings 128, 150, 152, 155, 159, 168, 171, 178, 246, 263
hearing loss 5, 191, 280
    see also deafness
Helvetica font 198
Hemingway Editor 106–07, 203
hiring practices 66, 76
hover effects 133
HTML 29, 31, 76, 136, 166, 195
human resources communication 72, 76

human rights model of disability 9
human transcription services 264
humour 205
hyperlink placement 132
hyperlinks 130–34, 141, 143–44, 152, 168, 171
hyphens 105

identity-first language 112, 114
image descriptions 137–38, 195, 196
images 136, 247
impairments 7
inclusion xiii, 15, 16, 61
inclusion, diversity, equity & accessibility (IDEA) 16
  see also accessibility; diversity; equity
inclusive language 90, 91, 92–93, 111–18, 119–20, 151, 188, 205–06
innovation 70, 285
Instagram 189, 191, 200, 208, 217, 234, 252, 278, 292
  see also Reels
instructional videos 240, 241
integrated descriptions 230, 237, 240–41, 242
intellectual disability 5
interactive content 164, 172, 193
  spreadsheets 160–61
  transcripts 262, 265
internal communication 39, 69, 72
internal review groups 116
International Association of Accessibility Professionals 74, 81
International Classification of Functioning, Disability and Health (WHO) 8
International Committee of the Red Cross 9
international phone numbers 105
International Telecommunication Union 105
investment 78
invisible disabilities 4
Ireland 46, 282
ISO (International Organization for Standardization)
  24495-1:2023 103
  24495-2 102
IT *see* technology (IT)
italics 125, 153, 245, 264

Japan 45–46
jargon 98, 102, 203
JAWS 13, 161, 171
JIS X 8341-3 standard 46
justified text alignment 140, 198

kerning 140, 151
key performance indicators (KPIs) 80
key visual elements 225, 241

keyboard alternatives 14
keyboard navigation 24, 28, 31, 79, 172, 192, 251, 266
keyboard shortcuts 249, 250, 267
Keynote 157–58
keyword search 153
Kurzweil 3000 14

labelling 31, 159, 160, 162–163, 172
Labrador 40
landing pages 126
language 10, 33, 49, 109, 153, 241, 255
  ableist 92, 112–13, 151, 206
  ageist 112, 113
  familiar 92, 241
  gender-neutral 92, 114–15, 151, 205
  gendered 112, 113
  identity-first 112, 114
  inclusive 90, 91, 92–93, 111–18, 114, 119–20, 151, 188, 205–06
  person-first 92, 112, 113
  podcasts 258–59
  video content 229–30
  see also action verbs; active voice; clear speech; clear versus complex words; clichés; jargon; 'official' terms
language settings 153
large language models 107
large print format 33
lawsuits 25–26, 35, 47, 189
leadership 63–65, 72, 83, 117
leading (line spacing) 140, 150, 151, 198, 246
left-aligned text 140
left-to-right content 126, 152
legal communication 100–02, 256
Legal Plain Language standard 102
legislation (laws) xvi, 22, 23, 33–49, 66–67, 189–90, 281–83
  see also lawsuits
letter spacing (kerning) 140, 151
level A WCAG 29
  see also alternative (alt) text
level AA WCAG 29
  see also captions; colour contrast; labelling
level AAA WCAG 30
  see also colour contrast
lighting xv, 226
line breaks 236, 263
line length 151
line spacing (leading) 140, 150, 151, 198, 246
LinkedIn 210, 215, 292
links (hyperlinks) 130–34, 141, 143–44, 152, 168, 171

lists 128, 129, 150, 171, 246
live streaming 191, 233, 235
low literacy 90
low numeracy 90–91
low vision *see* visual impairment

macOS 13
'Make Accessible' (Adobe) 173
'Manifesto for the Simple Scribe' (Radford) 94
manual testing 50, 69, 161, 170–72, 217
marginalized audiences 111
margins 150, 151
market position 25, 189
marketing communication 72
marketing training 76
marketing videos 239
medical model of disability 7, 9
mental anchors 231
merged cells 160, 178
messaging 10, 42
Meta 208
   See also Facebook; Instagram
metadata (document properties) 153, *154*
metrics (measurement) 66, 68, 79–80, 84
   engagement 190
   error reduction 77
   training effectiveness 77
microphones 226, 254, 255
Microsoft 25, 61, 188, 194
Microsoft Excel Accessibility Checker 161, 164
Microsoft Office Suite Accessibility Checker 173
Microsoft PowerPoint 166
   Accessibility Checker 157
Microsoft Teams 158
Microsoft Word 73, 78, 107, 166, 167, 174, 262
   Accessibility Checker 152
Ministry of Seniors and Accessibility 39
minus symbols 106
misgendering 114–15
mistakes, normalizing 77, 117
mobile content 126, 141
mobility issues 249, 280
motor disabilities 192
multilingual content 126
multimedia accessibility guidelines 32, 50–51, 73, 81, 156–57
multiple audio tracks 249
multiple hyperlinks 131, 133
music 231–32, 258, 261

narrative films 239
National Disability Authority 46

National Disability Employment Awareness Month 188
National Transition Strategy 45
NaturalReader 14
neurodiversity 4
   see also ADHD; autism
Newfoundland 40
Newton, Elizabeth 94
non-compliance 24, 25–26, 45, 46
   penalties 39, 43, 282
   see also lawsuits
non-verbal sounds 201, 236, 260
Northwest Territories 40
Nova Scotia 40
number (numeral) formatting 104–05, 126, 149
numbered lists 128, 129, 150
numeracy levels 90–91
Nunavut 40
NVDA 13, 69, 161, 171, 217

objective (goal) setting 68, 69–70, 71
observation 96
'official' terms 97, 98–99
Office for National Statistics 104
on-screen text 231
open captions 225, 234–35, 252
open-door policies 82
Open Sans font 139
OpenDocument format 166
OpenDyslexic 153, 155
operability 12, 28, 42, 67, 193
optical character recognition 167
ordinal number formatting 105
organizational values 62, 65, 83, 93, 190
Otter.ai 201, 264, 278
outcomes-focus 10
Overcast 269

paragraph breaks 141
paragraph structure 100, 126, 127, 137
Parkwood Entertainment 26
Pascal case 73, 203–04, 209
passive voice 96, 127
PDF Accessibility Checker (PAC) 31, 169, 170
PDF file sizes 169
PDF/UA standards 31, 169, 170
PDFs 31, 149, 165–72, 180, 262
penalties (non-compliance) 39, 43, 282
perceivability 11, 28, 42, 192–93
   see also alternative (alt) text; audio descriptions; captions; transcripts
person-first language 92, 112, 113
personalization 64
phone numbers 105

photosensitive epilepsy 246
physical accessibility 17, 32–33, 38
Plain English campaign 97, 100, 151
plain language 50, 79, 89–111, 118–19, 127–28, 151, 193, 202–03, 207, 290
plain text files 261–62
plans 36, 37
    actions plans 67–71, 84
platform native tools 209, 217
playback speeds 249, 251, 266, 267, 268
plus symbols 106
Pocket Casts 269
podcast introductions/ outros 257
podcast players 265–69
podcast practice 256
podcast recaps 258
podcast script structure 256–57
podcast summaries 258
podcasts 32, 73–74, 224–29, 253–69
policy making 65–67, 83, 117
pop filters 254
positive reinforcement 78
post-production audio descriptions 237, 238–40, 242
posters 17
POUR principles 11–12, 28–29, 192–94
'powwows' 114
presentations 73, 74, 149, 168, 178, 180
    see also slide decks
Prince Edward Island 40
print materials 32–33
private sector 36, 41, 43, 47
procurement 66
product development cycles 67
professional development 280
progress reporting 37
promotional videos 239
pronouns 114–15
proper names 105
protected characteristics 44, 96
psychology 8
Public Sector Accessibility Directive 46
Public Sector Bodies Accessibility Regulations (2018) 44–45
punctuation marks 215

Quebec 40

racially inclusive language 114
RAG reporting 142
reach 5, 24, 62, 64, 188–89
read-aloud functionality (PDFs) 170
readability 92, 106–07, 198–99, 203, 283
readability scores 106

reading order 31, 157, 167, 171, 177
real-life experiences 65
real-time captions 32
real-time subtitles 32
real-world training examples 77
reasonable adjustments 44
recognition 75, 80
redundant information 92, 135
Reels 191, 252, 292
regulations 22, 33–47, 189–90, 281–83
relevance 68, 103
reports 37, 65, 168
    annual 31, 81, 166, 177
    compliance 39
    RAG 142
responsive content design 141
retail sector 70
Rev 32, 201, 237, 251, 264
review groups 116
reward systems 75
Rhianna 26
right-aligned text 140
right-to-left web content 126, 140
risk, reputational 25, 26, 30, 47, 60–61, 64, 70, 189
risk management 64, 70
robustness 12, 29, 42, 193–94

sans-serif fonts 32, 139, 153, 156, 198, 200, 234, 245, 263
Saskatchewan 40
screen magnifiers 13
screen readers 13, 153, 166, 167, 171, 266, 268, 283
    social media 187, 197, 204, 208, 212–13, 215
    web content 133, 134
scrolling 126
segmented podcast episodes 257–58
sensory sensitivities 232, 247
sentence length 99–100, 127, 203
serif fonts 139
shared slide decks 158
sight loss *see* visual impairment
signage 17
Sim Daltonism 244
simulations 65
Siri 267, 268
Siteimprove 69, 80
situational disabilities 4, 10, 109, 192
slide decks 73, 155–58, 178
slide formatting 158
slide order 155
SMART goals 68, 71
Smart Speed 269

social factors 8
social media 25, 72, 73, 186–218, 235, 290–92
   see also Facebook; Instagram; TikTok; Twitter (X)
social model of disability 7–8, 9
Sonix 265
sound effects 231–32, 261
sound quality 226
sources citation 103
spacing 178
speaker identification
   captions 235–36
   podcasts 260–61, 264
special characters 105–06, 199
specificity 65, 68
speech 254–55
speech recognition software 13–14
Speech Tools 255
Spotify 268–69
spreadsheet instructions 160
spreadsheets 149, 158–62, 168–69, 178–79, 180
   see also cells; columns; header rows
stakeholder engagement 66, 82, 112
standards 22–23, 27–33, 47, 51, 66–67, 81
   JIS X 8341-3 46
   PDF/UA 169, 170
Starbucks 188
Starbucks Stories 188
static images 247
statistics 138
   see also number (numeral) formatting
Stories 191, 252
storytelling 64, 188, 280, 283–84
strategic alignment 61, 69–70, 82
streaming content 191, 233, 235
stress 110–11
style guides 74, 117
sub-headings 100, 128, 263
subject matter experts 69, 98, 102–03, 283
subtitles 32, 199–201, 249, 250
success celebrations 78
summaries 103
surveys 82, 116
switch systems 14

Tableau 164
tables 152, *154*, 163, 171
tags (tagged content) 31, 167, 177, 262
Tahoma font 139
TalkBack 13, 268
'tapper/ listener' experiment (Newton) 94
targeted messaging 10
team-building events 17

team meetings 82
team-work (collaboration) 71–73, 242
tech tutorial videos 226
technical terms 97, 258
technology (IT) 47, 72
   gesture-based 281
   see also AI (artificial intelligence); assistive technology; augmented reality; digital accessibility
templates 71, 74, 193
temporary (situational) disabilities 4, 10, 109, 192
testimonials 64, 80
testing 10, 49
   manual 50, 69, 161, 170–72, 217
   see also user testing
text 197, 208
text alignment 140, 198
text documents 149, 150–55, 180
text size 32, 141, 245–46, 248
text-to-speech software 14
they/them pronoun 115
thumbs-up emoji 213–14
ticketing machines 42
TikTok 189, 191, 200, 211, 217, 234, 292
time-bound goals 68
Times New Roman font 139
timestamps 263–64
Title I (ADA) 34
Title II (ADA) 34–35
Title III (ADA) 34
Title IV (ADA) 34
Title V (ADA) 34
titles 105, 153, 156, 160, 162, 168–69, 178, 250
tone of voice 91, 109, 205, 215, 258, 261
topic-based podcast scripts 257
Toro, Luis 26
TPGi Colour Contrast Analyser 159, 164, 198, 216, 244
training 48, 64, 71, 74, 75–79, 84, 116, 181, 283, 286
   see also e-learning; education; simulations
training participation rates 77
transcription services 264
transcripts 32, 50–51, 157, 178, 193, 201–02, 224, 227, 249–52, 259–65
transportation services 38
trauma 110–11
Trint 265
trust 70, 112, 189
tutorial videos 240
TV shows 239
Twitter (X) 188, 207, 208–09, 292
2i process 96

typeface 125, 133, 153, 178, 264
  see also capitalization; fonts; italics

UK 5, 6, 24
  Equality Act (2010) 44
  Equality Commission for Northern Island 45
  Office for National Statistics 104
underlining 126, 133
understandability 12, 28–29, 42, 95–96, 103, 193
unicode text 199
United Nations (UN) 9, 47, 105
United States (US)
  ADA (1990) 25, 27, 33–35, 48
  ADA (Amended) (2024) 189
  Department of Justice 34
  Digital.gov 104
URLs 126, 131
usability 48, 80, 103
  see also readability
user-centred content design (UX writing) xviii, 285, 286
user stories 95
user testing 50, 82, 95–96, 161–62, 169–70, 279, 286
  social media 216
  video content 236, 240, 242, 245, 246
  web content 141, 143

Valuable 500 61
Venngage 165
Verdana font 139
video content 24, 32, 73–74, 156–57, 188, 189, 207, 223–70, 292–94
  see also captions
video content warnings 247
video embedding 250
video players 248–53
video pre-production 293
video transitions 247
Vimeo 233, 235, 239, 250–51, 253
virtual reality 279–80
visible disabilities 4
visual accessibility 50, 73, 134–43, 144, 194–99, 227–28, 231, 243–48, 293
  see also colour contrast; fonts; images
visual impairment 5, 25, 26, 191, 249, 280
  see also blindness; colour blindness
visual layout 199
Voice Boost 269
Voice Pitch Analyzer 255
voice recognition software 13–14
voice search technology 13–14, 268, 281

VoiceOver 13, 69, 171, 217, 266–67, 268, 269
voiceover artists 240
VoiceView 269

WAVE 69, 80
Web Accessibility Directive (2016) (EU) 41, 43
Web Accessibility Initiative (WAI) 27
web content 42, 72, 78, 80, 81, 82, 124–44
  on-screen text 231
  sentence lengths 100, 101
  transcripts 262
  see also Web Accessibility Directive (2016)
Web Content Accessibility Guidelines (WCAG) 27–30, 35, 47, 48, 66, 67, 76, 78, 79, 216
  social media 192–94
  video content 244, 245, 246–47
Web Content Accessibility Guidelines (WCAG) 2.1 Level AA 35, 37
  DDA (Australia) 45
  EAA 42
  Ireland 46
  Japan 46
WebAIM 80, 174
  Colour Contrast Checker 133, 164, 198, 216, 244
webinars 74
white space 126, 151
Whocanuse.com 142
Windows 13
Wistia 251–52, 253
word spacing 140
workarounds 99
workflows 71–75, 81, 84, 190
workshops 65, 74, 76
World Bank 5
World Health Organization (WHO) xvi, 5, 8, 24
World Wide Web Consortium (W3C) 27

X (Twitter) 188, 207, 208–09, 292

YouTube 157, 200, 211, 228, 233, 235, 239–40, 249–50, 253, 278
  tutorials 174
YouTube Caption Editor 237
Yukon 40

Z-patterns 126
ZoomText 13

Looking for another book?

Explore our award-winning books from global business experts in Marketing and Sales

Scan the code to browse

www.koganpage.com/marketing

EU Representative (GPSR)

Authorised Rep Compliance Ltd, Ground Floor, 71 Lower Baggot Street, Dublin, D02 P593, Ireland

www.arccompliance.com

www.ingramcontent.com/pod-product-compliance
Lightning Source LLC
Chambersburg PA
CBHW071157081025
33734CB00028B/181